Headline Sheffield

The News ... The Views ... The Pictures Which Shaped the Sheffield Area

Headline Sheffield

The Star brings your past to life

The **Star**

PETER
GOODMAN

breedon **books**
PUBLISHING

Leisure ... Entertainment ... Sport ... Transport ... Weather ...
War ... Communications ... Tragedies

First published in Great Britain in 2000 by
The Breedon Books Publishing Company Limited
Breedon House, Unit 3, Parker Centre, Derby DE21 4SZ.

Acknowledgements

THANKS are due to the hundreds of local reporters and photographers whose words and pictures over the last 100 years or so have helped shape history and also made this book possible.

For many of these years, Sheffield Newspapers published an evening newspaper, *The Star*, and also an illustrious morning newspaper, the *Telegraph*. They had separate editorial staffs – it was healthy to preserve an element of competition – but, on the photographic side, the pictures were often shared between the two newspapers

Some of the photographs in the book, therefore, will have been taken by photographers whose work was principally for the morning paper.

The Star has had many name changes since its launch in 1887 (it was then the *Sheffield Evening Telegraph*) but, for ease of reference, it has been called *The Star* throughout the book. Similarly, the morning newspaper, which was known as *Morning Telegraph* when it closed in 1986, has known different titles and is referred to in the book as the *Telegraph*.

Reborn as the weekly *Sheffield Telegraph* in 1989, it is a thriving publication and carries on the *Telegraph* tradition for quality journalism.

Heartfelt thanks are also due to Susan Woods, Sheffield Newspapers librarian, and her staff for their immense help, patience and good humour, to Angela Furniss and Nicola Ball in the Photographic Department and also to Doug Hindmarch at the Local Studies Library, Sheffield Libraries, Archives and Information.

ISBN 1 85983 212 1

Printed and bound by Butler & Tanner Ltd., Selwood Printing Works, Caxton Road, Frome, Somerset.

Jacket printing by GreenShires Group Ltd, Leicester.

Contents

Fair, Foul and Frightening –
Our Weather Over The Years
Sheffielders Strip Off – But Still Maintain the Canons of Propriety!

YORKSHIRE TELEGF

92.1.

Sheffield Grilling in the Nineties.

RECORD HEAT.

No one in Sheffield can remember a hotter day than this, nor has there been one if records may be trusted.

August 9, 1911... and Sheffield sweated and strained through its hottest day since records had begun in 1882.

As the shade temperature at Weston Park nudged 92.1 at 2pm, The Star reported that residents "with faces bronzed as Arabs" were either walking down the shady side of the street or "existing indoors merely by shedding all the clothing which was not needed to maintain the canons of propriety."

The formal headlines on The Star's 1911 article are typical of those days and very matter of fact. It was to be many, many years later before "Phew, what a scorcher" came along!

The tropical weather caused something of a sensation at the House of Commons in London. The Star's report said that members of the Standing Committee on the Coal Mines Bill had actually removed their coats and sat in their shirt sleeves because the heat was so great!

YORKSHIRE TELEGR.

THANK GOODNESS !

Sixteen Degrees Cooler To-day in Sheffield.

HEAT WAVE RECEDES.

There has been a big drop in the temperature in Sheffield...

According to the next day's edition, the temperature at 2.30pm on August 9 had hit a blistering 92.3.

Twenty-four hours later, it was much cooler at 75 degrees, thanks to a cooling breeze from the north tempering the heat of the sun.

The hot weather of 1911 led to a drought and the low water level at Redmires Reservoir exposed an old smithy not seen for 36 years.

Region's highest temperature ever as heatwave continues

HOTTEST YET AS RECORD TUMBLES

By Patrick Gardner

IT'S a record-breaker! Scorching Sheffield was roasting in an all-time high temperature of 93F this afternoon.

Weather experts confirmed the city's long-standing 1911 record of 92.3F was toppled at precisely 2pm today.

And Gaynor Boon, who records temperatures at the Sheffield's Weston Park Weather Station, said: "It could get even hotter later this afternoon."

Today's temperatures beat the record of August 9, 1911, to become the highest in Sheffield since records began in 1882.

Into the **90's**

● History in the baking: P3
● Weathergirl goes for record: P5
● Fire risk shuts moors: P6
● Sweat it out...

Costa del Sheffield: holidaymakers Steven Thompson and Morven Sincla

The record of 1911 was to stand for another 79 years. Then, on August 3, 1990, the thermometer in Sheffield bubbled to 93 degrees.

Everybody sweltered. Ambulance crews were busy all day helping people who had collapsed with heat exhaustion, especially on buses. Peak Park rangers closed 100 square miles of tinder-dry moorland for a week because of the fire risk and fire crews fought to dampen grass and wood fires.

It fell to weather girl Gayner Boon, from Sheffield's Weston Park weather station, to record the historic moment.

A favourite pastime of drought-suffering Sheffielders up to 1947 was to go steeple-spotting at Ladybower Dam. When Derwent village was submerged as part of the Ladybower Reservoir extension, the church tower was left standing and during long periods of dry weather it was interesting to see how much of it was exposed when the water level dropped.

It was left so high and dry one summer that thousands of people were able to climb the wooden staircase inside. Derwent Valley Water Board decided this was no longer safe after its long immersion and ordered it to be demolished.

The move pleased former residents of Derwent village who felt it had been unseemly to leave the spire standing.

1976 was hot but not hot enough to shatter the 1911 record.

But as the temperatures soared, so did the spirits of pupils at Sheffield's King Edward VII Lower School. They were allowed home an hour and ten minutes early during the heatwave because of boiling classrooms…

Also sent home early was a Sheffield Crown Court jury after a be-wigged judge complained about the heat.

Some pubs in the area ran out of lager and greenkeepers got hot under the collar because the drought was ruining bowling and golf greens.

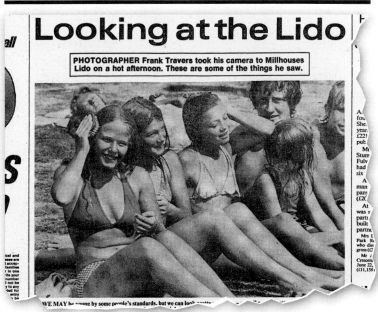

(Right) When the temperature rises, every editor wants good pictures to go with the heatwave stories. Photographer Frank Travers, a real Sheffield Newspapers pro who could read an editor's mind from 50 yards, probably went along to Millhouses Lido without being asked.

Sunny side up! Whit holiday crowds stretch out at the side of Hathersage Swimming Pool in May 1955.

Lunchtime in Fargate, Sheffield, on June 2, 1978.

The Sheffield Area is Just One Big Iceberg

Brrr...brrr...and even more brrr. At the other end of the thermometer, the Sheffield area was little more than one big iceberg in 1947 and 1963, the two winters most talked about by Star readers who sneezed, spluttered and shivered though one or both of them.

Both big freezes seemed to go on for ever but diligent research of the files during these two winters has failed to find a single "white hell" headline! That must have been an invention of the 80s or 90s.

But The Star's reporters, headline writers and photographers did, nevertheless, manage to capture all the bone-chilling horrors of '47 and '63, those two winters of our discontent...

Many years later, incidentally, the owner of a Derbyshire store selling camping equipment rewrote the famous Richard III quote and put a notice in his window saying: "Now is the discount on our winter tents."

SPRING IN JANUARY!

CAN Spring be far behind? Judging by these scenes, pictured by a cameraman of "The Star," winter has not long to run. Top, sunlight and shadows for the outing with nurse; below, Spring flowers on sale in the market; left, road signs are

January, 1947...and, as the month wore on, cock-eyed optimists in our part of the world could see Spring just round the corner.

We seemed to be getting away with winter very nicely, thank you. Rather than winter draws on, they were starting to come off. Clouts were being cast in all directions.

The story and pictures left, from The Star of January 21, 1947, captured the mood.

Judging by these scenes, said The Star, winter has not long to run...

It's the sort of throwaway line journalists sometimes use because it seems to make sense at the time and certainly makes people feel good.

Talk about tempting fate!

A few days later, straight from the Arctic, came the longest, fiercest blast of cold weather in living memory. Such was its ferocity and intensity that many genuinely thought the Ice Age had returned.

In one whole month, between January 26 and February 23, temperatures at Weston Park rose above freezing only twice, and then for no more than a few minutes. It was the longest continuous frost on record.

February's mean temperature was 28.3 degrees, nearly four degrees below freezing.

If you enjoy horror stories, wrap up warm, pour yourself a hot toddy and read on...

- Between January 23 and March 11, 1947, nearly 18 million tons of snow fell on Sheffield;
- Shipping in the North Sea was warned to keep clear of giant ice floes;
- The River Don froze over in Sheffield for the first time since 1895;
- Throughout our area, hills appeared where none had been before – hills of packed snow 20 feet high;
- On some roads, particularly in Derbyshire, you could just make out the tops of telegraph poles – the only indication that there was a road below;
- Workmen struggled night and day for weeks to keep roads, tram tracks and railway lines open, often fighting a losing battle;
- Water levels in Ladybower Reservoir dropped four feet, to 15 feet below peak, as springs and water courses on the moors froze up for five weeks;
- Coal stocks ran out in hundreds of Sheffield homes because trains had difficulty reaching the pits;
- Blocked roads prevented milk supplies getting through on several occasions;
- March 4 was the coldest March day on record, the mercury plummeting to 15.3 degrees;
- During a winter of many blizzards, one snowfall started on March 5 and lasted for 29 hours;
- Blocks of snow as large as a house and weighing six tons hurtled on to the Sheffield-Glossop road from surrounding hills;
- One hundred and fifty passengers were marooned all night on a Manchester to London via Sheffield train;
- Stock was ruined in a Wombwell, Barnsley shop, when bottles of ink froze solid and then burst.

A lane in the Ashbourne area in 1947.

Beautifully sculptured snow on Kinder Scout in 1947.

Clearing the Buxton and High Peak Railway after yet another 1947 blizzard.

A 1947 white-out in Dobcroft Road, Millhouses, Sheffield.

The "worst blizzard in living memory" hits the Sheffield area on February 4, 1947.

A bus driver and conductor were marooned for four days near the Fox House inn.

First customer for a week is the landlord's niece!

Yet another blizzard...February 26, 1947.

The Dreadful Winter of 1963 …

Ice Weather For Ducks!
BEER, PETROL, VEGETABLES AND CATS ALL FREEZE!

"Winter's tale" was the headline of January 19, 1963, over a story of skiers having to dig cars out of snowdrifts near Fox House.

And there were many more tales to come as the worst winter since 1947 held the region in its icy clamp.

SHEFFIELD HAS ITS COLDEST NIGHT SINCE MARCH, 1947

AN air temperature of 15.8 degrees—one degree lower than Monday night's reading—was recorded during the night at Sheffield's weather station at Weston Park.

It was the city's lowest night-time temperature in the air since the 15.3 degrees recorded on March 4, 1947.

But breakfast-time temperatures today were slightly higher than yesterday. The 9 a.m. reading showed 22.7 degrees, compared with 18.3 degrees at the same time yesterday.

Minimum temperature on the ground last night was 7.8 degrees—24.2 degrees of frost. Highest point reached by the thermometer yesterday was 28.6 degrees.

DUCKS GROUNDED

Twenty Muscovy ducks which grounded themselves in Endcliffe Park, Sheffield, today, because of ice on their wings, were thawed out by Sheffield R.S.P.C.A. Insp. Terry Watson and members of the park staff.

They managed to corner the waddling ducks in a tunnel at the end of a small stream and then carried them off to a park-keeper's hut, where they were given large helpings of mash and where they will stay until conditions improve.

January 23, 1963, was Sheffield's coldest night since March 4, 1947, the air temperature of 15.8 degrees being slightly above the 15.3 of 1947.

Everything and everybody froze, including the ducks on Endcliffe Park. Grounded because of ice on their wings, they had to be thawed out by RSPCA staff. It gave new meaning to the old phrase "like water off a duck's back."

Weekend skiers spend half day digging cars from snowdrifts

EIGHT people trapped by snow while on their way to spend the weekend ski-ing at Edale spent the first half of today digging out their cars from deep drifts on the Stoney Ridge-Froggatt Edge road.

They had completed the earlier part of their journey from their homes at Newark without difficulty, but ran into trouble on the exposed roads near Fox House.

One of three cars managed

P.M. ON TV

Power failures put hundreds of villagers in the dark

HUNDREDS of homes in the Sheffield area were without electricity for several hours today when snow and ice caused widespread power failures.

Worst hit was the Hope Valley, where thick ice on two 33,000-volt overhead power lines caused a short circuit.

Trouble began when one line supplying Bradfield was

battle through appalling conditions to trace the fault.

The snow-search for the engineers started at 5.30 a.m. today when lights flickered out over a wid

The St

SHEFFIELD, TUESDAY, JANUARY 22, 1963

It was so cold

Last night's temperature of 13 degrees F.—20 degrees of frost —achieved the spectacular—it froze diesel oil! It happened at Wood Lane, Canklow, depot of X.R.E. Transport, Ltd. Twenty of their trucks were immobilised early today when the drivers arrived at the depot to find their diesel fuel tanks frozen solid. And under the direction of General Manager, Mr. Peter Fenwick, they built bonfires round every truck in an attempt to thaw them out.

"This is the most fantastic thing I've ever seen in the business," said Mr. Fenwick. "And the worst of it is that either the tanks or the pumps must inevitably have been fractured, and will need extensive repairs when we have thawed them out." He said the trucks were mainly engaged on earth-moving operations for the Steel, Peech and Tozer Spear project, and said he understood that excavators on the site were also frozen up.

Frozen vegetables leave city markets with 'greens' famine

WHOLESALERS at Sheffield's Parkway Market to-day reported cabbages frozen like bricks and sprouts like balls of concrete as the city was plunged into a green-veg. famine.

By mid-morning some Sheffield retailers were out of either cauliflower or cabbage —and the only sprouts to be seen were tiny and frost-bitten.

One chain of greengrocers was not too badly hit. They were relying on produce from their own local nurseries.

Protected

A spokesman said: "We have protected our produce wherever possible. But we can imagine that supplies from out of town have been badly hit by the frost.

"We are advising our customers to soak their produce before cooking."

Another chain of green-grocers was without a green

Goodacre and Sons Ltd., the manager, Mr. W. Elsom, said: "There are no sprouts about. Cauliflowers are very dear and will be up to 2s. 6d. in the shops. These are Italian ones, and there are no Cornish ones about.

Plentiful, but . . .

"Cabbage is very scarce, too," added Mr. Elsom.

Mr. A. E. Bovill, of A. E. Bovill (Sheffield) Ltd., said there were plenty of fresh vegetables about the market because anything affected by the frost had not been bought.

Sprouts were frozen, but would come out all right.

Mr. Bovill added that he was expecting a plentiful supply of vegetables from Monday

THE STAR, SHEFFIELD, Saturday, January

The Star

No. 23,699   SHEFFIELD, THURSDAY, JANUARY 24, 1963   3d.

Now it goes to another EGGStreme—

AFTER the gas shortage, power reductions and the dried up taps — now it's the EGG FAMINE.

Snowed-up farms, frozen lorries and obstinate hens brought today's sad story for farmers, egg producers

and packers AND the housewife.

Supplies from farms— many completely cut off and isolated — have been cut by a quarter.

IMPORTS

A spokesman for one of the North's leading egg producing centres told The

Star that a meeting was being held by his firm in Sheffield tonight to discuss the serious situation.

A Yorkshire egg producing firm, which distributes about 1,500 30-dozen cases of eggs each week, are even having to import eggs from Finland, Den-

A tale of two cats

. . . ON A COLD TILE ROOF

THE CAT ON the cold tile roof just sat and stared . . . he found his 14-inch tail FROZEN firmly to the roof.

It was time to go home but Snowball the tomcat stayed where he was. And Sheffield bus conductor George Curr just couldn't coax him down.

He offered him meat, a saucer of milk, sweets and chocolates—but his cat refused to budge. Then George, of Gifford Road, Sheffield, telephoned for help.

Mrs. Edith Pyecroft, secretary of the Sheffield branch of the P.D.S.A., climbed a ladder and found the tomcat frozen to the spot.

'ANCHORED'—BY DEEP FREEZE

MAROONED—on an island of ice. Victim of the deep freeze is the Hull barge She entered Sheffield Ba?n a week ago, discharged h? ?eed from the i? fl? ?ee James Wal?en and

A Hull barge was trapped by ice in Sheffield basin for a week.

Sheffield freezing smog warning

NEW HAZARD TONIGHT

THOUSANDS of home-going motorists may face a fresh and alarming hazard by early this evening — thick, widespread, freezing smog.

And the forecasters expect it to be at its worst in Sheffield and South Yorkshire industrial towns.

This follows the coldest night known for several years in Sheffield—the city's official weather station at Weston Park recorded a minimum air temperature of 16.8F., the lowest since March 4, 1947.

At 9 a.m. today the temperature had risen to 18.3F.— but was still the lowest at that time of day for the whole of this winter.

Severe

The R.A.F. weather station at Bawtry reported that last night's minimum temperature in South Yorkshire was down to 13 degrees F. and will remain low today with severe frost tonight.

"The mercury could even fall lower," a forecaster warned.

"Thick and widespread patches of smog will develop quite early, mainly around the industrial towns and open water — if there is any open water left unfrozen!"

The only comparatively bright prospect on the weather front is that there is no more snow expected, at least within the next 24 hours.

A party of 24 teenage hikers from Manchester who have been marooned at Hartington, Derbyshire, which has been cut off by 10ft drifts for

TEMPERATURE IN PIT WAS 8 DEGREES BELOW

THE temperature in a pit where a miner collapsed from the cold was more than eight degrees below freezing point.

This was disclosed today by Mr. Bert Wynn, area secretary of the Derbyshire N.U.M., who are investigating sub-zero working conditions in a number of pits.

Mr. Wynn said the miner was found collapsed at Arkwright Colliery, near Chesterfield.

"He was immediately examined by a Coal Board doctor, who said his condition was due to cold, and he sent him home," said Mr. Wynn.

"A temperature reading was taken in the drift where he had been working and it showed 23.5 degrees Fahrenheit. There was also a terrific velocity of air at that point."

AND EVEN THE BEER FROZE...

THAT was the night that was—the night even the beer froze up!

It happened at the Netherton Workingmen's Club, near Barnsley, where Mr. Eddie Hill, the club's steward, and club members were today working to thaw out the seven pipes.

Mr. Hill, former landlord of the Alhambra Hotel, Barnsley, said: "The beer is frozen up in all the seven pipes. We are having to put hot cloths on the pipes and we have had to put some heat in the cellar. I have been connected with the trade all my life and I have never known beer freeze up."

MARIA CALLAS

City in grip of worst gas crisis since the war

By KEITH WALKER

SHEFFIELD is in the grip of the worst gas crisis since the war.

- Homes were blacked out by power cuts;
- Diesel oil froze;
- A cat was frozen to a house roof by its tail and couldn't move;
- The beer froze at a Barnsley club (there were no reported riots);
- Vegetables froze at Sheffield's Parkway Market – "cabbages were like bricks and sprouts like balls of concrete";
- The area faced gas shortages because of demand exceeding supply;

- A Hull barge was trapped by ice in Sheffield Basin for a week after delivering its cargo;
- A children's church choir was trapped for two hours on the Woodhead pass;
- Lung-bursting freezing smog enveloped the area;
- Frozen pipes caused taps to run dry;
- A miner collapsed at Arkwright Colliery, Chesterfield, when the temperature underground plunged to eight degrees below freezing.

SWIMSUITS IN THIS WEATHER 'SILLY' —CONTEST JUDGE

AFTER judging a beauty contest in Sheffield yesterday, Coun. William Whitby, aged 39, who was Cleethorpes' youngest Mayor when he held office in 1958, said: "Wearing bathing costumes in mid-January seems ludicrous."

"I would have preferred to see these girls in pretty dresses."

Coun. Whitby was one of four members of the Cleethorpes publicity committee who came to Sheffield with entertainments manager Mr. Arthur Ingham to judge the preliminary round of the Holiday Princess and Maid of Honour competitions.

Entrants

From more than 100 entrants, 50 girls were selected to take part in the finals which will be ~~held~~ at Cleethorpes during

Grange Lane, Maltby, near Rotherham, and Pat Mudson, Worsbrough Road, Birdwell, near Barnsley.

Finalists

For the title of Maid of Honour, the finalists from Sheffield region chosen were: Sheila Sorby, Blackstock Road; Loreen Smallwood, Blackstock Drive; Janet Tankard, Birley Spa Lane, Hackenthorpe; Lynne Shepherd, Atlantic Road, Greenhill.

Christine Ibbotson, Hall Road, Handsworth; Janice Theaker, Harrogate Road, Darnal~~l~~; Jacqueline Milligan, ~~Gre~~ Road, Heeley; Marg~~aret~~ Wort~~h~~

And at the height of the bleak mid winter, a Cleethorpes councillor helping to judge a Holiday Princess beauty competition in Sheffield, had some frosty comments for the organisers about the way the girls were dressed.

It was ludicrous, he said, that the contestants had to wear bathing costumes in the middle of January.

Avalanche Danger

One of the most dramatic stories of this crippling winter was the attempt to avert a life-threatening avalanche on the Snake Pass.

Five hundreds tons of frozen snow hanging dangerously over the road kept the Pass closed for a month as explosives experts waited for the right weather conditions to detonate it.

The Pass was shut because it was feared the slightest vibration, even the closing of a car door, could bring the snow and ice crashing on to the road.

Explosives experts may be called to avalanche scare on Pennines route

EXPLOSIVE experts may be called out to the Snake Pass near Sheffield where 500 tons of snow and ice are hanging perilously over the road.

The slightest noise or vibration could bring the huge avala~~nche~~ sweeping down across the

Heavy snow on the Snake Pass.

Carrying explosives on the Snake Pass.

Huge blocks of snow posed a real danger.

S'now joke. The blocked Hathersage Road at Fox House.

Unbelievable! The snow has almost reached the top of the signpost.

Sub zero temperatures and frozen water supplies meant that standpipes had to be used.

Fighting a way through heavy drifts was a constant battle.

There was so much snow in 1963 that it had to be emptied into the River Sheaf on Furnival Road.

1963 fun for some when this Sheffield stretch of water froze over.

The big freeze of 1963 and two-year-old Janet Halliwell, of Spout House Farm, Oughtibridge, plays with the two-day old lambs born on her grandad's farm.

A fountain at Weston Park, Sheffield, during a 1910 freeze.

A Fargate freeze-up in 1986.

1994 – this is all you need after a busy day at the office!

FLAMING JUNE! SNOW PUTS CRICKET OUT IN THE COLD

Here's something to tell the grandkids – snow stopped play **in June** in two county cricket games, Derbyshire v Lancashire at Buxton and Essex v Kent at Colchester, in 1975.

Winter 1991…and is this Sheffield's tallest-ever snowman?

Deep and crisp but not very even. Heavy snow caused drifts on the Totley to Holmsfield road on November 30, 1965.

This huge "teardrop" of ice fell out of the sky at Ecclesfield on March 14, 1997. To give an idea of its size, a 50p piece has been placed in front of it. It weighed 4lb.

SHEFFIELD – "CITY OF DREADFUL NIGHT"

5 HOURS' CONTINUOUS LIGHTNING

SCORES OF HOUSES STRUCK AND MANY FLOODED.

NIGHT OF AWE AND BRILLIANCE.

MINERS' CONFERENCE PROPOSAL FOR PENSIONS.

ALMOST the sole topic of conversation to-day in Sheffield and the district is the terrific thunderstorms which broke over this part of the country last night and early this morning. The play of the lightning was impressively magnificent, and it is generally conceded that never before in Sheffield has there been such a "display." Reports to hand to-day show that a good deal of damage was done, but in the main it was on a small scale. The heavy rain caused floods in some places reminiscent of the deluge of about a year ago.

PENSIONS FOR MINERS.

At the closing session of the Miners' Federation Conference at Folkestone to-day, a resolution was adopted on the motion of the Derbyshire district that the Executive should meet the Secretary for Mines with a view to the provision of a superannuation fund for workers in the industry by a levy of one penny per ton on all coal turned to provide the nucleus of a pension in addition to Old Age pensions.

BRIXTON TRAGEDY: DRAMATIC ALLEGATIONS.

Dramatic allegations were made by Mason, the man accused of murdering a taxi-cab driver, at the Old Bailey to-day. In the box he declared that he went to Brixton by arrangement and that when the taxi drove up he heard Vivian, a witness, disputing with the driver. He further spoke to hearing three shots fired and said he got away the best he could as he was "frightened to death."

CITY OF DREADFUL NIGHT.

Sheffield Violently Strafed by Storms.

THUNDER & LIGHTNING.

Buildings Damaged: Firemen Frequently Called Out.

When elderly folk talk, as they do, of last night's storms being the most awful within living memory, it is no mere hyperbole: they are speaking with sincerity and honest reliance on memory. The storms may not have been the worst from the point of view of the damage they caused; but undoubtedly they were the most violent in character for many years.

The first, which was between 7 and 8, was of a comparatively mild nature, but a warning, perhaps, of what was to follow. The second, which started between 9.30 and 10 o'clock, opened and developed in a unique manner. First the skies changed deliberately from a haze to a dull hue, and then huge clouds, of peculiar shades, some picturesque and others most evil-looking, moved slowly overhead, gradually darkened the heavens, until it was prematurely night-black; next rain ...ted in warm drops. Incidentally, during ... Government's

FLASHES AND BOLTS.

"Striking" Incidents of the Great Storm.

STORY OF A PONY.

At the house of Mr. H. Bishop, dentist, of 257, School Road, Crookes, Sheffield, when the thunder claps were terrible, the electric light was cut off, and there was an awful crash, which made the occupants of the house, to use their own words, "think the end had come." The house had been struck by lightning, the roof being stripped of slates, and considerable damage was caused to the furniture of the attic and other rooms.

In the case of Mr. H. O. Edwards, of 41, Fossdale Road, Millhouses, strange to relate, the family were not awakened by the storm. The first they knew of anything being wrong was the sound of rushing water down the staircase. The lightning had burst the water-pipe and flooded the house, and furniture, carpets, and fittings were damaged.

In the Highfield district many houses were struck, and numerous chimney-pots were displaced. One remarkable case was where the ...

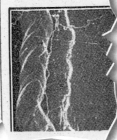

FLOODS AND F...

Reckless Storm's Tr... Damage.

SHEFFIELD INCID...

Serious Rush of Wa... Pitsmoor.

A lady living in Brocco Bank, ... describes very vividly a "fire ba'... states she saw at 2.10 this morni... there seemed to be a circle of fi... lightning of vivid blue, then in th... the phenomenal appearance of ... large star which quickly chang... red ball of flame, which, in the... informant, "fell right down the r...

Chimney Pots Dis!...

Damage was done to the back attic by lightning at 30, Coleri... pied by Martha Harwood.

A picture was broken in the McCague's house—next door... also done to the front bed...

At 251 Don Road, the hou... th front bedroom window-sill wa... a numbe rof bricks in the wall w...

Lightning caused a slight fire at Street, occupied by Harold Ingb... front and back bedroom and damaged and the chimney-pot w... Thos. Hardy's house next door and damage was done to the ...

A chimney-pot was knocked o... ceiling was cracked at 12ct. 2ha... Street, occupied by Albert Crowd... The chimney-stack and roof we... the house of Thomas Straw, 44...

After being struck by lightning pot at 19, Marshall Street, in the Alfred Hill, fell through the roof The lightning ran down the fall a hole in the living-room wall.

Three feet of plaster was strip... wall at 5, Writtle Street, occupie... and a gas globe was damaged.

Slates were loosened and damaged at houses in Writtle Str...

Lightning passed down the chin... out the fireplace in a bedro... Jerroll's house, 119, Wincobank

At 48 and 50, Wincobank La... lightning was also done.

The house of Mrs. Jessie Andr... Street, was struck and a slight f...

An unoccupied house, 82, Batle... a bedroom fireplace torn out... chimney damaged.

Lightning struck a chimney-s... through the attic of 19/5 Sorby S... Houses, 28, and 25, Addison ... Rothay Road, were struck.

Probably the worst damage wa...

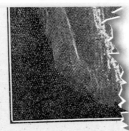

[Photo: Brindley. Block: ... A photograph taken at No...

factories, and other buildings stood ... against the glare; and then each ... the scientific sequel—thunder. ...r—sometimes in sharp, crackling more frequently like a dreadful rolling ... drums—gradually drawing nearer, a final crescendo, it seemed to shake foundations of buildings and send ... tremors though the earth.

Terrible and Fascinating.

...ghtning was dangerous; the thunder ...; the two combined struck terror, fear, ...ead into the hearts and minds of some; ... it appealed as an awe-inspiring, ...g, spell-binding spectacle—all according ...rament. To civilians it recalled nights ... during war-time when Zeppelins and aeroplanes used to make their visits on ...f merciless destruction; to soldiers and ...emen the constantly recurring electric ... resembled, more than anything else, ...an, a violent "strafe" on the Western ... dred ... of guns on each side

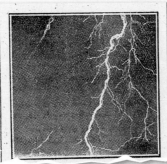

The Star used two photographs to illustrate the severity of the lightning, which started as "an expansive flash that transformed darkness into apparent daylight."

It was the worst Sheffield storm in living memory and, after drying themselves out, The Star's headline writers, not wanting to be wet blankets, penned such memorable creations as "City of Dreadful Night" and "Night of Awe and Brilliance" for The Star's edition of June 13, 1923.

Their imagination had been stirred by five hours of continuous lightning, frightening thunder and torrential rain.

Many people stayed up all night, either too terrified to go to bed or just to marvel at the spectacle.

And, like the water that poured into houses all over the area, The Star's reporters were also in full flow. One wrote:

"The impression of the phenomenal night will ever remain in the memory of Sheffield as some mighty force which raided the city in atmospheric cycles, hurling devastation and something like terror in its path, only to return with greater vigour and intense fireriness after its first terrible blows had been spent.

"Truly, the nearest likeness to the storm has been a city subjected to a colossal attack from the air for several hours together, or of the gathering of massed batteries prior to an attack on some fated part of a late-war battle front."

All over the Sheffield area, houses were struck by lightning and many were flooded. A dentist living in Crookes "thought the end had come" when lightning struck his house and stripped the slates from the roof.

The Brightside and Attercliffe areas took a particular battering and in Owlergreave Road the occupants of four houses stranded in their bedrooms had to be rescued by firemen as flood water reached the tops of downstairs living room windows.

A thunderbolt struck the Royal Hotel, Attercliffe, passing through the bedrooms and down into the bar. The licensee and his family escaped injury.

The Penistone Road area was also badly hit, with flood water table high in some houses.

In the Hope Valley, hailstones "as large as peas" fell and cows, sheep and lambs were killed by lightning.

"REAL" RAIN COMES IN TIME TO SAVE THE CROPS

Heavy rains which started during the night and continued persistently to-day in Sheffield and in a wide surrounding area, "well and truly" broke the drought which had lasted for nearly three months.

IN North Derbyshire, Notting-hamshire and South Yorkshire farmers rubbed their hands with glee as they watched rain pouring steadily from the cloud-laden sky.

"This has come in time to save the situation—and to save us from great financial loss," was a comment made on all sides by farmers to-day.

"Vegetable crops will receive a ... of benefit"

More Rain Likely

The weather forecast for Sheffield and district for the next 24 hours, issued at noon, is:—

Light east winds, backing north-east; dull, with rain at times; fair periods later; rather cold.

A complex area of low pressure extends from S.W. England to Germany and a ridge of high pressure ...

NO RAIN FOR THREE MONTHS

"RAIN IS NEWS", said the headline of May 18, 1938, and it was, because they hadn't seen any to speak of for nearly three months.

Farmers throughout the area were jubilant. The downpour, they said, had come just in time to save them from financial crisis.

It started at 1am and, by 10am, 0.46 inches had fallen – equal to the total for the whole of March and April. February had also been a very dry month.

---

aph & Star

ATING THE "SHEFFIELD MAIL") LONDON: TELEPHONES CENTRAL 6909 PUBLISHING; MUSEUM 9841 ADVERTISING

IELD, TUESDAY EVENING, AUGUST 11, 1931. REGISTERED AT THE POSTAGE INLAND

owden After Hastening

ISES IN IA.

r Gandhi to ondon.

VICEROY.

hreat to Table.

PREMIER.

Angry Seas at Scarborough.

A holiday crowd at Scarborough sheltering from the mountainous seas which broke over the sea wall.

CRASH TO DEATH VIOLENT EAR

Scarborough was the place to be on August 11, 1931, for a pleasant, calm summer's day!

WALSHS Ladies' TAIHO HATS
Each 29/11

The Star

STEREOPHONIC SOUND
PHILIP CANN
DIXON LANE, SHEFFIELD.

No. 22,323 WEDNESDAY, JULY 2, 1958 A KEMSLEY NEWSPAPER. 3d.

TERROR by NIGHT   HAVOC by DAY

FLOOD PLIGHT GRAVE

COUNCIL TO REHOUSE HOMELESS FAMILIES | MILLHOUSES PARK IS DEVASTATED | HOUSE OF WIDOW, 83, SLIDES INTO RIVER

Next hours critical for Sheffield

SEVERAL SHEFFIELD FAMILIES WILL HAVE TO BE REHOUSED FOLLOWING THE TERRIFYING STORM WHICH BROUGHT HAVOC TO THE DISTRICT TODAY.

LINES TO SOUTH BLOCKED

Tragedy of Yard 4 ct.

Hoffmanns

MORE PICTURES

WOMAN, 83, RESCUED AS HOUSE CRASHES INTO RIVER

A dramatic front page picture in The Star summed up the misery caused by a "terrifying storm" on the night of July 2, 1958.

Families on Suffolk Road had to be rehoused when floodwater swamped their homes and this picture was taken after residents had struggled to rescue furniture and clothing.

An 83-year-old woman had an amazing escape when the Yarborough Road home she had lived in for 50 years collapsed into the River Sheaf. She had been taken from the house only minutes earlier and had to be pulled over the doorstep when she refused to leave.

Floodwater had undermined the foundations, plunging the roof, walls and furniture into the swirling river.

Her biggest concern was for the savings she had stored in a sideboard...

There were flood alerts all over the area. Millhouses Park, The Star reported, had been badly damaged by a four feet high wall of water sweeping through it and the Derbyshire village of Hathersage had been devastated by a river of flood water pouring through the village.

It reached tablecloth level as it rushed through the restaurant of the George Hotel, leaving a half-inch layer of mud on the plush carpet.

A bridge collapses in the children's paddling pool at Millhouses Park.

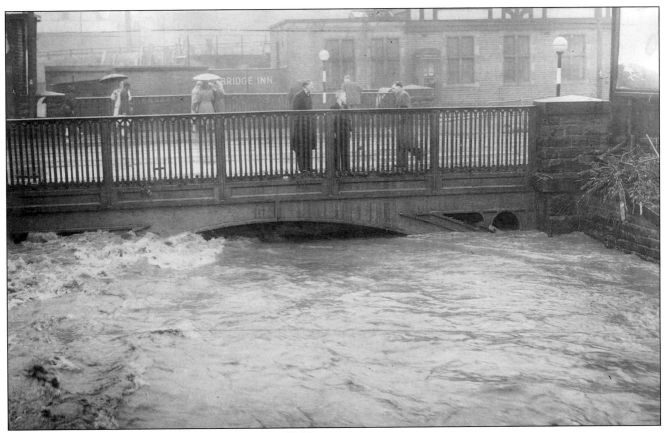

The River Sheaf perilously high under Heeley Bridge, Sheffield.

Water, water everywhere. Looking over the flooded fields along the banks of the River Rother towards Woodhouse Mill.

A lorry, its wheels half covered by floodwater, braves the flooded Chesterfield Road at Dronfield.

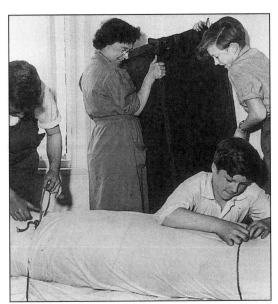

Homeless because of the floods, mum, dad and their two boys are moving into Burngreave Vestry Hall, Sheffield.

A widow, 83, escapes as home tumbles into river

FLOOD CHAOS IN VILLAGE COST £10,000

IN a miracle escape from her crumbling home, 83-year-old widow, **Mrs. Evelyn Rowland**, today cheated death. Minutes after she had been carried from the Yarborough Road home she has lived in for half a century, her four-roomed house cracked and crashed into the swirling River Sheaf.

Her rescuers, her next door neighbour and daughter-in-law, **Mrs. Lottie Rowland**, another neighbour, Mrs. Annie Williams and Mr. J. Cotton had rushed into her home when they heard warning shouts from workmen on the opposite side of the river who had seen the house cracking and slipping.

The old woman's home, built steeply up from the river, lost its foundations in the swirling waters. Roof, walls and furniture plunged into the water and

furniture from the home and a police official paid tribute to his three helpers—**Thomas Squires**, of Walkley Road, **Reginald Banks**, of Eccesall Road, and **Eric Rhodes**, of Kersley Road.

Of the rescue, Mrs. Lottie Rowland said it was a miracle that all three of them had escaped. "I was in the yard, cleaning up mud that had accumulated during the night when I heard these men shouting, 'Get out! Get out.' Your house is coming down."

Reluctant . . .

The widow's younger daughter, Mrs. Edna Horsepool, who works at Laycock's firm from where the warning came, said it was the third disaster that had struck the house. About 1928 the house had its foundations similarly undermined. During World War II it was bombed

FIRST estimate of damage caused by a two-foot deep river of flood water that battered its way through the Derbyshire village of Hathersage early this morning is put at more than £10,000.

When dawn came to the village it revealed the desolation the flood had left— buildings swamped, windows smashed and a carpet of mud and rubble on the streets.

The water ripped up two-inch thick chunks of road surface on its way down from the Surprise, and for a terrifying half-hour tore down Main Road.

It smashed through the back windows of the George Hotel, quickly reached table-cloth height in the sumptuously

MILLHOUSES PARK IS DEVASTATED—DAMAGE IS £6,000

MILLHOUSES PARK, a Sheffield show piece, lay battered and broken today after a savaging from the flood-

Residents of Broadfield Road, Nether Edge, Sheffield, survey floodwater outside their homes in 1958. Not many wellies to be seen but plenty of high heels!

Our area was also deluged on August 20, 1954. It was time to get the wellies out for these children on flooded Surbiton Street, near Broughton Lane, Attercliffe.

Exciting times for children paddling at Firth Park terminus in August, 1954...but not for stranded car drivers.

ALTHOUGH it was opening time, there were no customers at the Railway Inn, Beighton, near Sheffield. Seen looking from the upper floor of the premises are the landlord and his family.

No customers were lucky enough to find themselves marooned when floodwater surrounded the Railway Inn, Beighton, in 1951.

Crown Square, Matlock, after heavy rain in December, 1965.

Sheep had to be rescued at Woodhouse, Sheffield, in December 1965.

Stumped by the weather in May, 1967. Definitely no play today at Worksop Cricket Club.

It had to happen! It's Sod's Law (or should that be Sodden's Law?) that if you stick a "Help Save Water" information caravan in the middle of Sheffield it's going to throw it down...

And it did in January 1976. The Yorkshire Water representative in the doorway of the caravan has that "what on earth are we doing here" look about him.

This taxi, with passenger silhouetted in the back, is clearly determined to make it through these May, 1979, floods but the car pulling the caravan has decided otherwise. The driver is turning round and going back.

A splendid piece of initiative by the photographer in 1977, persuading these children to pose under the Water Bus sign at Conisborough, near Doncaster!

London Road, Heeley Bridge, Sheffield, is notorious for flooding. Perhaps no one told these drivers, stuck after a storm in June, 1993.

High water at Ladybower Reservoir in February, 1977, brings out the sightseers in their cars.

The splendour of Derwent Dam after heavy rain in December, 1992.

Believe it or not, this rainbow pictured over Sheffield on March 14, 1994, stretched into the Guinness Book of Records. It shone continuously for six hours.

Hurricane Leaves Four Dead

The Star's page one headline of February 16, 1962, said it all. The worst hurricane our area had ever known left four people dead as it swept through with terrifying force.

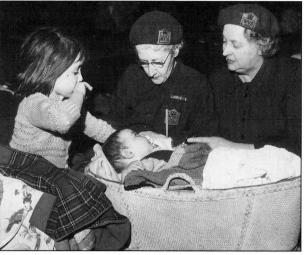

The emergency services were magnificent and the WVS helped people to settle into refugee rest centres throughout the area. Receiving tender loving care from (left) Mrs I.Dyson, who was in charge of the Cemetery Road Vestry Hall centre, and Mrs D.Thomas, Deputy County Borough Organiser of the WVS, are six months old Adrian Wright and his sister Susan, aged six.

This was The Star's front page picture. Joe Platts stands among the wreckage of his prefab at Sky Edge, Sheffield.

Homes were wrecked and this pathetic sight was typical.

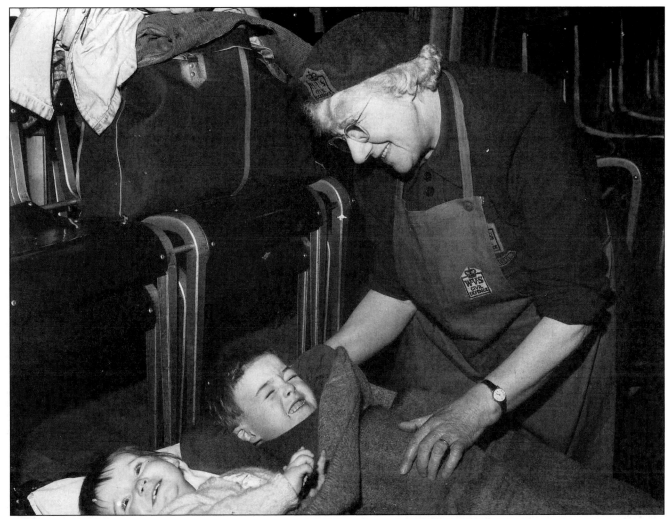

WVS helper Mrs A.Dale tucks up one-year-old Dawn Hydes and brother Russell, aged three, at Cemetery Road Vestry Hall.

Refugees David and William Trigg, and pet dog, settle into a school reception centre.

Having evacuated her home, Mrs Josephine Ellar looks over her two sleeping children, Anthony, aged two, and one-year-old John, at Hurlfield Secondary Boys School, Sheffield, which was turned into an emergency centre.

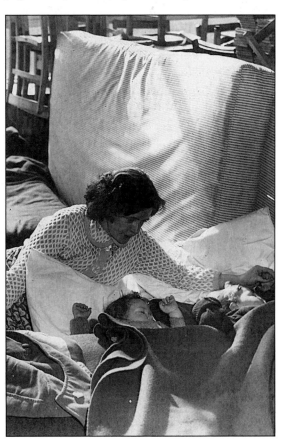

The school meals staff at Hurlfield Secondary serve food to the homeless.

Refuge at last. Mrs E.Hallam, of Arbourthorne, 15-year-old daughter Pamela and dog Rover arrive at Hurlfield Secondary School.

High winds also caused havoc in February, 1983.

...and again in 1984.

Out and About – How We Enjoyed Ourselves

FRESH AIR FOR SHEFFIELD CHILDREN.

AN OUTING AT OUGHTIBRIDGE.

A BOTANY CLASS

TEA-TIME

BAGS OF BREAD-&-BUTTER, & CAKE & BUNS.

IN THE CRICKET MATCHES, THERE WAS NO LACK OF FIELDERS

Sheffield, the city with the golden frame, has always made the best of the countryside surrounding it and none more so than when it provided a welcome, and healthy, escape from the choking confines of its fume-filled industrial areas.

Back in the early 1900s, a Fresh Air Fund was set up to help pay for outings into the countryside for poor children.

So imagine the excitement when, in July, 1907, more than 600 of them set off for a trip to Wharncliffe Side.

They travelled by special train to Oughtibridge Station and an artist from The Star went with them to record the day's activities for the next edition of the paper.

Angling has always had a passionate following in South Yorkshire and Sheffield fishermen were responsible for the first Act of Parliament passed to protect coarse fish.

The Mundella Act of 1878 gave coarse fish a legal status and fixed a close season from March 15 to June 16. In drawing up his Bill, Anthony John Mundella, MP for Brightside, Sheffield, embodied the ideas of Sheffield Anglers.

It seems odd in this day and age that some of these anglers from the Exchange Works Fishing Club, pictured in 1914 at a match in Ely, are wearing collars and ties.

morality—about what is locally and universally the right Moral End—they are, before long, almost certain to fall immorally fighting.—"Daily Mirror."

UGLY PLACES.
One for Barnsley.

Dear Sir,—You mentioned a day or two back, something about ugly places. I don't know what the general view is, but I think Barnsley is the ugliest place I was ever in.

I hope you will not disclose my address to any Barnsley person, but that is my deliberate opinion, and I have seen one or two spots.—Yours truly, Sheffield, Sept. 22nd.   TRAVELLER.

PATIENTS AT WADSLEY.
Another View.

Sir,—I have read with interest about patients at Wadsley and the suggestion of a classification scheme wanted by "Interested," in which he states he does not reflect on the doctors or attendants.

The writer of this letter to The Star in 1908 seems hardly likely to choose Barnsley for a day trip!

Mixed bathing in Sheffield! It caused quite a stir when it was introduced at Glossop Road Baths in 1912 and was sufficiently newsworthy to attract the attention of The Star's cartoonist.

day to put a stop to the whole thing.—Yours, etc.,   MAGGIE.
Sheffield, June 21, 1911.

MIXED BATHING.

Sir,—A married man asks "Is mixed bathing immoral?" He is afraid of appointments, etc. My opinion is that if appointments are made they are as likely to lead to good results as evil ones.

As to mixed bathing causing legal separations and divorces, suppose married men wore rings like the ladies the moral would be obvious. A danger zone would be created from which some men would gladly escape. Saving life is heroic; bath swimming commonplace.

Mixed bathing at sea is to be extolled, but bathing (mixed) in confined spaces, whilst not immoral, is of doubtful utility, and may be classed along with whist drivies as promiscuous and interesting.

Eliminate horseplay and swimming is useful and spectacular.

Ladies, I would add, can be taught swimming by female instructors.—Yours, etc.,
Sheffield, June 21, 1911.   J. C. T.

Husbands and Wives.

Sir,—I was pleased to see "A Married Man's" letter in answer to mine of the 17th inst. I may be wrong, but the reading of the letter suggests that it is from a married woman, who, not being a swimmer and having no intention of learning, thinks her husband might indulge in mixed bathing with other women in her absence.

I did not suggest that a married man should indulge in mixed bathing, leaving his wife at home. What I want is that husbands should take their wives and teach them to swim, and, by so doing, introduce a beautiful, joyous, healthful, and clean form of recreation.

My motto is the same as "A Married Man's"—"what is good for the goose," etc. Why should a married man have his delightful half-hour's swim and not encourage the wife who has been less fortunate than our girls of to-day in having an opportunity of learning?

It is not every woman, married or single, who can afford to pay for admission to baths and another 1s. per lesson for private tuition, or even join a ladies' club, although I admit some ladies of Sheffield are making great strides to encourage swimming amongst their own sex.

I think after a few years' careful coaching some of our City Fathers...

Mixed bathing created quite a splash in The Star's readers' letters column. Would it lead to divorces?

TELEGRAPH AND STAR, TUESDAY EVENING, JUNE 18, 1929.

FAMILY GATHERINGS AT GLOSSOP ROAD BATHS.

A large number of Sheffield families are now taking advantage of the mixed bathing facilities at Glossop Road Baths to enjoy a cool evening.

By 1929, it had become much more acceptable for swimmers of both sexes to jump into the pool together.

DISCORD OVER SUNDAY MUSIC IN SHEFFIELD PARKS

But if mixed bathing was controversial, a proposal that live Sunday music should be allowed in Sheffield's parks was even more of a talking point.

Some people saw it as the work of the devil and others regarded it as an ideal way to brighten up a dull Sunday.

One letter writer to The Star thought it would "keep many people from going into the country and getting beer."

Another thought that if music was allowed, it wouldn't be long before people would be asking for Sunday football and cricket...

The Star took a poll among its readers and the majority were against. Eventually, the Council vetoed the proposal by 39 votes to 12.

SUNDAY MUSIC.

Shall Bands Play in the Parks?

COUNCIL DISCUSSION.

Arguments For and Against the Proposal.

The agenda of business to be transacted at the Sheffield City Council, which was held at the Town Hall this afternoon, was not a very heavy one, and a long sitting was not expected.

The question of outstanding importance was the proposed scheme of the General Purposes and Parks Committee for the provision of band performances in certain parks on Sundays, which has created so much controversy throughout the city.

A shoal of protests against the proposal had been received from religious bodies and other rigorous adherents of Sunday observance, and it was generally felt that the committee's recommendation would be rejected by the Council.

It was mentioned that 122 petitions, containing 13,671 signatures, against Sunday music had been received. The petitions included one sent on behalf of the parishioners of Walkley, containing 222 signatures.

A resolution was read from the British Socialist Party supporting the proposal.

Alderman Senior introduced the question. "I expect we shall have a lot of talk on this resolution," he ———ly re———rked. "before we have

SUNDAY MUSIC IN THE PARKS.

Sir,—Where I come from, seven miles this side of Manchester—Denton and Haughton Green—we have had bands in the open spaces on Sunday afternoons for above thirty years, and I have seen occasions when we have taken about £10 for the benefit of the Manchester Royal Infirmary and Hospitals.

I see no harm in having bands playing in the parks in Sheffield, and it would keep many people from going into the country and getting beer.

There are some folk who never go to a place of worship, and plenty of the men of Sheffield who have to work on Sundays would be glad to hear the music when they have finished their work.—Yours, etc.,   AN OLD BANDSMAN.
Sheffield, July 8, 1912.

Bands, and What Then?

Sir,—My only objection in regard to Sunday band performances is because of the small selection of places where the bands will play and the price to be paid to go to hear them. The beginning of such performances means more than music; it means all kinds of meetings to follow, as they will claim such right as ratepayers.—Yours, etc.,   A. F.
Sheffield, July 8, 1912.

The Services at Kirk Braddon.

Sir,—I have read your letter from "Reform," who asks for services and congregations similar to those seen at Kirk Braddon, Isle of Man. I am astonished. Does he mean it seriously? I . . . . . . ice the opinion

SUNDAY BANDS.

Sir,—I wonder if it has occurred to those who favour Sunday bands how many more shops it will cause to open on the first day of the week. I allude to the "sweet" shops in the vicinity and upon the routes to the various parks.

Yesterday I saw several small boys devouring ice-cream sandwiches outside a sweet shop, and whilst wondering why such shops were permitted to defy the law by opening on Sundays, it occurred to me what a quantity of ice-cream, sweets, tobacco, etc., will be bought on Band Sundays, which otherwise would not be, for it is just the people who would flock to a Sunday Band Concert (I speak of the majority, not the exceptions), who would have no hesitation in buying these unnecessaries on Sunday, and, further, who would make the streets and parks hideous with the litter of paper wrappers and empty cardboard boxes.—Yours, etc.,   REST-DAY.
Sheffield, July 8th, 1912.

Southport and Sheffield.

Sir,—With regard to Sunday music, is Southport, with its well-known spirit of Evangelicanism, really more irreligious than Sheffield? If not, how is it thousands of people have the opportunity of listening to the municipal band or of visiting the picture palaces on Sunday evenings after the churches are cleared?

Surely the people of Sheffield as a whole cannot subscribe to the narrow spirit of those who fear the baneful effects of good Sunday music on church attendance. Let them determine to cater for the wants of the people in every legitimate form, and ignore the present-day representatives of Snodgrass, Pecksniff, and Co.—Yours, etc.,   MEERSBROOK.
Southport, July 8th, 1912.

GRAPH AND STAR, THURSDAY EVENING,

THE CITY COUNCIL MEETING

ALL ABOUT SUNDAY MUSIC

AW NIVVER RI-MEMBERS A MOOR 'EATED DISCUSSHIN - JUST T'SOORT O SUBJECT TO SET EM ON END!

A SERMON

AT TEA

OUTSIDE

WHILE IN THE THROES OF THE DISCUSSION COUNC. BESCOBY FEELS FOR HIS RECENTLY DISCARDED BEARD

Blackpool, Cleethorpes, the Derbyshire countryside? A John Watts (Lambert Street) works outing in 1919 but the destination is not recorded.

Phone Message to "Star."

FIELD DAY AT DRONFIELD WOODHOUSE.

A happy band of children from Hanover Street Chapel, who enjoyed the field day frolics at Dronfield Woodhouse, on Saturday. The Gloopers sign is much in evidence.

Fun and frolics at Dronfield Woodhouse in 1929.

NO 10.30 DRINKS.

Sheffield Justices Refuse to Extend Closing Hour.

MINISTERS WIN.

All Denominations Join in Opposing "The Trade."

Ministers and clergy of all denominations attended the Sheffield Licensing Sessions, to-day, to oppose any extension of licensed hours. An equally strong body of representatives of the Trade were present to protect their interests,

Telegraph and Star.

Saturday, July 20, 1912.

THE WEEK-END HABIT.

WHENEVER clergymen or denominational ministers foregather there is not long to wait for a denunciation of the nation's growing "love of pleasure" and a recital of the direful effects which it is supposed must inevitably follow. At such a gathering this week special reference was made to the increasing popularity of what has come to be known as the "week-end habit." This, it is asserted, is the "mad pursuit of pleasure" in its worst form. Let us look at the matter dispassionately. To begin with one might imagine from the speeches of some of these worthy gentlemen that the majority of people spent the week-end away from home, whereas it is only a minority, and a small minority at that. The habitual week-ender is usually the man who is in a position to finish his week's business early on Friday and resume it on Monday or Tuesday. Comparatively few men are so happily placed. Their "week-end" example may be good or it may be bad, it all depends on the point of view.

What those who denounce the "week-end

Four Hundred Sheffield Drunks In Three Nights

Closing time at Sheffield pubs in 1921 was 10pm and when the brewery trade applied for an extension until 10.30pm, the churches lined up to object.

The trade's grounds for the application were that many workers, particularly in the east end of the city, worked 2pm-10pm shifts and couldn't get a drink when they finished.

An extension would also be beneficial to those who had been to cinemas and theatres.

The objectors said they did not want to go back to the bad old days before the war when there were long hours of opening and, in the evenings, "a great deal of drunkenness."

They also claimed there had been in increase in drunkenness since the closing time had been extended to 10pm.

The objectors had taken a count in the city centre over three Saturday nights and the number of drunks had totalled more than 400.

The magistrates unanimously agreed to turn the extension down.

Weekend visits to the seaside and country were becoming more popular in 1912 but the church wasn't entirely happy about the "weekend habit", fearing that it would lead to a decline in church attendances.

In its leader column, The Star took a sympathetic line towards the trippers, saying it could see no harm in people wanting a change of scene and plenty of fresh air.

"However loud the lamentations of the churches and chapels may be in regard to this Sunday exodus, we fail to see how they can break the people from the habit they have acquired."

Sheffield and Betting.

Sir,—I read with great interest the remarks made by Inspector Denton at the recent commission, and can heartily endorse what he said. It is simply appalling to see the amount of betting going on in this city and mostly the offenders are those who cannot afford either to lose or be fleeced of their money. For a long time now it has been a well-known fact that almost the sole topic of the buzz of talk one hears at the Relief Pay stations is racing. I have heard a crowd of boys from 15 to 16 in Campo Lane animatedly discussing the prospects of certain horses, and also the amounts of their bets on same. But we cannot expect otherwise seeing that the parents of these boys are encouraging them in the habit.

It is simply awful to think of food tickets being sold for money in order to bet whilst half-starved and nearly naked children are at home. And now the mania is actually extending itself to women! Fancy a mother of a family discussing the merits of certain horses and spending badly-needed money in that way instead of darning the numerous holes in her husband's socks and attending to the wants of her family. Such people want hounding out of the city, and certainly are not fit to claim the sacred

culosis, for instance, goes up when foodstuffs are dear, and comes down when foodstuffs are cheap and plentiful."

ARCHBISHOP AND SEX QUESTION.

The Archbishop of York, addressing a men's gathering at Scarborough, yesterday, on "A National Crisis," said it was no exaggeration to say that the crisis affecting the moral health of the community was whether they were to retain the Christian standard or give way to the pagan on the sex question. Sexual instinct and indulgence was being invested with a sort of romantic interest, and in certain circles with a very great and absorbing scientific interest.

His Grace said they must educate those instincts as part of the normal education of the child and this education must be early, frank and pure. Some of them would be a great deal surprised if they overheard the conversation of multitudes of educated young men and women on this particular theme, and equally surprised at some of the conclusions to which some of them came.

"CHARLIE'S" LITTLE LOVE AFFAIRS.

Betting was causing great concern in 1923, as this letter to The Star illustrates.

The "sex question", much of a taboo subject in those days, was raised by the Archbishop of York in 1923.

Star Beauties!

The Star's in-paper beauty competitions had great appeal in the early 1900s and attracted entrants from throughout the paper's South Yorkshire, North East Derbyshire and North Notts circulation area.

Entrants had to submit their own photographs and for this competition in 1923 there was a top prize of £100 (big money in those days) for the overall winner and £10 for the girl winning her division.

Presumably, having a photograph good enough to submit must have been something of a problem at that time. Hence the "important notice" at the foot of the entry details which warned that some of the pictures sent in couldn't be reproduced successfully enough to give the competitor a fair chance.

The minimum age limit was 15 and there was no upper limit.

BARNSLEY, MEXBORO', AND BASSETLAW BEAUTY CONTEST.

M.383—Miss Nellie Mason. M.384—Mrs. A. H. Hewitt. M385—Miss Annie Laurence. BL.386—Miss S. Sutton. BL.387—Miss Gwendoline Bagaley. BL.388—Miss Dollie Bagaley. BL.389—Miss A. Elliot. BL.390—Mrs. E. ...Gree... BL.391—Miss Edith M...timer. B.392 Miss Elsie Fletcher.

OLD-FASHIONED

How People of Sheffield Spent the Yuletide.

IDEAL HOLIDAY.

Heavy Fall of Snow Makes City Like the Festive Cards.

FEAST OF PLEASURE.

Sheffield has had an ideal Christmas. On Monday evening, Christmas Eve, the centre of the city was crowded with people; in the main thoroughfares pedestrians moved about with great difficulty; the pavements were thronged with people, and the roads were literally packed with crowded tramcars, taxis, and other motor vehicles.

The shops had a great time. From morning until late at night most of them were full of people, and the huge parcels which fathers and mothers carried home were evidence of the heavy purchases which many of them had made, mostly for the Christmas table or for the children. There were many indications that money was much more plentiful this year than it was twelve months ago, and this in spite of the fact that there are still something like 20,000 workers unemployed or only partially employed in the city.

Places of amusement were packed, and the "Aladdin" pantomime at the Theatre Royal had a great send-off.

Frost and Sun.

Christmas morning the weather was delightful; sharp air m

playing for Newark Town against Notts For

FESTIVE CITY.

Christmas Spirit in Streets of Sheffield.

HOLIDAY TRAFFIC.

Possibility of Fine Weather To=morrow.

CROWDED SHOPS.

All records for Christmas traffic have been broken this year, and the excursion trains leaving London to=day for the Midlands, Scotland and other parts were packed.

In Sheffield thousands of workers began a week's holiday to=day, and the festive spirit was apparent everywhere.

Happy dense crowds thronged the principal streets of the city to-day. Workmen accompanied

Even with 25,000 people out of work in Sheffield, Christmas 1923 was a joyous occasion according to a report in The Star and on Christmas Eve "happy, dense crowds thronged the principal streets of the city".

There were 150 weddings over the Christmas period and the better-off spent the festive period at the East Coast resorts.

And it was a White Christmas, with heavy snow falling on Christmas Day afternoon.

Out on a ramble in 1925 are these girls from Sheffield's Sharrow Lane School.

The Star organised a matinee of "Peter Pan" at the Lyceum Theatre in February, 1926.

SINGALONG WITH THE STAR

Easter 1927 and so many Sheffielders wanted to get away because of the warm, sunny weather that 15,000 descended on the Midland Station on Easter Monday.

More than 1,000 who had opted for Blackpool were turned away because the trains were full.

From Sheffield Victoria Station, more than 10,000 had left before noon for Cleethorpes, Scarborough, Bridlington, Harrogate, Manchester and Wetherby (for the races).

Thousands more boarded trains at the Midland Station for Derbyshire.

And as an Easter treat for stay-at-home football fans, The Star organised a programme of mass singing for the Wednesday v Burnley football match at Hillsborough.

There were 16 songs and the newspaper printed the words of all of them. They ranged from "O God, our help in ages past" to "Trot-Trot-Trot-Trotter, Score a little goal for me."

Jimmy Trotter was a Wednesday favourite at the time and finished top of the country's goalscoring charts that season with 37.

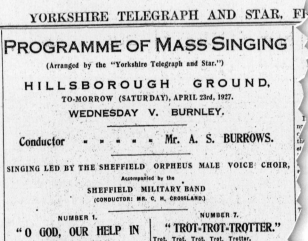

The Star organises community singing at Hillsborough.

Overwhelming

DEMAND EXCEEDS TRAIN SUPPLY.

1,000 FARES RETURNED.

CARNIVAL OF HOLIDAY SPORT.

FOOTBALL---RACING---FLYING.

THE one thing needful—perfect weather—crowned the hopes of Easter Monday holidaymakers to such a degree as to bring about phenomenal scenes.

The demand for travel rose to such a height that at one time something like 15,000 were crowded in and around the L.M. and S. Station in Sheffield, and about 1,000 people who had booked for Blackpool could not be carried and had to have their fares refunded.

These conditions were reflected with lesser emphasis at the L.N.E.R. Station.

The sports element in the day's attractions was at full strength, and there was a full programme of football.

PHENOMENAL EASTER SCENES.

Train Facilities Exhausted at Sheffield.

passengers had been dealt with some sixteen special trains would be required.

Station Jammed with People.

From the L.N.E.R. Victoria Station some 10,000 people were taken before noon to Scarborough, Cleethorpes, Market Rasen, Weatherby (for s) Brid on (five trains carrying

Fifteen thousand people at Sheffield Midland Station.

What the girls were wearing on the beach at Easter, 1927. The weather was "perfect".

EASTERTIDE TREK TO SEA AND COUNTRY.

BEST ROUTES.

(By the Sports Editor).

Honk, honk! Tinkle-inkle! Bzzz! Wo-OOST
It is all jazz nowadays, even the Song of the
Road. When I was a boy out for my first
tourlet, with a shilling (borrowed), and
rackety bicycle loaned by a far too trusting
friend, accompanied by a schoolmate mounted
on his sister's Dreadnought, the road was silent
except when we fell off. In ten miles we might
pass a farm waggon, or a doctor's trap, and
that was about all.

Those were the
days, but we sha...

How writing styles change! The
first paragraph of this Easter 1927 article, about
days out for cyclists, would no doubt make The
Star's present sports editor wince...

BOUND FOR SKEGNESS.

SHEFFIELD DAILY TELEGRAPH'S ANNUAL OUTING FOR SHEFFIELD'S CHILDREN

No. 4 603

The scene on Victoria Station, Sheffield, this morning, where 500 Sheffield children were given a send-off by the Lord Mayor and Lady Mayoress, on the first of the outings to Skegness under the auspices of the "Sheffield T..." side excursions scheme.

Both Sheffield papers, The Star and the Telegraph, have always played a leading
role in the community over the years, showing great enthusiasm for charitable
activities and deserving causes.

Here, children set off for Skegness in June, 1929, as guests of the Sheffield
Telegraph seaside excursions scheme. Even the train driver and fireman get in
on the action.

"ICE-CREAM STRIKE."

Rotherham Sellers' Complaint.

An "ice-cream strike" was declared at Rother-
ham to-day by 21 men, of whom 18 are single.
They are employed by the Eldorado Ice-cream
Co., who have a branch depot at Clough Road,

The strike has been declared on the grounds
of "excessive" low wages, and also that the men
who sell the product of the company in the
streets are held responsible for "softs," which
is ice-cream that has become practically liquid
and therefore is not purchased by consumers.

The men are paid 3s. per day for a seven-
day... plus... in the £ bonus. Till a recent

Just as the summer of 1929 was hotting up, ice
cream salesmen at Rotherham went on strike.
They were grumbling about low wages and the
fact that they had to stand the cost of "softs" –
ice cream that had gone runny and couldn't be
sold.

YORKSHIRE TELEGRAPH AND STAR, TUESDAY EVENING

OPENING OF THE SHEFFIELD PARKS BAND SEASON.

A section of the crowd which gathered in Weston Park yesterday to hear the City of Sheffield Police Band and the Apollo Quartette, who gave the opening performance of the season's music in the parks.

| BEN TURNER. | A DOCTOR'S VIEW. | SNAKE BITES. |
| NEW SECRETARY FOR | Is Educational System | ZOO KEEPER' |

The new 1929 music in the parks season started at Weston Park in June and
attracted a large crowd.

The Star's photographer went to the seaside on August Bank Holiday, 1931, and snapped this happy bunch of streetwise Sheffielders.

SHEFFIELD GIRLS LEAVE FOR THE ORCHARDS.

Another party of Sheffield unemployed girls departed to-day for fruit picking in Lincolnshire. They numbered 15, and they were conveyed in a lorry by Mr. K. Beezley, a fruit grower, of Long Sutton, by whom they will be employed for the next three or four weeks.

At one time the Lincolnshire fruit-growers nearly always had London girls to assist them in the seasonal rush, but in recent years they have had a preference for girls from the provinces. Mr. Beezley apparently finds the young women of Sheffield satisfactory workers, as this is the third time he has undertaken their transport to Long Sutton.

To-day they travelled via Cranwell, and it was intended to halt there in order that the girls could see the aerodrome and watch the aero-

Off to pick fruit in 1929 – and also to watch aeroplanes.

A trip organised by The Star and Sheffield Telegraph to see the Cunard liner Samaria at Liverpool in 1929 was popular with readers and there were long queues for tickets outside Thomas Cook and Son an hour before the office opened.

The staff of Messrs. Thos. Cook and Son, Ltd., dealing with the rush of applicants for tickets this morning.

BIG BOOKINGS FOR TRIP TO GREAT LINER.

Coupon for Next Thursday's Excursion Now Available to "Star" Readers.

THE opportunity afforded readers of the "Sheffield Daily Telegraph" to inspect the Cunard liner, Samaria, at Liverpool, on Thursday next, is now

may go on the excursion, and under these circumstances it will not be possible to make arrangements for tea. Visitors will have to make their own arrangements in this respect.

Below: 1932…and no games in Sheffield's parks on Sundays.

1946 – and Sunday games in Sheffield's parks get the go-ahead at last, but only after 2pm.

The motion was approved with a majority of one after a long debate, with objectors claiming that the quiet of the parks would be "atomised" by the playing of games.

On August Bank Holiday, 1946, thousands poured into Derbyshire, a group of girls splashed about in a local bathing pool.

pleaded "Not guilty" to driv

The Young Train Spotters Were a Little Too Keen

A BOOK of engine numbers and pictures of trains was handed to Mr. Brian Pye-Smith, chairman of Sheffield Juvenile Court to-day.

He glanced through it, then asked its 13-year-old owner: Was the siding near Aston Street a good place for engine-spotting.

It was, replied the boy.

Then he and the four boys with him—two aged 13 and the others 11 and 12—were each fined 2s. 6d. for trespassing on the railway and warned not to do it again.

'YOU DON'T CARE'

A 12-year-old boy, one of five accused of housebreaking, was told by Mr. Pye-Smith: "You don't care one bit for the feelings of your father."

The boy, stated to have appeared before the court twice previously, was said by his father, an invalid, to be quite well behaved at home.

With another boy, aged 11, he was sent to the remand home for three weeks, the period for which the case was adjourned. The othee three boys, all aged 12, were allowed to go home.

They all admitted stealing a pair of binoculars and two pen-knives worth £2 15s. and 15s. in cash from the house.

BROTHERS ACCUSED

Two brothers, aged 14 and 11, and another boy aged 10, were stated to have stolen money and articles from cubicles at Hillsborough baths on a number of occasions.

The two younger boys admitted stealing 10s. in money, and a watch and fountain pen, worth £3 1s.

All three admitted stealing a watch worth £2 4s. and 1s. 4d. in money, and asked for other other offences to be taken into consideration.

The case was adjourned for a fortnight for a probation officer's report

You set off to go train-spotting – and finish up in Juvenile Court. Hard lines for these young "anoraks" – the word hadn't been invented then – in 1950.

Annie Gets He Day At The Sea

Eighty - nine - year - old Mrs. Annie Ogden, of Attercliffe. gave a tug at her bright green cardigan, straightened her beads, and after a glance at the countryside from the Cleethorpes-bound train, said: "What am I going to do when I get there? Why, go on the roundabouts!"

SHE was the oldest of 350 old-age pensioners who went to the seaside today e first trip of the year

The Telegraph and Star Old Folks' Fund is still going strong after 50 years and this trip for 350 pensioners in July 1950 was the first it organised to the seaside.

Whether 89-year-old Annie Ogden finished up on the roundabouts is not recorded.

Lunchtime rock 'n' roll sessions at the Locarno Ballroom, Sheffield, were popular in 1957. Putting on the style are these two young jivers dressed in the latest fashion, close-fitting tartan and brightly coloured slacks.

Rock 'n' roll was sweeping the country in the Sixties and The Star and Telegraph, always keen to keep abreast of the latest trends, organised a contest for local rockers in August, 1960. Having a swinging time in the finals are the winners, Adrienne Gregory and Derek Burbeary.

Nodding-off grandads in jackets and trilbies, babies with sand in their eyes and everywhere else...and hardly a spare inch of space anywhere. Scarborough beach in 1966. And what's the betting that at least half of them were from our region?

Stepping out into the new year are these youngsters at Sheffield's Endcliffe Park, photographed on January 1, 1967.

Sheffield's Millhouses Park in 1968.

The model boat lake at Sheffield's Firth Park in 1969 and this lad is trying to retrieve his yacht with a plank of wood.

Sheffield Midland Station 1971 and holidaymakers head for the seaside and sunshine (hopefully).

Don't you rock me, daddy-O. Just look at those sideburns...and that jacket...and those drainpipes. Sheffield and District Vintage Rock 'n' Roll Society members all shook up in 1976.

South Yorkshire people letting their hair down on holiday on the East Coast have been the subject of many a feature in The Star over the years and in 1975 a reporter and photographer went to Skegness to interview landladies. The beaming, welcoming smile of one of them, Mrs Joyce Faulkner, of Algitha Road, proved irresistible for the cameraman, Stuart Hastings, who is still going strong at Sheffield Newspapers.

Meat and two veg, a pot of tea, apple pie...then off to the disco. Funsters (as newspapers used to call them in those days) pictured at an East Coast holiday camp, so popular with South Yorkshire holidaymakers, in the early 1980s.

Paddling pool here we come! Millhouses Park, 1983.

Then Along Came the Wireless... and the Telephone... and the Telly

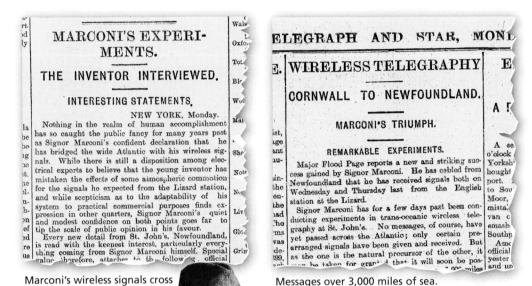

MARCONI'S EXPERIMENTS.

THE INVENTOR INTERVIEWED.

INTERESTING STATEMENTS.

NEW YORK, Monday.

Nothing in the realm of human accomplishment has so caught the public fancy for many years past as Signor Marconi's confident declaration that he has bridged the wide Atlantic with his wireless signals. While there is still a disposition among electrical experts to believe that the young inventor has mistaken the effects of some atmospheric commotion for the signals he expected from the Lizard station, and while scepticism as to the adaptability of his system to practical commercial purposes finds expression in other quarters, Signor Marconi's quiet and modest confidence on both points goes far to tip the scale of public opinion in his favour.

Every new detail from St. John's, Newfoundland, is read with the keenest interest, particularly everything coming from Signor Marconi himself. Special value, therefore, attaches to the following official

Marconi's wireless signals cross the Atlantic.

ELEGRAPH AND STAR, MONL

WIRELESS TELEGRAPHY

CORNWALL TO NEWFOUNDLAND.

MARCONI'S TRIUMPH.

REMARKABLE EXPERIMENTS.

Major Flood Page reports a new and striking success gained by Signor Marconi. He has cabled from Newfoundland that he has received signals both on Wednesday and Thursday last from the English station at the Lizard.

Signor Marconi has for a few days past been conducting experiments in trans-oceanic wireless telegraphy at St. John's. No messages, of course, have yet passed across the Atlantic; only certain pre-arranged signals have been given and received. But as the one is the natural precursor of the other, it may be taken for granted that it will soon be possible...

Messages over 3,000 miles of sea.

Marconi in Newfoundland on December 12, 1901.

Picture courtesy of Marconi Wireless Telegraph Co Ltd.

S is for Signals Across the Sea

It was one of the most significant stories for years and thoroughly deserved the amount of space The Star gave it on December 16, 1901.

Italian Guglielmo Marconi had managed to bridge the Atlantic with wireless signals, confirming the discovery he had made five years earlier that messages could be carried by electric current without wires.

Before leaving England for St John's, Newfoundland, the modest young inventor had arranged for the long-distance wireless station at the Lizard, Cornwall, to signal him the letter S repeatedly for three hours.

Once over there, he cabled Cornwall to say he was ready. The article in The Star quoted Marconi as saying: "On Thursday, I received indications of the

signals at 12.30 and with certainty and remarkable clearness at 1.10 when quite a succession of S's were received with distinctness."

It was a remarkable breakthrough and laid the foundations for the communications revolution we are experiencing today.

Now who would have imagined that Marconi's discovery would lead to this – a portable wireless to take with you on a picnic? All you had to do to listen in before getting stuck into the potted meat sandwiches was "sling an aerial lightly across a convenient branch."

This 1923 advert from The Star boasts that the Marconiphone is "easily packed along with the other picnic appliances." Even in those days, the marketing men knew how to come up with a slick selling line…

But, at £22 8s (about £3,300 in today's money), how many takers would there have been?

Take a Marconiphone with you

This summer no outing is complete without a jolly Wireless entertainment contributed from a distant Broadcasting Station and heard to perfection through the popular Marconiphone. A Marconiphone is easily packed along with the other picnic appliances. To listen-in, all you have to do is to sling an aerial lightly across a convenient branch.

Take a Marconiphone with you. Its absolute reliability is attested by the signature "G. Marconi" on the case.

In consequence of the reduction in the price of Valves and Telephones, the Marconiphone V2 can now be purchased for £22 8s. complete with headphones, valves, batteries, etc.

The Marconiphone
The Triumph of the Master Mind

Your local dealer can supply you. In case of difficulty apply to:

MARCONI'S WIRELESS TELEGRAPH COMPANY, LIMITED
Marconiphone Dept., Marconi House, Strand, London, W.C.2
Coates Building, Castle Street, BELFAST; 2 Ludgate Hill, BIRMINGHAM; Principality Buildings, Queen Street, CARDIFF; 41 St. Vincent Place, GLASGOW; "B" Building, The Temple, Dale Street, LIVERPOOL; 10 Cumberland Street, Deansgate, MANCHESTER; 38 Northumberland Street, NEWCASTLE-ON-TYNE.

CHRISTMAS RUINED BY 'AMATEURS'

The invention of the wireless was not without its teething problems and interference ruined Christmas listening for many in our region in 1923.

The interference came from "unskilled users" of valve sets who received them as Christmas presents and were trying them out for the first time.

The writer of one article in The Star wrote pleadingly: "The lifelong gratitude of all listeners would be earned by the inventor of a device which, when attached to a valve set, would absolutely prevent radiation taking place from it."

Listeners were also disturbed by "loud irregular cracklings", caused by wireless waves originating from the sparks of passing trams.

This was especially bad for people living near tramway junctions with automatic points.

But the growth of wireless was phenomenal and, through its columns, The Star played a leading part in the development of facilities and improved reception.

Dealing with Some Intrusive Noises.

SCREEN DEVICES.

Special Difficulties for City Receivers.

(By H. Lloyd, M.Eng.)

It is very regrettable that the Christmas programmes from the Broadcasting Stations have been completely spoiled to many listeners on account of interference from unskilled users of valve sets. This trouble has been experienced all over the country, owing no doubt to the large number of newly acquired sets being tried out for the first time at this period. The lifelong gratitude of all listeners would be earned by the inventor of a device which, when attached to a valve set, would absolutely prevent radiation taking place from it. Incidentally, if such an attachment were made compulsory, as it most certainly should be, and a patent were secured on it, the inventor might retire on his fortune very quickly. Here is a chance for the wireless experts with which the country seems to abound.

Another trouble which many city listeners are encountering immediately they instal a wireless receiver is also one due to noises which do not form part of the transmissions from the Broadcasting stations. Sometimes these noises consist of loud irregular cracklings, and sometimes they consist of a continuous buzzing sound. The former

Christmas spoilt by interference.

WIRELESS MAD.

Sheffield Dealers Tell of Rush for Sets.

GREAT GIFT HUNT.

Crystal Sets Being Favoured by the Ladies.

("Yorkshire Telegraph & Star" Special.)

Keen in their search for suitable Christmas ... Sheffield ... to the city an ...

Sheffield goes wireless mad in 1923.

Response to Demand Voiced in "Star."

("Yorkshire Telegraph & Star" Special.)

The announcement that wireless enthusiasts in Sheffield are to have better facilities than those at present in existence will be received with great pleasure by all who are interested in this popular subject. It has been frequently explained in the columns of the "Yorkshire Telegraph and Star" that Sheffield, being so far from a broadcasting station, was debarred the advantages enjoyed by other important centres, despite the fact that Sheffield has interested itself in wireless probably more than any other city of its size.

It was stated in these columns only a few days ago that people in other towns, by using a

The Star campaigned strongly for the development of wireless broadcasting in the area.

Hill, Sheffield.
Tel.—Central 1287.

BROADCASTING.

To-day's Programmes from the Stations.

SHEFFIELD OPENING.

SHEFFIELD RELAY STATION (350 metres). Official opening:—

8. 0.—James Hoskins, 'cello solo, playing Aberdeen, will be relayed to Sheffield.

8.10.—Sir William Clegg, C.B.E., will open proceedings.

8.30.—The Lord Mayor, Alderman A. Blanchard, will officially open the station.

8.40.—Dorothea Rodgers, L.R.A.M., will sing from the Sheffield Relay Station.

8.50.—A short address by the Master Cutler, James Neill, Esq.

9. 0.—Gertrude Johnson, soprano, singing from Bournemouth, will be relayed to Sheffield.

9.10.—Mr. J. C. W. Reith will introduce Major-General Sir Frederick Sykes, G.B.E., K.C.B., C.M.G.

9.20.—Major-General Sir Frederick Sykes, G.B.E., K.C.B., C.M.G., will be simultaneously broadcast to all stations.

9.30.—Vote of thanks to be proposed by President of the Chamber of Commerce and seconded by Mr. H. L. Cooper, editor of the "Yorkshire Telegraph and Star."

MANCHESTER.
(385 metres, call 2 ZY.)

3.30-4.50—Concert. 5.0—Women's hour. 5.Farmers' weather report. 5.30—Children's hour. 6.Orchestra. 7.0—News: "Seen on the Screen," S.B.London. 7.45—Orchestra. 8.0—Elsie Cochran, soprano. 8.15—Orchestra. 8.45—G. W. Kerr, B.A., LL.B. "Anticipations: or, What will the World be like in 2000 A.D." 9.0—Silvio Sideli, bass. 9.10—Cochran. 9.20, Major-General Sir Frederick Sykes, G.B.E., K.C.B., C.M.G., speaking at the opening of ... from Sheffield. Silvio Sideli.

Sheffield got its own relay station to improve reception in November, 1923, and this was the first day's programme.

SHEFFIELD WOMAN'S FEAR.

Landlord Might Hear Her on His Wireless Set.

In the Summons Court at Sheffied, to-day, the appicant for an ejectment order stated that the tenant (a woman) had refused to pay her rent because her landlord had put up a wireless aerial on her house, and she refused to pay until it was removed, as the landlord could hear what she was talking about in her house.

The Worksop Farmers' Union has passed a resolution urging Parliament not to extend the Daylight Saving Act or make it permanent as it was detrimental to farmers and agriculturists.

Not everyone was happy with the new invention!

PIER CONCERT FROM BLACKPOOL.

Northern listeners will hear a concert by the Royal Follies from the Central Pier, Blackpool, to-night.

NORTH REGIONAL (626 kc/s., 479.2 metres).
5.15—Children's Hour: Tom, the Keeper, tells us about poachers and such like.
6. 0—Weather and news.
6.30—Bulletin for Northern English farmers.
6.35—Eccles Borough Band; C. Jones and H. Mallinder (cornet duet); Klinton Shephard (baritone).
8. 0—Mr. H. Fairbank: The Northern Garden.
8.20—Tom Vernon's Royal Follies; Sam Brough's (Ardwick Empire) Band; Sam Rayne, Stan Paskin, Nan Kennedy, Anna Clive, Kitty Prince, William Aspden, Harry and Mac, and Cecil Reid; from Blackpool.
9. 0—London Regional.
10.20—Weather and news.
10.35—North of England news.
10.40-12.0—National.

NATIONAL NORTH REGION (995 kc/s., 301.5 metres).
5.15—Northern Studio Orchestra. 6.0-9.15—National. 9.20-10.30—National.

NATIONAL (193 kc/s., 1,554.4 metres).
5.15—Children's Hour. 6.0—Time (Big Ben), weather, news, and bulletin for farmers.
6.30—Time; The Italian and Spanish songs of Wolf, sung by Winifred Radford (soprano) and Sumner Austin (baritone). 6 50—"Pride and Prejudice," read by Mr.

Ronald Watkins. 7.20—The weekly bulletin of special notices. 7.30—The Past: "Encumbrance or Inspiration" by Mr. H. C. Wood.
8.0—Suitable Songs, Part 7, arranged and produced by Gordon McConnel, with Parry Jones, Garda Hall, Foster Richardson, and Edgar Lane (compere); Walter Randall at the piano; the Revue Chorus, and the B.B.C. Theatre Orchestra. 9.0—Time, weather, and news. 9.15—Shipping. 9.20—The Way of the World, by Mr. Vernon Bartlett.
9.35—Kate Winter (soprano); Angus Morrison (pianoforte): 10.30-12.0—B.B.C. Dance Orchestra. (Time at 11.30.)

NATIONAL LONDON REGION (1,148 kc/s., 261.3 metres).
5.15—North National. 6.0-9.15—National. 9.20-10.40—National.

LONDON REGIONAL (842 kc/s., 356.3 metres).
6.0—Weather, News, and Bulletin for Farmers.
6.30—Regional Bulletin for Far... 5—North ... 8.0—...

A typical night's wireless programmes in 1932.

A new studio, on Castle Street, Sheffield, opened in April, 1925, 15 months after the relay station, and special rooms were provided for artists taking part in the programmes.

The opening ceremony was told that Sheffield had 64,000 people with the facility to listen to the wireless.

A young listener is all wired up. Just look at those headphones...

Sheffield Relay Station in 1931.

The Early Days of Television

An Ekco radio from the 1930s.

New technology 1909 style.

A Sheffield radio detector van in 1947. It was estimated that of the city's 170,000 radio licences at the time, at least 15,500 were attributable to the van's activities.

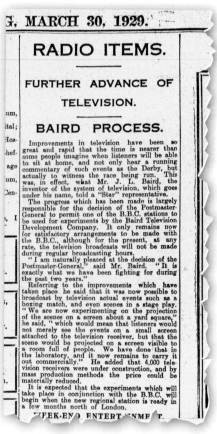

G, MARCH 30, 1929.

RADIO ITEMS.

FURTHER ADVANCE OF TELEVISION.

BAIRD PROCESS.

Improvements in television have been so great and rapid that the time is nearer than some people imagine when listeners will be able to sit at home, and not only hear a running commentary of such events as the Derby, but actually to witness the race being run. This was, in effect, what Mr. J. L. Baird, the inventor of the system of television, which goes under his name, told a "Star" representative.

The progress which has been made is largely responsible for the decision of the Postmaster-General to permit one of the B.B.C. stations to be used for experiments by the Baird Television Development Company. It only remains now for satisfactory arrangements to be made with the B.B.C., although for the present, at any rate, the television broadcasts will not be made during regular broadcasting hours.

"I am naturally pleased at the decision of the Postmaster-General," said Mr. Baird. "It is exactly what we have been fighting for during the past two years."

Referring to the improvements which have taken place, he said that it was now possible to broadcast by television actual events such as a boxing match, and even scenes in a stage play.

"We are now experimenting on the projection of the scenes on a screen about a yard square," he said, "which would mean that listeners would not merely see the events on a small screen attached to the television receiver, but that the scene would be projected on a screen visible to a room full of people. We have done that in the laboratory, and it now remains to carry it out commercially." He added that 4,000 television receivers were under construction, and by mass production methods the price could be materially reduced.

It is expected that the experiments which will take place in conjunction with the B.B.C. will begin when the new regional station is ready in a few months north of London.

WEEK-END ENTERTAINMENT.

HE'S INVENTED SOMETHING CALLED TELEVISION...

You can just imagine the conversation in pub tap rooms throughout our region on the night of March 30, 1929.

Some bloke called Baird had invented a system called television and had told a representative from The Star how quickly the system was developing.

So quickly, he said, that the time was nearer than people imagined when it would be possible for listeners to sit at home listening to a horse race commentary AND watch the race being run on a screen.

Pie in the sky or what? It would certainly have been a talking point for the regulars down at the Dog and Duck.

Warming to his theme, Mr Baird went on to tell our reporter that it was now possible to broadcast by television actual events such as a boxing match "and even scenes in a stage play."

He added that 4,000 television receivers were under construction and the price could be materially reduced by mass production methods.

We know the rest of the story. Pie in the sky was to turn into satellites in the sky and no self-respecting Dog and Duck was to be without its telly in the tap room.

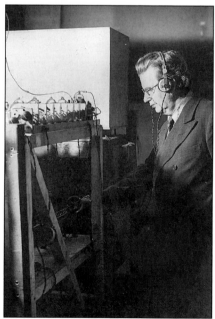

Here he is...Scottish electrical engineer John Logie Baird, the man who started it all.

An early television set.

LIMITATIONS OF TELEVISION.

Problem of Finding Subjects to Fill the Bill.

Imagine Size of Figures in a Football Relay.

FILM HANDICAPS.

(BY ALBERT SHAW.)

TELEVISION has arrived. Technicians have triumphed, and have made it possible for us to see events at a distance at the moment they happen.

It is marvellous, but when we have finished expressing our admiration we come to the all important question of how to use this modern marvel. It is not sufficient to provide a medium, and the sterner task of providing programmes for conveyance by this method remains to be explored.

At the moment we can be quite frank and admit that television is and will remain for some time the rich man's toy; i...

be used—that usually described as "interest films," travel and sports pictures, as a rule. These will undoubtedly be used, and it is even possible that eventually the B.B.C. will possess its own film unit for the making of such pictures. But these films are limited in their appeal, and cannot possibly provide anything like a major portion of television programmes.

EXISTING PROGRAMMES.

We are thus left with existing radio programmes. Glance through any programme and pick out ...would li...

But did television have the great future predicted for it? This certainly occupied the thoughts of a writer in The Star in 1931.

Television was, he said, the rich man's toy and a novelty everyone was curious to see, hence the enormous crowds at Radiolympia.

"But the time will come when the general public will be expected to join in the fun and purchase television receivers. What then?

"Before expending £50 or even £10, the general public will require convincing that television can provide entertainment. Novelty soon passes; entertainment is the need.

"When a man puts down his £10 today for a radio set, he knows that it will give him varied entertainment at most hours of the day. Can television do the same? It must before it becomes anything like as universal as radio."

By the middle and late 1950s, television sets were becoming a "must" with most families, although only the more affluent could afford one when the Queen was crowned in 1953.

Special Coronation parties were held in the homes of the "haves", with the "have nots" sitting there mesmerised during the lengthy ceremony at Westminster Abbey, cup of tea in one hand and a salmon paste sandwich in the other.

What this 1950s family was watching is not known, but it looks gripping. Mind you, it could have been the test card – or even a goldfish swimming round in a bowl. All in black and white, of course.

each, with the alternative of five days' imprisonment.

TELEVISION STATION OPENED.

Statement on Possibilities "New Art."

Television history was made, to-day, when the proceedings at the opening ceremony of the B.B.C.'s Alexandra Palace service were televised.

Major G. C. Tryon, the Postmaster-General, performed the ceremony.

Mr. R. C. Norman, Chairman of the B.B.C., who presided, said they were confident that television held the promise of unique, if still largely uncharted opportunities of benefit and delight to the community. British television was undoubtedly ahead of the rest of the world.

Lord Selsdon, Chairman of the Television Advisory Committee, said it was possible to conceive of the "new art" being applied not only to entertainment but to education, commerce, the tracing of wanted or missing persons, and navigation by sea or air.

In the light of experience they would proceed with the location of a second and subsequent transmitting station according as public interest justified the course. Technically Britain led to-day.

Television history is made in November, 1936, when the opening ceremony of the BBC's Alexandra Palace was televised.

TV KEEPS CHILDREN UP LATE

MANY children are far too receptive of everything that comes out of the television set, says a schoolteacher.

They no longer make up their own games, exercising their imaginations. And they do not read to themselves as much as they should.

These points are made by the teacher in the parish magazine of Sheffield's William Temple Church, at Manor Park.

In his article on "The Effects of Television Viewing," he goes on:—

THEIR HOMEWORK

"Far too many children are allowed to stay up late, straining their eyes in darkened rooms, while older children dash off their homework in careless haste, so as not to miss their favourite programme."

The writer adds that there is a similar effect on adult viewers—it discourages reading, sewing and many other profitable occupations.

Monday, October 10, 1955

Tonight TV Test First Colour

VIEWERS of B.B.C. television transmitted from Alexandra Palace will see the first experiments with colour television if they keep their sets switched on after eleven o'clock tonight—but they will of course receive pictures in black and white.

The B.B.C. has emphasised that these transmissions—likely to continue for months—will in no sense be a public service and are not an indication of any early start with colour TV.

The experimental pictures will be mainly still patterns, demonstration films and simple studio shots, all designed to provide technical information.

First colour tests in 1955 – but viewers will only see them in black and white!

October, 1955 – and they are still saying the same about the effects of television 45 years later.

A typical advertisement for television sets from 1962.

Tonight's TV and Radio

TELEVISION

B.B.C.

5. 0—Children's Television.
6. 0—News. 6.20—The Burns And Allen Show. 6.45—Tonight.
7.25—News. 7.30 — The George Mitchell Glee Club. 7.50 — The Phil Silvers Show.
8.15—"This Is Your Life." 8.45 — Panorama.
9.30—Picture Parade.
10. 0—News. 10.15—Come Dancing. 10.45—Orson Welles Sketchbook.
11. 0—News.

A.T.V.—MIDLAND
(Channel 8)

5. 0—Seeing Sport — Fencing.
5.25—Popeye. 5.55—News.
6.10—Dr. Christian. 6.40 — The Last Word

7. 0—Shadow Squad. 7.30—Tell The Truth.
8. 0—Jack Hylton's Monday Show. 8.30—International Celebrity Festival.
9.30—Murder Bag.
10. 0—It's a Woman's World. 10.15—Melody Ranch. 10.46 —News.
11. 0—Epilogue

GRANADA
(Channels 9 & 10)

5. 0—Seeing Sport. 5.25—Popeye 5.55—News.
6.10—Private Secretary. 6.40 — The Last Word.
7. 0—Shadow Squad. 7.30—Tell the Truth.
8. 0—Monday Show. 8.30—International Celebrity Festival
9.30—Murder Bag.
10. 0—Out of Step. 10.15—Melody Ranch. 10.46—News.
11. 0—Alfred Hitchcock Present — "Conversation Over Corpse." 11.30—Sailor of Fortune.

SOUND RADIO

NORTH REGION
(434m. VHF Holme Moss 93.7 Mc/s.)

5. 0—Children's Hour. 5.55—Weather.
6. 0—News. 6.30—Reginald Dixon's Half-Hour.
7. 0—Music to Remember.
8. 0—Workshop. 8.30—The Goon Show.
9. 0—News. 9.15—"Christophe" (Play).
10.45—Today in Parliament.
11. 0—News. 11.6—Market Trends.

LIGHT
(1.500m. 247m. VHF Holme Moss 89.3 Mc/s.)
News summary every hour

9.15—Song Hits of the Century. 9.45—By the Fireside.
10. 0—Jack Jackson's Hit Parade 10.30—Pete Murray's Top Pops.
11. 0—Taking Points. 11.05—The Bible Christian Programme 11.15—Frank and Ernest 11.30—The World Tomorrow.

DISTRICT SEEKING

If you were around on March 3, 1958, this is what you might have watched on television and listened to on the radio. "This is Your Life" was going strong even then!

COLOUR TELEVISION FOR GRAND HOTEL

VISITORS to the Grand Hotel may soon become the first people in Sheffield to enjoy colour television outside the dealers' shops.

For the hotel general manager, Mr. F. W. Cockbaine, has decided to have a colour TV set installed in the television lounge, and although no date has yet been fixed, it will definitely be there by the end of the month.

"We are hoping to be the first people in Sheffield, apart from dealers, to have a colour set." Mr. Cockbaine said.

He explained that as soon as he heard that colour television was on the market he decided that his guests should have the opportunity of seeing it.

And his idea will probably be taken up by all the Frederick - Excelsior hotels, the group to which the Grand belongs.

The television lounge is open

Today's youngsters will find this 1967 headline unbelievable. Yes, having a colour telly WAS headline news in those days.

NOW THAT RINGS A BELL...

By 1923, not only businesses were realising the value of the telephone. It was starting to find its way into private houses as well and in April, 1923, a new telephone exchange costing £80,000 was opened in Sheffield to cope with the increasing demand.

The city also had one of the most extensive public kiosk services in the country.

But by 1938, the "scourge of the telephone bell" was having its effect on the country and an MP asked the Postmaster General to come up with something that didn't disturb invalids and children.

What he had in mind was a "more euphonious" type of bell or a buzzer, or a phone that lit up. The word "euphonious" – meaning "a pleasing sound" – has largely fallen out of use but it must have sounded good at the time.

An enterprising reporter from The Star asked famous singer Gracie Fields what she thought of the idea and was stunned into silence by her reply: "Eh, lad, I'm sick and tired of answering the telephone. My idea of the perfect telephone bell is a silent one which never rings at all and therefore never worries me."

CITY ORNAMENT.

The New Automatic 'Phone Exchange.

WORK'S PROGRESS.

To Make Communication Much Easier.

("Yorkshire Telegraph & Star" Special.)

"An ornament to the city."

This was expressed to a "Yorkshire Telegraph and Star" reporter to-day who called on the clerk of works (Mr. C. J. Bassett) to see what progress had been made with the construction of the automatic telephone exchange which is being erected on the long-vacant Bow Street site.

An imposing building, with several floors fronting busy Bow Street, ideally ventilated, roomy, and light, the projected Central Telephone Exchange is to cost something like £80,000, and is to be completed—under a condition imposed by the Sheffield Corporation—before two years have elapsed.

It is to be more than an ornament, of course, the main object of the automatic exchange being the speeding up of telephonic communication to bring us more up to date, and somewhat on the lines of the American system, which is so encouraging that the majority of American households consider it a very ordinary necessity to be on the 'phone—instead of, as is the case in England, having to look upon the telephone as an unmitigated evil.

After long and patient excavation work worthy

New telephone exchange, April, 1923.

THE 'PHONE HABIT.

Remarkable Increase in Sheffield Subscribers.

("Yorkshire Telegraph & Star" Special.)

The number of people indulging in the "telephone habit" is increasing in a remarkable manner every week. The value and utility of a telephone seems to be coming more widely realised in these days not only by business firms, but by private householders, and considering the state of trade in Sheffield, the weekly increase in telephone subscribers is surprising.

Mr. C. E. Smith, manager of the telephone department in Sheffield and district, states that the average number of new subscribers in his area during one week in fifty-five.

He also points out that the number of street kiosks in the city had been greatly increased, and are being widely used. In some cases there has been delay in fitting up these kiosks, but they have now been practically all completed, and there are few cities which have such a valuable and extensive street telephone service.

A correspondent writes:—

I suppose my memory is right when recalling that it was somewhere in the 'eighties that Mr. John Tasker first brought his Telephone Exchange into being. He was a little bent man with a wide vision, and one who built up a big business, having to do with the introduction of electric light into the town as well as the telephone. The latter was looked upon with much misgiving, and for a long time the communication was faulty, but the work was persevered with, until to-day Sheffield is very well served by a thoroughly good system. It is one which may at times create worry, but generally speaking I think I am right in suggesting that the service leaves little to be desired, save, perhaps, in its still substantial cost, and rather irritating penny farthing.

I was having a telephone installed at home a week or two ago; it is perhaps significant that within a fortnight of the order being placed the instrument was installed.

A moment's reflection will show what this sudden interest in the telephone means, and how very much more nearly to the American Sheffield is becoming in its desire for inter-

1923 sees a "remarkable" increase in subscribers.

Dumb-bell Wanted by Gracie!

A SUGGESTION to free householders from the scourge of the telephone bell will be made in the House of Commons on Monday.

The Rev. R. Sorensen (Lab., Leyton, W.) is to ask the Postmaster-General whether he will arrange to supply domestic and other telephone subscribers, when requested, with an alternative more euphonious type of bell or with lights, soft buzzers or some device for calling subscribers less liable unnecessarily to distract the household, or to disturb invalids and children.

A COOING CALL

Mothers, whose children will awake on the slightest provocation, or none at all, are not the only ones who will welcome this movement for a quieter Britain.

Harassed business men, instead of being jerked back to wakefulness by the strident rattle of the telephone, will be gently awakened by a hellifluous cooing sound.

By 1938, people were complaining about the loudness of the telephone bell.

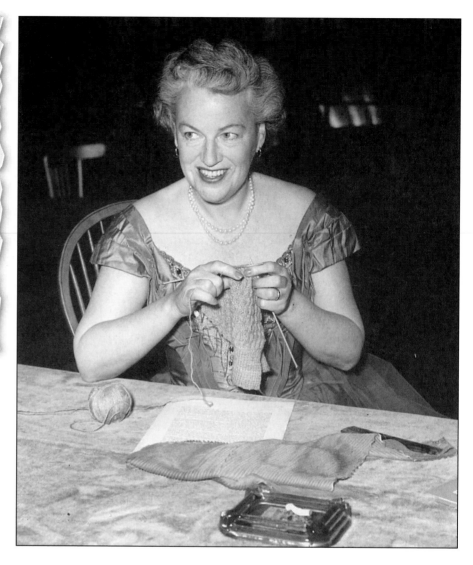

Not a telephone in sight. Gracie Fields knitting in the dressing room at Sheffield City Hall in 1954.

THE STAR IMPROVES ITS COMMUNICATIONS

THE STAR, Monday, June 6, 1949

"GREEN 'UN" IS FIRST TO GO BY AIR

A NEW and speedy service for sports enthusiasts began on Saturday when an aircraft left Sheffield carrying copies of the "Green 'Un" to Lincoln, Cleethorpes, Skegness, and Boston.

The plane, a small, silver Auster monoplane, left from a disused open-cast coal site near Richmond Park Road, Sheffield.

Next week and onward a larger Miles Messenger aircraft will be used.

Sports enthusiasts in Lincoln were reading the "Green 'Un" little more than 20 minutes after the aircraft left Sheffield.

Mr. Derek Allison, managing director of Boston Air Transport Ltd., the private air charter company which has contracted to deliver the "Green 'Un," said:

HOURS EARLIER

"I think this is an excellent idea, and a good business proposition. I know of no other

Snarey, a former R.A.F. pilot and test pilot for Westlands, where he flew Lysander and Whirlwind aircraft, remained at Lincoln for only three minutes.

Cleethorpes was reached in 14 minutes, at a few minutes to seven. Normal delivery time is an hour and a half later.

A slight mishap to the undercarriage prevented this experimental test run being completed. Copies of the "Green 'Un" were sent to Skegness and Boston by road. They arrived at Skegness to appear on the streets for the first time at 9.30 and at Boston a few minutes later—fully 12 hours ahead of normal delivery times.

WILL CONTINUE

Although the flight was considered an

The Star's Green 'Un sports paper, legendary throughout our area for the speed of its operation with Saturday football results and reports, grew even more wings in 1949 and became the first Saturday special in the country to deliver copies by air.

An aircraft took copies to Lincoln and the East Coast and sports fans were reading the paper in Lincoln 20 minutes after the plane left Sheffield.

"TEST" PICTURES MAKE HISTORY

THESE pictures of the Test Match from Headingley make history. They are the first to be wired direct to "The Star" at Kemsley House, Sheffield.

By JOHN B. HUGHES

"CHAMPAGNE" cricket was for a delighted crowd of Leeds today.

First Pollard dismissed Bradman in the second over of the day and then got Miller to a most amazing catch.

Crowning achievement of the morning came when 19-year-old Neil Harvey got a century in his first Test match.

He helped Miller to put on 121 in 95 minutes for the fourth wicket.

Showing no signs of nervousness, he hit all round the wicket without giving a semblance of a chance. He missed a ball from Laker when 112 and was bowled.

Don Bradman had made only two runs today from a no-ball when a delivery from Bedser came off sharply and hit him low on the body.

Bradman doubled up and play was held up while the England players gave him attention.

However, he quickly resumed, limping in apparent pain, to see Hassett lose his wicket to Pollard's ball.

This page one picture in The Star on July 24, 1948, was historic – the first photograph to be "wired" direct to The Star's Sheffield office. It was also unusual in that it showed legendary long-stay Australian batsman Don Bradman actually being bowled out! It makes this photograph something of a collector's item…

Curtain Up! It's Entertainment Time

THESE NEW FILMS ARE ALL TALK...

Are talking films here to stay? Or will they prove to be one of those novelties which will attract public interest for a time and then gradually subside into the background?

With the benefit of hindsight, that is probably the daftest question The Star has ever asked its readers.

But, in June, 1929, when silent films were an established and very popular form of entertainment, it was fair to raise doubts about this new development.

As The Star pointed out on June 17, 1929, the day the first "talkies" were to be shown in Sheffield, there was no disputing the fact that "astute cinema producers will not risk the spending of thousands of dollars on something which may prove a temporary craze."

The two films to be shown were "Showboat" at the Regent Theatre and "The Singing Fool" starring Al Jolson at the Central Picture House.

A reporter from The Star attended a private preview of "Showboat" and came away "impressed with the picture both from the acting, talking, orchestral and singing standpoints."

The reporter's overall verdict was: "If all talking pictures are on the same level as 'Showboat', it is safe to predict that there is a future for the industry." Wise words, indeed!

Members of Sheffield's Education Committee and their wives went along to the first performance of "The Singing Fool" and were impressed with the film and also the curtain raisers – a movietone news production featuring the Boat Race "and all the cheering of the crowds" and the Trooping of the Colour with accompanying military music, the shouting of commands and the sounds of marching troops.

Two weeks later, another Sheffield cinema, The Cinema House, announced that, for the time being, it would be remaining a "silent house."

A statement said that the "close personal touch between the manager and staff and the patrons had enabled the directors to ascertain the type of entertainment the patrons wanted and, after many reports and investigations, it had been found that a great number of patrons would prefer the theatre to remain a silent house."

The decision had been based on the quality of the silent films they had booked and the quality of the "fine" orchestra which played during performances.

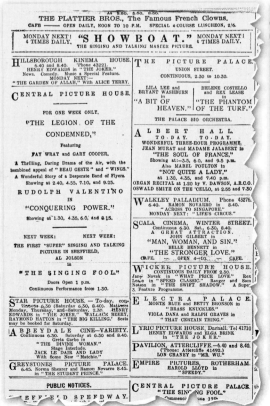

The talkies come to Sheffield on June 17, 1929.

An advertisement on The Star's entertainment page on June 13, 1929, heralds a new cinema era.

July, 1929 and The Cinema House, Sheffield, decides to remain a "silent" house for the time being.

Al Jolson, who played the part of a singing waiter in "The Singing Fool."

PHOTOGRAPHED SOUND.

Moving Picture that Talks and Renders Music.

THE PHONOFILM.

New Possibilities for the Silent Drama.

A moving picture film that talks and renders music was described by Dr. Lee de Forest, inventor of the audion tube, to the New York Electrical Society, and a demonstration of the apparatus, which is called the "phonofilm," was given.

Dr. de Forest speculated, says the New York correspondent of the Central News, as to the future use in the theatre of the phonofilm, which is in all respects like an ordinary motion picture film except that sound is photographed on the edge, and by an ingenious process is reproduced.

The action and sound are photographed simultaneously and reproduced simultaneously, overcoming the weakness of some past attempts at talking drama, where the words have not harmonised perfectly with the action. The sounds are reproduced with great fidelity.

New Screen Drama.

There had been a hint in The Star six years earlier that "talkies" were on the way. A story said that Dr Lee de Forest, inventor of the audion tube, had demonstrated to the New York Electrical Society an apparatus which showed a "moving picture film that talks and renders music". He called it a phonofilm and claimed that an entirely new form of screen drama could be worked out, taking advantage of the possibilities of introducing music and voice and appropriate acoustic effects.

Now there was a clever boy! Why didn't he become a household name?

The biggest competition Sheffield cinemas had in 1927 was from... local churches!

Cinema proprietors were furious because places of worship were showing films. One stormed: "These people are exempt from rates because they are places of worship and, under the guise of religion, they are conducting shows for profit in competition with legitimate traders. This is decidedly unfair.

"It is sometimes said that only religious films, or films which are out of date, are shown at these places but this is not so."

CINEMA STORM.

"COMPETITION OF PLACES OF WORSHIP."

SHEFFIELD MOVE.

Sheffield cinema proprietors are up in arms against what they term the unfair competition of places of worship which have cinematograph apparatus installed.

According to "The Cinema," the trade paper, the subject was discussed at the last meeting of the Sheffield branch of the Cinematograph Exhibitors' Association when Mr. E. W. Bassil called the attention of the meeting to the fact that films were being shown at the Attercliffe Wesleyan Hall on Saturday evenings. The prices of admission were 6d. and 3d., and the building accommodated over 2,000.

Mr. H. Bramwell pointed out that this sort of thing had been occurring in the centre of the town for some time.

Mr. W. Bryan said that the action they had taken before had been to ask renters not to supply these establishments with films, but Mr. Newton argued that if the renters could get the money they asked for the films they would not give the custom up.

Mr. Graham said the only way was to compel the hall to be brought under the Cinematograph Act, and in this way they would be rated in the same way as the houses to which they were in opposition. In Sheffield rates were enormously, and people such as the king advantage of the...

YORKSHIRE TELEGRAPH & STAR, December 2, 1933.

FURNITURE
OF EVERY DESCRIPTION BY
EASY WEEKLY PAYMENTS
FROM THE
EXCHANGE COMPANY
LIMITED.
Free Delivery on First Payment.
136, BRAMALL LANE,
SHEFFIELD.

SHEFFIELD: TELEPHONE 22055 (FIV

NO. 14,698.

Attendant Badly Ma

FIGHT WITH BEAST ON STAGE.

| ANIMAL DASHES INTO CELLAR. | FORCED OUT BY USE OF FIRE HOSE. |

RECAPTURED AFTER EXCITING HUNT.

LOCKED IN THE BAND ROOM.

AN intense drama of real life was enacted at the Sheffield Empire, to-day, when an attendant was

Front page drama at the Empire Theatre.

blue crepe de Chine, and fawn hat, and carried a sheaf of lilies.

The bridesmaids were the Misses Freda Jenkinson and Sarah Moxon.

Mr. Fred Moxon was the best man.

Escaped Tiger.

THRILL FOR WOMAN.

Left Cellar Just Before Tiger Entered.

(Continued from Page 1.)

For a time when the animal first got loose there was something approaching a panic in the theatre, in which there were about six Sheffield women, who were cleaning the auditorium. Two of them were actually in the pit on a level with the stage, the others being in the circle and gallery, and all fled when the alarm was given.

One of the women employees, Mrs. Florence Hirst, of 14, Bishop Street, Sheffield, had gone into the cellar to mash some tea a few minutes before the animal bolted down the steps.

She heard the screams of the injured man rising above the roars of the infuriated animal, and ran up the steps, where she was met by a Corporation electric meter man, who had been in the theatre attending to the meters. He was running frantically into the street to give the alarm, and collided with her, both falling down the steps into the cellar, and rushed out

Some thrill !

ROARS GALORE FROM THE EMPIRE – BUT IT'S NOT LAUGHTER!

Like most variety theatres of its kind, the old Sheffield Empire in Charles Street, which closed in 1959, attracted all the big names over the years and gave the public the best in live entertainment.

But none of it quite matched the drama played out there on December 2, 1933, when a tiger ran amok for four hours.

The Empire was staging a circus at the time and an attendant cleaning out a cage looked up to see the tiger leaping at him. It knocked him to the floor and clawed him, causing serious lacerations to his neck, shoulders and back.

Attracted by the man's screams, other attendants rushed up and beat the tiger off with iron bars and shovels.

They managed to drag the badly-injured attendant out of the way and the frenzied tiger, enraged by the blows from the iron bars and shovels, stampeded round the stage of the theatre before rushing down some steps into a cellar.

The cellar doors were quickly shut and attendants stood guard until the police and fire brigade arrived.

A reporter from The Star, admitted to the theatre through the stage door, said in his story, which took up most of the front page that day, that he found one of the attendants holding the cellar door for all he was worth. Behind it, the snarls of the tiger could be plainly heard.

It took police, firemen and attendants another three and a half hours to get the beast back into its cage.

Discovering that the tiger was in a cellar pit used for storing meat for the circus animals, they bravely descended into the cellar and managed to drive the tiger out of the pit and into a corner by playing water on it from a hosepipe.

When the animal rushed into the band room under the stage, the door was slammed to and attendants built a tunnel of iron cage sections, lashed together with rope, around the band room door and up the steps into the animal's cage.

The door was then opened and the tiger driven up the tunnel by the hose back into its cage.

The reporter, who watched the action, wrote: "While the men were working, the tiger could be heard stampeding in the band room and it was afterwards found he had wrecked the room, overturning instruments and ripping the upholstery off the chairs."

Six Sheffield women were cleaning the auditorium when the tiger first broke loose and one of them had actually been in the cellar mashing tea a few minutes before it dashed in there.

Hearing the attendant's screams, she came running out and

The Empire Theatre, scene of the drama.

collided with a electric meter reader who was dashing frantically into the street to raise the alarm. They both finished up, Laurel and Hardy fashion, falling down the cellar steps.

A big crowd gathered, attracted by the tiger's roars, and the incident caused so much interest that the theatre was packed for that day's matinee performance.

Coolest man throughout it all was one of the theatre attendants who, while helping to get the tiger out of the cellar, accidentally dropped his pipe on the animal's back.

He waited until it was safely locked in the band room, went into the cellar, retrieved the pipe...and came out smoking it!

ENTICED INTO CAGE.

SCREAMING women, theatre attendants, keepers and police officers figured in an amazing scene at the Sheffield Empire Theatre, to-day, when a tiger got loose, badly mauling one appearing at the theatre this week; and finally took refuge in a cellar, from which it was recaptured after defying attendants and Sheffield policemen and firemen for four hours.

Screaming women…and a tiger on the loose for four hours.

An entertainer called Professor John Popjie amazed a huge Sheffield crowd in July, 1931, when he drove blindfold through the city centre in a car.

Thrills of Professor Popjie's Drive Among Sheffield's Traffic: Crowds Amazed.

And no one was more staggered than a reporter from The Star who had the job of tying the blindfold on before the professor left the Empire Theatre for his journey through the city's busiest streets.

Before the prof set off, the reporter tried on the blindfold himself – three thicknesses of velvet and a black hood over that – and couldn't see even a glimmer of light.

At one stage the car carrying the reporter had to accelerate to keep up with the professor, who said later that he had done it with the aid of mental pictures of the route.

But how could he have had mental pictures of the traffic, asked The Star man, concluding: "The method of achievement must remain a mystery and a marvel."

STARS OFF SCREEN.

Laurel and Hardy Pay a Visit to Sheffield.

When the two famous film favourites, Stan Laurel and Oliver Hardy, arrived in Sheffield at noon, to-day, there was an unrehearsed comedy, which delighted the fun-makers as much as the tumultuous greeting accorded them.

As the comedians were standing posed for their photograph against the train which brought them from Leeds, a tiny woman in blue hurriedly brushed past the renowned couple in her anxiety to catch the train. She glanced neither to the right nor left, and totally ignored the film stars. They joined in the general laughter after she had passed by.

To-night they will appear on the stage of the Cinema House, Fargate, at 6.50 and 9 o'clock approximately.

Laurel and Hardy are laughter-makers in real life as much as they are on the screen. They kept a small party of friends amused in a sitting room at the Grand Hotel where they are staying.

In real life Laurel's features seem plumper, and his style of hairdressing is changed. In real life, as on the screen, Hardy still remains his genial friend.

"Since we arrived in England, we have been virtually prisoners in the hotels," Laurel confided to a "Star" reporter.

He said that after lunch, however, he was going to slip away with Hardy and buy some silverware for Mrs. Hardy in the warehouse of one of the city's famous silversmiths, and do other "shopping."

While at the hotel Oliver Hardy received a gift of some golf clubs presented by George Nicholl, Ltd., iron makers, of Leven, Fifeshire. Each iron is stamped with a typical photograph of Hardy and the name of the donor. Hardy is an enthusiastic golfer.

Laurel has not visited Sheffield since 1909.

LIFE MAKES LAUREL HARDY!

At Sheffield Theatres

THE genius of Laurel and Hardy is that their comic situations are based firmly on reality.

The things that happen to them could happen to anybody—or almost anybody—but their treatment of events is highly individual. In fact, they turn life inside out.

Their sketch at the Empire, Sheffield, is a good example of their art.

Ollie, forever trying to smother his partner's social errors, weightily lands them deeper in the misunderstandings on which they thrive.

Stan, the quavering droll, is the starting point of inspired idiocy.

"BURGLARY"

On the whole they translate well into the atmosphere of live theatre.

The two scenes of the sketch

STAGE STUDIES By HEAP

character which Reginald Birks gave to Henry Fanshaw Beringer, would have suffered, and so, by comparison, would the David Brown of Charles Lepper.

They hold the stage for the major portion of the time as successful and would-be successful author whose pact to exchange manuscripts causes so much confusion.

There is also neat, quiet comedy from Ella Atkinson, put over without fuss, and a pleasant performance by Ursula O'Leary, to say nothing of some real forthright comedy by Sally Lahee.—B. C. D.

the same quality then I should rank it among the best "Maria Martens" I have se

So Refreshing

Stage studies by The Star's cartoonist Harry Heap when Laurel and Hardy appeared at the Empire in July, 1952.

That's another fine mess you've got me into, Stanley. Classic Laurel and Hardy pose during their 1952 visit.

THE BEST SILVER FOR MRS HARDY

When famous comedians Laurel and Hardy came to Sheffield in 1932 for a one-night appearance at the Cinema House on Fargate, they received a "tumultuous greeting" at the Midland Station.

The Star reporter there to interview them said that they were laughtermakers in real life as much as they were on screen.

Before the show, they visited the warehouse of one of the city's famous silversmiths (The Star report didn't say which one) to buy some silver for Mrs Hardy.

Laurel told the reporter he had not been to Sheffield since 1909, when he appeared at the Empire with Charlie Chaplin and Fred Karno. The 1932 visit to the city was believed to be Hardy's first.

The pair came several times after that and always played to packed houses.

Brilliant Scenes At

HALL WORTHY OF GREAT CITY.
—Alderman A. J. Bailey.

CULMINATION OF 16-YEAR EFFORT.

CELEBRATION BY MUSIC, SONG AND SPEECHES.

DEDICATORY PRAYER BY THE BISHOP.

SHEFFIELD'S new City Hall, considered one of the finest in the country, was formally opened to-day by the Lord Mayor (Alderman T. H. Watkins).

Alderman A. J. Bailey gave a review of the efforts of the past 16 years which had resulted in the provision of a public building, which, he said, "was worthy of this great city; a monument to municipal vision, foresight, enterprise, and achievement."

The event was attended by an immense gathering.

The Lord Mayor headed a civic procession from the Town Hall, and was accompanied by most of the members of the City Council.

Future citizens of Sheffield were represented at the ceremony by the attendance of scholars from city schools.

The Oval Hall, where the formal proceedings took place, accommodates about 3,000 people, and those attending were fully representative of every phase of activity in the city.

The proceedings were broadcast on the North Regional wave-length.

SHEFFIELD: TELEPHONE 22055 (FIFTEEN LINES). INCORPORATING THE "SHEFFIELD MAIL." LONDON: TELEPHONES CENTRAL 6909 PUBLISHING; MUSEUM 9841 ADVERT

SHEFFIELD, THURSDAY EVENING, SEPTEMBER 22, 1932.

At Opening Of Sheffield's Half

"Star" photo., the first to be taken, of the magnificent Ballroom in the Sheffield City Hall. Two ounces of gold leaf were used in the decoration of each of the sixteen pillars.

UTURE USEFULNESS. "GOING TO CUT OFF OUR EARS." METHODISTS A

Poignant Appeals From

The official opening of Sheffield City Hall on September 22, 1932, was one of the biggest events in the city for years.
The hall, described as Sheffield's finest building, cost nearly half a million pounds.
Nearly 70 years later, nearly £2m is to be spent on essential repair work.

THEATRE ROYAL GUTTED.

ONLY THE BLACKENED WALLS REMAIN.

LYCEUM AT ONE TIME IN DANGER.

DISASTROUS FIRE IN SHEFFIELD.

THE Sheffield Theatre Royal is gutted. Now only the four blackened walls and the property room remain after a disastrous fire which was discovered early to-day.

So fierce was the blaze that the Sheffield Lyceum Theatre, a few yards away, caught fire—but not seriously. The Adelphi Hotel, opposite, was in real danger, and even now the outside wall of the theatre opposite this hotel is unsafe.

Sunday is the only night when a fireman is not on duty at the theatre.

MANAGER AS FIREMAN.

The Theatre Royal is one of the few variety houses in the country where contracts have been placed until next December.

Mr. Arthur Holland, the manager, worked at the fire in fireman's helmet and which donned af

some money right away. I had a sort of premonition a month ago," says Castelli.

"That is why I insured my instrument for fifty quid. I wish all of you had done the same. Anyway, don't lose heart . . . I'll wire some friends straight away . . ."

Castelli leaves the room. I follow him (writes a "Star" reporter).

There in the hall, Castelli brushes tears from his eyes.

"I can't let them see me upset," he tells me. "They depend on me for a lead. But what can we do? We have been out of work for two weeks . . . everybody has spent up on the Christmas festivities . . . we have at least seven consecutive weeks' booking before us . . . and now this happens.

"Everything has gone. There's nearly £500 worth of instruments melted away. There's r to In fact the girls ha

How the news broke…

CITY'S OLDEST THEATRE DESTROYED BY FIRE

1936 was just 24 hours away when a fierce blaze, one of Sheffield's biggest fires for years, destroyed the city's oldest theatre and marred the New Year celebrations.

Flames leapt 150 feet into the air only minutes after the fire was discovered at 3am by the licensee of the Adelphi Hotel across the road.

The Theatre Royal, at the junction of Arundel Street and Tudor Street, was the city's best loved theatre and had been standing for more than 160 years. But, in three hours, it had gone…

At the height of the fire, slates were crashing down 30 and 40 at a time from the 80 feet building and The Star's report said that the flames had eaten up the plush, covered seating as thought it had been paper.

(Left) The Theatre Royal fire at its height, dramatically captured by a Sheffield Newspapers cameraman.

LINK WITH FAMOUS NAMES.

| Long History of Sheffield's Theatre Royal. | The Last of the Old Playhouses. |

SYMBOLS UNTOUCHED BY THE FIRE.

THE Sheffield Theatre Royal, which was to-day destroyed by fire, has a long and interesting history. It is the oldest theatre in Sheffield and one of the oldest in the provinces.

It was erected in 1773 at the corner of Arundel Street and Tudor Street and was rebuilt with the exception of the outer walls in 1854-5, at a cost of £3,000.

Its history, however, really goes back another 10 years, for it was in 1763 that the town first became possessed "of a theatre worthy of the name."

This was built back-to-back with the Assembly Rooms, the frontage being to Norfolk Street and the back to Tudor Place. It was described in 1764 as "large and commodious, capable of containing 800 spectators, handsomely decorated, and having some very good scenery." It was rebuilt on a larger plan in 1773.

Despite the drastic changes both internal and external, there remained in the front of the building the "spirited" profile of [Shake]spea[re and] some dramatic symbols

Shakespeare's plays appear to have been great favourites. Famous players of the time in these were Edmund Kean, S. Butler, Charles Young, and John Litton.

It is said that people rushed for three nights to see Maria Foote, whose fame as the heroine of a breach of promise case in which she obtained £3,000 damages from a Mr. Hayne conferred on her a popularity beyond her talents as an actress.

Charles Kean was another actor, and famous singers included Mesdames Catalini, Braham and Incledon.

The Sheffield public of those days evidently liked strong amusements, and some old play-bills give an idea of the tastes of the day.

At a benifit for Mr. Carter and Mr. Clarke, in 1811, there was given Beaumont and Fletcher's "Rule a wife and have a wife." "The celebrated Mr. Wilson" performed the "extraordinary feat of walking from the stage wheeling a real wheelbarrow to the gallery and down again," and also gave a wonderful performance on the tightrope.

In comparatively recent years Sir Henry [...] Terr[...] ulia N[...] Fred

The Theatre Royal had been standing since 1773.

(Below) Daylight breaks to reveal the colossal damage.

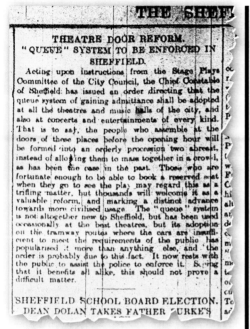

THE SHEF[FIELD]

THEATRE DOOR REFORM.
"QUEUE" SYSTEM TO BE ENFORCED IN SHEFFIELD.

Acting upon instructions from the Stage Plays Committee of the City Council, the Chief Constable of Sheffield has issued an order directing that the queue system of gaining admittance shall be adopted at all the theatres and music halls of the city, and also at concerts and entertainments of every kind. That is to say, the people who assemble at the doors of these places before the opening hour will be formed into an orderly procession two abreast, instead of allowing them to mass together in a crowd, as has been the case in the past. Those who are fortunate enough to be able to book a reserved seat when they go to see the play may regard this as a trifling matter, but thousands will welcome it as a valuable reform, and marking a distinct advance towards more civilised usage. The "queue" system is not altogether new to Sheffield, but has been used occasionally at the best theatres, but its adoption on the tramway routes where the cars are insufficient to meet the requirements of the public has popularised it more than anything else, and the order is probably due to this fact. It now rests with the public to assist the police to enforce it. Seeing that it benefits all alike, this should not prove a difficult matter.

SHEFFIELD SCHOOL BOARD ELECTION.
DEAN DOLAN TAKES FATHER BURKE'S

A new idea was introduced at Sheffield's theatres and music halls 100 years ago...QUEUEING!

Acting on instructions from the Stage Plays Committee of Sheffield City Council, the Chief Constable issued an order directing "that the people who assemble at the doors of these places before the opening hour will be formed into an orderly procession two abreast, instead of allowing them to mass together in a crowd, as has been the case in the past."

Our sister paper, The Sheffield Telegraph, said that thousands would welcome it as a valuable reform marking a distinct advance towards more civilised usage.

(Right) Now who is this new young performer earning the praise of The Star's critic at Sheffield Empire in 1927? None other than George Formby playing his ukelele.

PANTOMIMES IN SHEFFIELD.

CHRISTMAS ARRANGEMENTS.

The proprietors and managers of two of the Sheffield theatres are now busy completing the final arrangements for the production of the Christmas Pantomimes. At the Theatre Royal the fairy tale of "Cinderella" will be re-told, whilst "The Forty Thieves" will be presented at the Alexandra. There will be some departure from the usual custom at the Lyceum Theatre. In the place of pantomime Mr. John Hart has arranged for the presentation of "Alice in Wonderland" during Christmas week, and following this will come D'Oyly Carte and the Carl Rosa opera companies. Early in February Mr. Hart will send his only pantomime, "The Sleeping Beauty," which will run for a fortnight.

"Cinderella," at the Theatre Royal, will be under the stage management of Mr. Lonnen Meadows, the author and inventor, and, at Mr. Purcell's request, Mr. J. F. Elliston will produce the pantomime. Mr. Elliston's name will be well remembered in connection with last year's successful "annual" at this house. The pantomime will be on a grand scale of magnificence, quite in keeping with the usual gorgeous shows that the proprietor of the Royal has given to the public in years past. There will be no

Christmas, 1903, and panto season has arrived. "Cinderella" is showing at the Theatre Royal and "The Forty Thieves" at the Alexandra Theatre on Blonk Street.

"Formby Seeing Life" at the Empire.

The name of George Formby is familiar to all Sheffield audiences, and memories of the late comedian were conjured up by seeing on the bill the name of his son, George Formby, who is carrying on the great traditions of his father. He appears at the Sheffield Empire this week in a revue entitled "Formby Seeing Life," an excellent comedy production, in which mirth, melody, and dancing are all admirably presented. Playing the title rôle, George Formby is the central figure of the revue, and as principal comedian causes endless laughter in a variety of scenes. His singing, too, is a great success, especially his number with the ukelele.

There is a strong supporting company, including Percy King, comedian, Jenny Howard, comedienne, the Four Conshords, and Six Olraces, who give an excellent diversion in the form of an acrobatic display, and the Ten Grainger Girls.

The settings are good, and with plenty of catchy music and rapid change from scene to scene, there is never a dull moment.

The case of Mr. Le Mesurier

The case of Mr. Le Mesurier, who appeared personally, was that he had interested himself in the cause of the natives, and that in all he had done he was actuated by honest motives.

Defendants pleaded justification.

Plaintiff, in cross-examination, said that one of the advantages of being a Mohammedan was that a man could marry four wives. (Laughter.)

His Lordship: I do not at all see that that is an advantage. (Laughter.)

The jury stopped the case, and gave a verdict for the defendant.

PLEASURES OF THE CITY

Varied Phases of Entertainment at Sheffield.

RETURN OF "CARNIVAL."

"Carnival," which attracted so much patronage when it first came to Sheffield, is again at the Lyceum Theatre this week. It is a play which loses nothing of its appeal and glamour on further acquaintance; indeed it is one of the few productions which is really worth seeing a second time. The wonderful third act—the scene in a theatre green room—with its tense, thrilling incidents, was played last night with rare force and discretion. Throughout "Carnival" is presented with great cleverness by a skilful company. The exacting role of Silvio is in the hands of Mr. C. Skillan; that of the wife, Simonetta, in those of Miss Margot Drake; and that of Count Andrea in those of Mr. H. C. Hewitt. A word is also due to Felicity Garratt, a clever actress; Miss Blanka Stewart, and Mr. H. Cochran.

Dramatic Thrills at the Royal.

Drama of the most effective order characterises "Out to Win"—the Courtneidge success which is being played for the first time in Sheffield at the Theatre Royal this week. A capital plot is countered by a series of arresting situations. The play is cleverly acted, and thoroughly well mounted. Mr. E. Hamilton Jordan's ability is emphasised in a dual role, and his excellent support all round.

Variety at the Empire.

There is an excellent variety programme, including a heap of fun and music, at the Empire this week. At the head of the bill is Arthur Prince and "Jim" in a clever ventriloquial playlet, "The Love Affair of Yussif Hassan." Harmony is provided by the Henry J. Corner Musical Ensemble. Stanelli and Douglas are a clever and amusing couple of fiddle fanatics, whilst Leslie Strange shows talent. Other good turns are provided by Les Nosselas in the latest Parisian novelty, the Three Sisters O'Hara songsters and the Hanlon-Charles Troupe of Aerial Stage Gymnasts.

Revue at the Hippodrome.

The success of "Come On, Steve!" at the Hippodrome is reflected by the retention of this amusing revue for a further week. Scott and Whaley are responsible for most of the humour, which was well done. The show is attractively staged and should bring large audiences during the rest of the week.

Powerful Romance at the Cinema.

At the Cinema House, Sir Gilbert Parker's well-known romance, "Behold My Wife!" heads the bill of fare. A practical newcomer to the film-world is Mabel Julienne Scott, a petite brunette with remarkable dramatic ability and her portrayal of "Lali," a native squaw, and "Lali," the daughter-in-law of a proud old English general, are a striking contrast, and intensify her versatile personality. Milton Sills is ever a popular screen hero. "The Toreador" is one of the most amusing and original comedies shown for some considerable time.

Strong Bill at the Electra.

The Electra programme last night was one of the strongest that has been put on at this popular house for some time. "The Girl in Number 29" leaves the beaten track and takes the path of sound comedy of a high order. "The Trevor Case" is also a thrilling story. It strikes a popular appeal with molested lovers, a vicious husband, and alien plotters who strive to bring about the downfall of the hero, only to be foiled in the end. It is pure melodrama, and runs at a great pace throughout, the action being smooth, yet full of excitement.

Spiritualistic Thrills at Albert Hall.

"The Other Person," from Fergus Hume's novel, which is one of the exclusive films at the Albert Hall during the first half of the week, is a long story, lasting about an hour, and yesterday it kept large audiences absorbed from start to finish. It is a story of family feud and fratricide, and in its development spiritualism plays a leading part. Throughout the film she ... of "The Other

The entertainments scene in Sheffield in 1922.

STAGE AND SCREEN

YORKSHIRE TELEGRAPH AND STAR. SATURDAY EVEN[ING]

(1) ESTELLE BRODY IN "MADEMOISEL LE PARLEY VOO" AT THE ALBERT HALL. (2) NORMAN GRIFFIN IN "THE YELLOW MASK" AT THE LYCEUM. (3) DEREK WATERLOW IN "HER CARDBOARD LOVER" AT THE THEATRE ROYAL, SHEFFIELD. (4) MISS FELICE LASCELLES IN "SUNNY" AT THE EMPIRE. (5) "THE MERRY WIDOW" AT THE CENTRAL PICTURE HOUSE. (6) NORMA TALMADGE IN "THE WOMAN DISPUTED" AT THE REGENT. (7) "BEAU SABREUR" AT THE SCALA CINEMA. (8) "ROSE OF THE GOLDEN WEST" AT THE ELECTRA.

The stars of 1922.

CLEAR

Margaret Lockwood Crowd Scene

Miss Margaret Lockwood surrounded by crowds this afternoon as she entered Kemsley House, where she saw "The Star" being produced.

Margaret Lockwood, the most famous British film star of her time, visits The Star's office in 1947 to watch the paper being produced.

Empire staff plan 'epilogue'

MEMBERS of the staff of Sheffield's Empire Theatre, which is destined for demolition within a month, are hoping to organise an annual re-union.

Mrs. Teresa Slim, housekeeper to the theatre's 80-strong staff, said today: "It would be a wonderful idea to help us remember the old place."

Mrs. Slim is one of the few people who are staying on at the Empire to complete the final arrangements before the theatre is officially handed over on June 1.

VOCAL WREATHS

The theatre, Sheffield's "home of variety," died on Saturday, aged 64.

The "last-night mourners, who handed pea-can labels over the counter to hear the theatre's swan song, stayed behind to lay vocal wreaths in the silent auditorium.

And members of the staff slipped quietly in to manager John Spitzer's office to speak of their personal sorrow.

Earlier, most of the staff had gathered on the stage after the last performance of Smedley's "Theatre Night" to a tremendous ovation from the packed audience.

SOUVENIR

One who didn't go on stage was dark-haired Mrs. Florrie

1959 and it's lights out for the last time for Sheffield's Empire Theatre. Comedian Albert Modley reflects on the good times...

wife tried

lice
pen
of a
ent,

are,
nths
g an
cer's
n a

ar-old
condi-
after
ck by
rmer
n she

GIRL WINS
D ON HER
E DEBUT

field girl, Patricia Wood, carried off trophy for the best actor or actress Sheffield Drama Festival on Saturday Patricia's stage debut.

She won the trophy for her performance in the Denys Edwards Players' produc'io

● Top recording group, the Beatles, take time off during their City Hall concert to look at The Star's great TOP STARS SPECIAL.

And their verdict—it's a HIT!

Packed with pictures and stories of the greats of showbiz, the TOP STARS SPECIAL is great entertainment value. It's on sale at all newsagents' and selling points. Order your copy NOW!

IT'S A RIOT
AS BEATLES

THE FAB FOUR COME TO TOWN

The Beatles played Sheffield City Hall in May, 1963 and this picture was a bit of a scoop for The Star's photographer who snapped them reading Top Stars Special.

Produced by The Star, this excellent monthly music supplement was launched to reflect the incredible pop boom of the 1960s and in many ways it was well ahead of its time.

The Star's critic said the Beatles' performance was top notch but their numbers were drowned by continual screaming from the fans.

Several appeals were made to the audience for order but it had no effect.

Second on the bill was Roy Orbison and, said the critic, he deserved much more appreciation than he got.

The Beatles were back at the City Hall in November, 1963, and so were their fans.

Just the ticket!

Paul is presented with an oil painting by a fan.

John reads Sheffield University students' rag magazine "Twikker."

When the Bay City Rollers came to town

FAN FAINTS THREE TIMES – AND GOES BACK FOR MORE!

ROLLERMANIA hit Sheffield in May, 1975, resulting in 12 Bay City Roller fans going to hospital and another 100 receiving on-the-spot treatment during a City Hall concert.

A first-aid man defined Rollermania as "fainting bouts and hysterics brought on by the atmosphere of the occasion."

Some fans had leg and rib injuries caused by the crush but most of those treated were just completely overwhelmed by sheer excitement.

One girl fainted three times but each time went back into the hall for more…

its cats

the rabies
ts and
1974,
all
eign

pok-
memo
aboard
e rabies
extremely

CORRIDORS turned into casualty stations at Sheffield City Hall last night . . . and 12 young fans were rushed off to hospital after frenzied scenes at the Bay City Rollers concert.

At least 100 more received on-the-spot treatment for injuries caused by the crush and sheer hysteria.

One teenage girl was unconscious for 15 minutes after being carried from the packed hall

Young fans are rushed to hos...

Silent screen

By Charmaine Spencer

Credits roll as last rides into the sun

THE Classic Cinema has screened its last picture show. Next in line for the darkened screen is Studio 5.6.7. It closes next Saturday.

Sheffield viewers will then have a choice between five cinemas and 11 screens — res-

The Classic was the last of the great old cinemas. It opened in 1911 as the Electra Palace and was transformed into the Sheffield News Theatre 34 years later. It was re-named the Classic in 1962 and started showing feature films again.

The Electra/Classic survived serveral outbreaks of fire — the

dressed in Chinese costumes, a gong was sounded and incense was swung before each performance.

Disastrous

It managed to survive three disastrous fires, including one in 1967 which caused £50,000 worth of damage.

A year later hundred

The Star announces the closure of two more cinemas in 1982, the Classic and the Studio 5, 6 and 7.
It brought Sheffield's total down to five cinemas and 11 screens. Back in 1957, before television took a hold, there had been 50 picture houses.

May, 1991, and Sheffield's new £34m entertainments venue, the Arena, is launched by international pop star Paul Simons.

Cliff Richard in Sheffield in 1962...and again in 1994 when he met fan Hayley Maude, then 13, at Sheffield Arena.

Crowds gather outside Sheffield Cathedral to look at the wreaths.

From a humble working class home in Sheffield, Marti Caine rose to become an international superstar. Yet she never lost that "girl next door" touch and it endeared her not only to South Yorkshire folk but also to millions throughout the world.

Her death robbed us of a great talent and a great girl and The Star's headline captured it perfectly. She was, simply, "our Marti".

Marti in a 1974 production of "Funny Girl." The show title couldn't have been more apposite.

When schoolgirl Tina Wild wrote to Marti in 1982 and invited her for lunch at Lowedges Junior School, Sheffield, it was no real surprise when she accepted.

We're on the Move – By Road, Rail, Air and Water

Sheffield's first electric tram, 1899.

(Left) Real horse power, circa 1898, on the Endcliffe Wood, Hunters Bar, Ecclesall Road route.

RKSHIRE TELEGRAPH AN

SHEFFIELD'S ELECTRIC TRAMS.

OFFICIAL OPENING.

SUCCESSFUL RUNS.

GREAT PUBLIC ENTHUSIASM.

The great day has arrived, the members of the Corporation, with their wives, and many other guests, have ridden in the electric cars, and with enthusiastic "good speed" Sheffield in its thousands has seen the new tramcar system fairly launched on its career. There have been great days in Sheffield before, especially when it has been visited by members of the Royal Family, and great crowds have been gathered together, and have displayed their loyalty to the reigning house, but never, it is safe to say, has any great town's movement been formally inaugurated amid such widespread public rejoicing. For this, of course, the nature of the movement is to a large extent responsible. The acquisition of a water supply or the municipalisation of an electric light works, are not events that, in the very nature of them, lend themselves to spectacular display, but the first running of tramcars on a new system is of itself, without any extraneous aid, a development of the resources of the city that at once admit of the expression of popular interest. And Sheffield took full advantage of the opportunity... enthusiasm. The

STAR. TUESDAY EVENIN

THE ELECTRIC TRAM CARS.

TO-DAY'S USE BY THE PUBLIC.

HEAVY TRAFFIC.

To-day the public service of electric tramcars on the Tinsley to Nether Edge section was opened, and anticipations that the traffic would be heavy were amply fulfilled, notwithstanding the somewhat unfavourable character of the weather during the forenoon. The new system of traction comes with all the charm of novelty, and as it will take some time for that to wear away, an abnormal traffic will for a certain period have to be dealt with. There was a rush for the cars all day, notwithstanding that nine were running between High Street and Nether Edge, and nine between the Haymarket and Tinsley. Perfection cannot at first be reasonably hoped for, and that on both routes the traffic at one time became disorganised caused little surprise. Shortly before noon the controller of one of the cars on the Nether Edge section went wrong, a block resulted, and people in the centre of the city were at a loss to understand where the cars had gone to. The disabled car—there was never any danger to the passengers—transferred its living cargo, and made for the sheds, but the delay thus occasioned accounted for the scene witnessed in the city shortly before noon—five or six loaded cars coming from Nether Edge close to each other. A five minute service on both routes was what was aimed at, and as far as possible this was achieved.

DEATH OF A CRIMEAN VETERAN

Alfred King, a prominent socialist, and an intimate friend of the late Charles Bradlaugh, died at

A rush for the new tram cars all day.

An "electric" day for the city.

THE ATMOSPHERE WAS ELECTRIC!

Sheffield had never seen anything quite like it.

Thousands of people near the Town Hall – a crowd described by The Star at the time as "an unbroken mass of humanity, closely packed from side to side of the street and reaching from the top of Fargate to St Paul's Church" – watched in awe on September 3, 1899, as the city's first electric trams set off on their inaugural run.

Bedecked with bunting, six double decker tramcars carried the civic party, headed by the Lord Mayor, Ald. W.E.Clegg and the Lady Mayoress, and the crowd, estimated at 15,000 "on a moderate computation" raised cheers that were "spontaneous and hearty."

The Star reporter wrote colourfully: "As the Lord Mayor made his way to the tram car through the lines of people, a hearty cheer went up from the great crowd assembled in the square and from the large numbers of people occupying windows and other points of vantage on all the surrounding buildings."

The public had to wait until the next day to use the electric trams but some, out of sheer enthusiasm, came close to jumping on board and joining the civic party.

Said The Star: "There was not a large staff of police on duty and they had some difficulty in keeping the crowd back and preventing ratepayers anxious to have an early ride from boarding the cars a day too soon – for the public running of the new system is not to commence until tomorrow."

A deputation from Sheffield Council's Tramways Committee had visited towns and cities in France, Germany, Holland, Italy, Austria and England before recommending that the city should have an overhead electric system of traction to take over from the horse drawn tramcars.

The Tinsley to Nether Edge section was electrified first because the route presented "every variety of gradient to be encountered in Sheffield and will therefore show the fitness of the system for the city as a whole."

A reporter from The Star waxed enthusiastically about the introduction of electric trams, saying: "There have been great days in Sheffield before, especially when it has been visited by members of the Royal Family, and great crowds have been gathered together, and have displayed their loyalty to the reigning house, but never, it is safe to say, has any great town's movement been formally inaugurated amid such widespread public rejoicing."

As expected, the public flocked to use the new electric trams the following day. Nine were running between High Street and Nether Edge and nine between Haymarket and Tinsley and there were teething troubles shortly before noon.

One of the trams became "disabled", resulting in a blockage on the Nether Edge section. People waiting in the city centre were "at a loss to understand where the cars had gone to". Then five loaded tramcars arrived from Nether Edge close to each other.

But apart from that blip, the service achieved its objective – a tram every five minutes.

plague were reported there yesterday, and one death occurred

EXCITING INCIDENT IN SHEFFIELD.

CHILD PLACED IN FRONT OF AN ELECTRIC TRAM.

DRUNKEN MOTHER'S ESCAPADE.

At the Sheffield City Police Court this morning, Messrs. S. G. Richardson and R. A. Hadfield investigated a charge of drunkenness against Mary Ann Ward, married woman, residing at 104, Thomas Street.

On Monday afternoon this woman created considerable sensation by her remarkable conduct with regard to her child. She had been drinking during the morning, and by afternoon had got very drunk. Whilst the Lord Mayor and his friends were taking part in the ceremony of opening the new electric traction system, this woman was in Cemetery Road, just at the bottom at the junction with Ecclesall Road. As an electric car was approaching she walked to the rails and either deliberately placed her infant child on the track or let it fall. At any rate, the incident caused the greatest excitement. A woman rushed forward and took the little one from its perilous position. Later in the day P.c. Kirk found the woman in Bridgefield Road. She was very drunk and making a great noise. The officer heard of the incident in Cemetery Road, and also learned that the mother had been trying to bury the child alive. He arrested her for drunkenness, and she will most probably be proceeded against for cruelty to her child.

The woman expressed her sorrow for what had occurred, and the magistrates imposed a penalty of £1, including costs, or one month's imprisonment in default of payment.

ANOTHER LOBENGULA.

inasmuch as you do unto one of these my brethren so ye do it unto Me."—Yours, etc.,
Sheffield, June 21, 1911.   OBSERVER.

Sunday Trading.

Sir,—Does your correspondent, "A Christian," do nothing worse than ride in a car on Sundays? I am afraid he does. What do the cars run for on Sundays—pastime for the drivers or what? We all must be pleasing the devil who ride on Sundays.

I daresay "A Christian" is one of those who does not look to his own faults, but only watches other people.

How can he tell if they are so-called Christians or not who are riding in the cars on Sundays?—Yours, etc.,   SUNDAY RIDER.
Sheffield, June 20, 1911.

QUERIES ANSWERED.

"Don't Know."—The coin you name is of no

Is it sinful to ride on tramcars on Sundays? This contributor to The Star's letters column on June 21, 1911, had strong views.

The great celebration heralding the launch of the new electric tram came close to being marred by tragedy.

On the day the Lord Mayor and his party joined in the opening ceremony, a woman created "considerable sensation by her remarkable conduct with regard to her child."

A Sheffield Magistrates Court was told that the mother had been drinking during the morning and, as an electric tram approached the Cemetery Road/Ecclesall Road junction, she walked to the rails and "either deliberately placed her infant child on the track or let it fall."

Another woman rushed forward and "rescued the child from its perilous position."

A policeman found the mother "very drunk and making a great noise" later in the day. She was subsequently fined £1 by magistrates.

TRAMS DRIVEN "FURIOUSLY"

While Sheffield was getting used to its brand new electric trams in 1899, four Blackpool tram drivers faced prosecution for "furious" driving.

Police marked out 235 yards on a Blackpool street and constables were stationed at each end with stop watches.

All four were caught breaking the speed limit of 8mph and the worst offender, who was clocked doing 12mph, was fined 20s and costs.

HORSE BACKS INTO TRAM

A "startling occurrence" in London Road, Sheffield, on the morning of December 16, 1903, left an errand boy shaken when his horse shied at a passing electric tram and then backed into it.

Both the horse and rider were flung to the ground and The Star described it as an "exciting collision" in its headline!

Not quite the word the errand boy would have opted for, no doubt…

A BRIDGE TOO FAR

A traction engine owner appeared at Sheffield Police Court in August, 1911, in what the prosecution called a "new class of case."

He was charged with wilfully causing his traction engine and three trailers to obstruct the roadway on Brightside Lane, Sheffield.

The first trailer was too high to pass underneath the railway bridge and got stuck, blocking the tram lines for more than an hour.

The defendant pleaded Guilty but must have got the surprise of his life when the court chairman said: "Do you ask us to convict because this trailer happened to be a bit higher than defendant thought and therefore would not pass under the bridge? We shall not do so. The case will be dismissed."

This tram terminus at Lydgate Lane, Crookes, Sheffield, was opened in 1901.

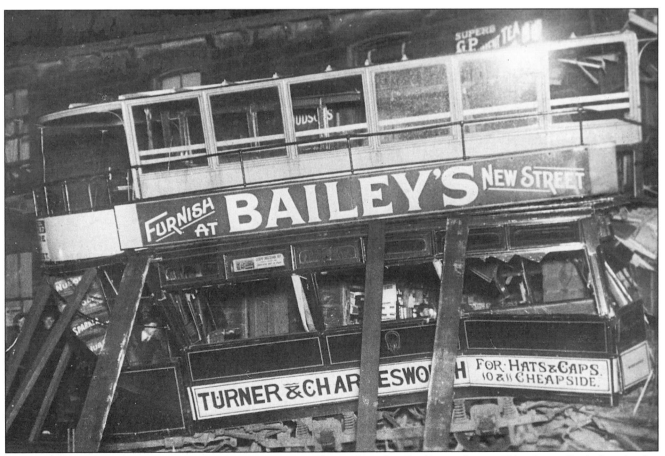

Two people were killed and five injured when this tram came off the rails and crashed into a shop on Eldon Street North, Barnsley, in December, 1914.

Last rites in the rain for city'

A sad moment, but Sheffield rings out trams in cup-tie style

By BRYAN DUNTHORNE

SHEFFIELD said farewell to its trams with a display of fervour that even torrential rain could not dampen, as the procession of 15 trams made its final sentimental journey through the city.

Cheers, rattles and bells, more often heard at a cup-tie, the hooting of motor-car horns, and music, sped them on their way to Tinsley, and eventually the breakers' yard.

Significantly, as a mark of respect, someone hung a wreath on the last tram, No. 510, as it moved slowly from Town Hall Square on its way east.

For museum

It was a symbol only, for this car in which the Lord Mayor and Lady Mayoress, Ald. and Mrs. H. Slack, the Master Cutler, Mr. and Mrs. C. H. T. Williams, and other civic guests rode in is to be preserved by the Tramway Museum Society at Crich.

Not so car No. 503, in which I travelled with Mr. Theodore Santarelli de Brasch, of Boston, Mass., president of the Trolley Society in Maine, who after a 4,000-mile flight arrived in Sheffield just before the procession moved off.

He was welcomed by the Lord Mayor and Ald. Sidney Dyson, chairman of the Transport Committee, and invited to attend the civic dinner at the Town Hall.

His diminutive little banker over the rails from

AN ENTHUSIAST places a coin on the lines to get a souvenir as last tram No. 510 passes Tenter Street depot.

Lang Syne" as 510 gradually moved away

The crowds surged round those last trams trying in vain to watercatch for a last ride

Transport Department, proposing the toast of Sheffield Transport Department.

"I only hope that in 1962 when Glasgow scraps its trams it can do it in such an unforgettable manner."

Good service

Municipal transport through the years he said had given good service to the public, and it had been untouched by the various shades of political opinion.

It was fortunate indeed for municipal undertakings that they had public spirited men willing and anxious to provide such services, not for £500 a year as they would be paid by the British Transport Commission.

They did it out of public spirited mindedness, and were backed by loyal staff and workers.

Replying, Ald. Sidney Dyson said this indeed was a proud if sad night, and the two sons of Mr. Arthur Fearnley, "father of Sheffield Transport," Mr. C. R. Fearnley and Mr. R. A. Fearnley, who were present, must indeed be proud men.

Proud city

Sheffield was proud that for so many years it had rendered good public service with its transport department, and of the people who had served it so well.

It would in the new era endeavour to continue to give that same efficiency.

He would be so bold as to say that if any future Government though nationalising

nent from the chairman of the committee.

Ald. Turner said Ald. Dyson, was once a 1s. per week horse boy at the Heeley tram depot, and had risen to give the city wonderful service, so appropriately he presented him with a silver horseshoe.

But this was not quite the end, for Mr. C. F. Burgin, driver of the last tram, presented the Lady Mayoress and Mr. De Brasch with buttons from his uniform.

Souvenir tickets

For those who took part in that last ride there were souvenirs in the form of special tickets, and a brochure, specially prepared for the occasion.

But while the trams have disappeared from public service it will be some time before those not being preserved are broken up.

They will remain in the Tinsley depot until they are taken one by one on a special track across the road to the breakers' yard.

The overhead wires and poles will also be scrapped, and within a year all traces of the trams will be removed from the city.

A WREATH FOR THE LAST TRAM

In the same way that thousands had packed Sheffield's streets in 1899 for the first electric trams, the crowds were out again for the last ones in October, 1960.

It was an emotional night and someone hung a wreath on the final tram to leave Town Hall Square, number 510.

They may not have known that this one was to survive the breaker's hammer and is preserved in Crich Tramway Museum, Derbyshire.

The Star devoted the whole of its leader column to the fond farewell.

SHEFFIELD is full of memories today.

In the centre there is feeling of nakedness.

Why?

Because this is our first working day in 87 years without our famous trams.

And for many thousands of Sheffielders the memory of them will never pass.

True, they have been raved at and cursed at by a large section of the public for a long time.

SALUTE

It is also undeniably true that as a form of public transport trams have had their day.

But on Saturday night the city showed just what place the trams had in the heart of almost every Sheffielder, whatever unkind thoughts he may have sometimes uttered.

Thousands of people packed the streets to pay their last respects in a fantastic demonstration of sentiment and nostalgia.

Lines of motorists who had hooted angrily at them often enough before now hooted in salute.

For everyone there it was an unforgettable moment of real history.

The trams moved to the breakers' yard through a positive barrage of camera flashes.

REGRET

Specially decorated for the occasion.

Torrential rain failed to stop the crowds saying goodbye to what had become trusted old friends.

Just like a pit pony after a lifetime's work, Sheffield's last tram has found a peaceful resting place. Number 510 pictured in the snow at Crich Tramway Museum.

End of the line for number 531, pictured in the scrapyard of T.W.Ward Ltd at Tinsley, Sheffield, on October 10, 1960.

After 1960, it was 34 years before the next tram came along. But super smooth Supertram was well worth the wait, even though the city centre traffic chaos caused by track laying seemed to go on for ever. Ironically, workmen discovered some of the old tram track while laying the new. A smiling Dave Bridges had the distinction of being the first Supertram driver.

(Right) Blue Riband Day for Sheffield as the first Supertram moves off.

15-minute ride into history books as network launched
BLUE RIBAND DAY FOR SUPERTRAM

Journey's end . . . Supertram breaks the tape as it arrives on Commercial Street after its first journey

Photo: Dennis Lound

By Bill Brotherton

Four different kinds of transport – trams, trains, cars and lorries – intermingle near the Wicker Arches, Sheffield, in April, 1955.

SHEFFIELD SETS 5 MPH SPEED LIMIT

A campaign to suppress the "dangerous" speed of heavy motor vehicles in the city was launched by Sheffield Corporation in August, 1912.

And it resulted in several defendants facing the wrath of a Sheffield court. They must have trembled in their well-polished boots when the prosecution solicitor rose to his feet to say that things had got to such a pass that vehicles which ought not to be driven at a speed of more than FIVE miles an hour had been driven at speeds approaching SEVEN miles an hour.

He thundered: "The cars carried very heavy loads and, apart from the danger to other traffic, the roads were being seriously damaged."

The court threw the book at several drivers. One vehicle, carrying a load of bricks, covered a measured distance of 110 yards on Chesterfield Road, Sheffield, in 40 seconds, which worked out at five and a half miles per hour.

He was fined 20s, a lot of money in those days.

Another driver was fined 40s for travelling at six and a half miles an hour.

YORKSHIRE TELEGRA
THE SPEED LIMIT.
Heavy Motor Vehicle Drivers Fined.
SHEFFIELD TRAPS.

The Sheffield Corporation have started a campaign to suppress the dangerous speed at which many of the heavy motor vehicles are driven in the city. Several summonses against defaulters were dealt with at the City Police Court to-day, convictions being recorded in each case.

Mr. J. Varley, from the Town Clerk's Office, appeared to prosecute, and stated that the cases had been brought under the Heavy Motor Car Order of 1904, which made it a punishable offence if heavy motor-cars were driven at a speed exceeding five miles an hour. Things had got to such a pass, said Mr Varley, that cars which ought not to be driven at a speed of more than five miles an hour had been driven at speeds approaching seven miles an hour. The cars carried very heavy loads, and, apart from the danger to other traffic, the roads were being seriously damaged.

Bernard Farman, of 11, Harbord Road, was summoned in respect of an offence on Chesterfield Road. It was found that he travelled over a measured distance of 110 yards with a load of bricks in 40 seconds, this being at a rate of just over five and a half miles an hour. Defendant was fined 20s including costs.

For driving over the same distance at a rate of nearly 6½ miles an hour, Percy Vamplew, of 231, Chesterfield Road, was fined 40s including costs.

Alfred Gosney, of Rivelin Glen, fell into a trap that had been set on Langsett Road. He covered the measured distance of 110 yards at a rate of nearly seven miles an hour. He was fined 40s., including costs.

Thomas Ellis, of 5, Brier Street, had to answer two summonses, one for an offence in Holme Lane, Hillsborough, when he covered the measured distance at a rate of about 6½ miles an hour, and the other for an offence in Langsett Road, when he travelled at a rate of nearly seven miles an hour. The magistrates—Sir Frank Mappin, Bart., and Mr. C. J. Whitehead—imposed a fine of 20s., including costs, in each case.

Robert Brown, of 270, Edmund Road, was fined 40s and 10s. costs for driving a motor-car to the danger of the public in the Haymarket on the 9th of August.

The evidence was to the effect that the defendant was driving in the direction of Waingate. A tramcar was standing at the corner of Castle Street, and instead of proceeding on the near side, the defendant, who it was alleged was driving at a rate of 15 miles an hour, "switched" his car to the off side, practically monopolising the whole of the road. He eventually ran into the kerb of the road opposite the Royal Hotel. Defendant, who contended that he was not driving at a rate of more than six miles an hour, said he was compelled to divert his course owing to other traffic.

THE VACANT VICARIATE.

Not ideal for a rainy day but the admiring glances of the cloth-capped onlookers seem to suggest that seeing this on a Sheffield road was a bit out of the ordinary.

THE "ALIENS'" ARRIVAL.

Taxi-Cabs in Sheffield.

WILL THEY OUST THE GROWLER?

"Yorkshire Telegraph and Star" Special.

It was in Church Street this afternoon (writes a "Star" man) that I made my first acquaintance with the taxi-cab, the new vehicle which in London has practically killed the "growler," and which promises to make a similar revolution in the provinces It stood amongst the four-wheelers, proudly conscious of its smart appearance, and positively shining with aggressive newness. The horses attached to the cabs on the ranks seemed to droop their heads a little lower, as if painfully aware of the shortcomings of their vehicles.

The driver of the "taxi," in smart grey uniform with white metal buttons, guessed a "fare," and holding open the door displayed an invitingly comfortable interior. "A shilling's worth anywhere," I said, as I jumped in. The chauffeur dropped the little red metal flag, and with a throb of the motor we were away.

It is early to say whether the taxi-cab has come to stay in the provinces, but judging from the comfort and rapidity of this mode of conveyance, it is highly probable. The car presents a handsome exterior, and inside the cushions are the last thing in comfort.

From inside, the taximeter can be seen by the passenger. The moment a "fare" is registered the price for one mile, 1s., is indicated; every additional quarter of a mile, threepence is charged. The driver is practically "on his own," and takes 25 per cent. of the fares.

There are three cabs at present in use in Sheffield. One cab is on the Church Street rank, one in Fitzalan Square and another Barker Pool. It

---

Our Gallant Firemen.

Sheffield's Splendid Brigade.

AN INTERIOR VIEW.

("Yorkshire Telegraph and Star" Special.)

The man in the street, as he sees the picturesque Reference to the officers of the brigade brings one to the information that all have been com

The Star published a special feature on Sheffield's "gallant" fire brigade in 1908, describing it as a model of what efficient administration and enterprising development can accomplish.

SHEFFIELD'S FIRST TAXIS

Taxicabs, three of them, arrived in Sheffield for the first time in July, 1908, and a reporter from The Star was among the first to use one.

He jumped into it in Church Street and was immediately impressed by the luxury.

He wrote: "It is early to say whether the taxi-cab has come to stay in the provinces but, judging from the comfort and rapidity of this mode of conveyance, it is highly probable. The car presents a handsome exterior and inside the cushions are the last thing in comfort."

Our reporter seemed fascinated by the method of payment – "From inside, the taximeter can be seen by the passenger. The moment a 'fare' is registered, the price for one mile, one shilling, is indicated; every additional quarter of a mile, threepence is charged."

The two other cabs were based in Fitzalan Square and Barker's Pool, and when the article appeared on July 17, 1908, the city was expecting another 20 the following week.

DOGS CAUSE SWERVE AND CRASH

DOGS, playing in the street, were directly responsible for this road crash in Sheffield to-day.

A van belonging to Sheffield Corporation Electricity Department swerved after getting out of control in Penistone Road, and collided with a tram standard.

JUST MISSED WALL

The driver, Alfred Sherratt, of 38, Oakland Road, Sheffield, was lucky to escape with only slight injuries, for the van missed crashing into a wall only by inches.

On the other side of the wall is a drop of 15 feet into the Don.

A number of dogs suddenly ran into Penistone Road out of West Don Street, and one of them ran into the nearside front wheel of the van.

The steering wheel was jerked out of the driver's hands, and he was unable to prevent the van swerving across the road into the tram standard.

Sherratt was taken to the Royal Infirmary suffering from abrasions, but was not detained.

A story about dogs and a post.

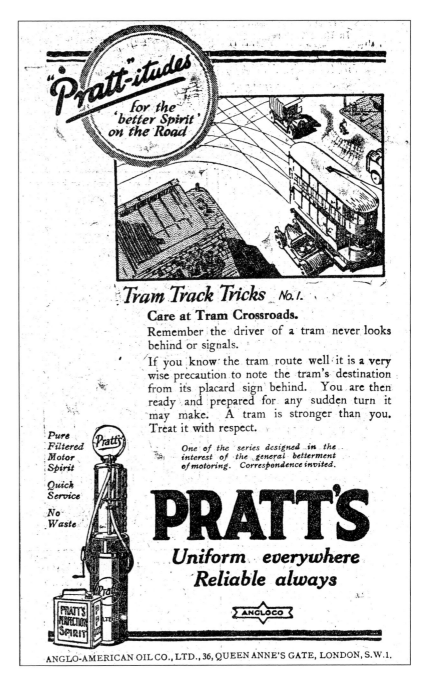

"Pratt-itudes" for the 'better Spirit' on the Road

Tram Track Tricks No. 1.

Care at Tram Crossroads.

Remember the driver of a tram never looks behind or signals.

If you know the tram route well it is a very wise precaution to note the tram's destination from its placard sign behind. You are then ready and prepared for any sudden turn it may make. A tram is stronger than you. Treat it with respect.

One of the series designed in the interest of the general betterment of motoring. Correspondence invited.

Pure Filtered Motor Spirit

Quick Service

No Waste

PRATT'S

Uniform everywhere Reliable always

ANGLOCO

ANGLO-AMERICAN OIL CO., LTD., 36, QUEEN ANNE'S GATE, LONDON, S.W.1.

A rather unfortunate name for a company offering advice on good driving! That was 1923. In this day and age, Pratt-itudes is a suitable word for describing the intentions and actions of bad drivers!

A COMING FALL IN HOLIDAY COSTS?

[Photo: Babington. Block: Leng.

A possible drop in holiday expenses is foreshadowed by this picture, which shows a party leaving Sheffield to-day for London by road, at a return fare of 10s. 6d.—a record in road transit.

Sheffield to London and back for 10s 6d in 1923.

Road Hogs.

Sir,—Spring has arrived, and with it has come the road hog, although as yet it is rather too early, chilly, and damp for the young bloods to be out and about.

We, however, came upon one on Monday in Derbyshire, and not being satisfied with coming round a bend at 20 miles per hour, giving no warning, trying to upset an orderly club, riding on its extreme left, he had to use obscene language, and this in the presence of lady members.

Needless to say, the matter has been reported to the proper quarters, and we hope to see him dealt with in the strictest manner possible at some future date.

The advent of the general road hog is coming shortly, and I feel sure I cannot do better than impress upon all club members to take the numbers of these pests' machines and cars and report them immediately to the first constable, and also to their respective unions. It is our only way to make it safe for our lady members to ride with us.—Yours faithfully,

C. S. ELMER, Hon. Secretary,
Sheffield Unity Cycling Club.
96, Greystones Road, Sheffield.

Summer Time.

Sir,—I think "Hadenough" is to be com-

A 1930 preview of the new Morris Minor for readers of The Star.

Sheffield Unity Cycling Club complain, through The Star's readers' letters section, about bad driving and obscene language from a 1923 road hog.

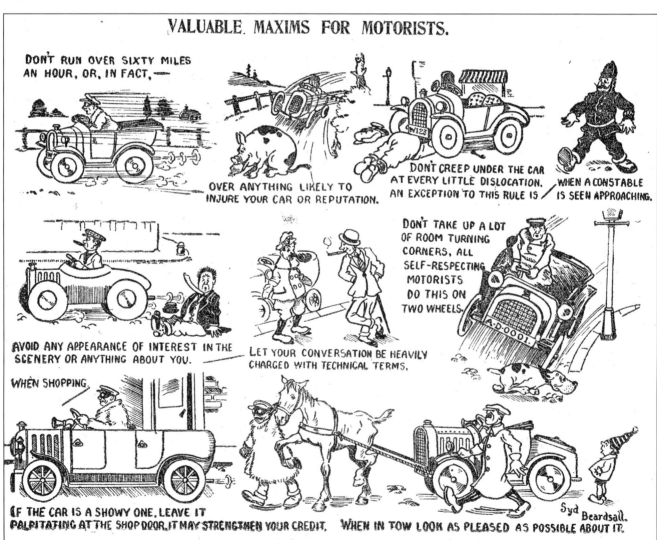

The Star's artist offers some tongue-in-cheek advice to motorists in 1923.

Roadside check for ALL cars planned for early summer

By JOSEPH TOBIN

THE Government have decided to go ahead with plans for roadside checks of cars and the compulsory testing of motor vehicles for road worthiness is expected to start after Easter.

A White Paper will be issued shortly by the Minister of Transport, Mr Harold Watkinson, which will give full details of the scheme to set up...

The first announcement in 1958 that MOT testing of motor vehicles was to start in this country.

RIVAL DOUBLE=DECKER PASSENGER TRANSPORT.

[Blocks: Leng.

With the growth of municipal passenger services in various towns special interest attaches to these two new photographs of the new rivals. Above is seen the double-decker closed-in motor 'bus, which the Sheffield Corporation Tramway Service is...

New buses for Sheffield in 1924.

THURSDAY EVENING, J

SILENCE CHARTER.

New Regulations for Motorists.

NOISE BAN.

Putting a Check on the Road Nuisance.

The Ministry of Transport announced last night that the Motor-Cars (Excessive Noise) Regulations, dated June 3rd, and applying to all heavy motor-cars, motor-cars, and motor-cycles, will come into force on August 1st next.

The regulations have been framed after careful consideration of the recommendations of a conference and in consultation with the Home Secretary.

The new regulations make it an offence for any person to use or permit to be used a motor-car or a trailer drawn by a motor-car which causes any excessive noise as a result of any defect in design or construction or lack of repair or faulty adjustment. It is also an offence under the regulations to use a vehicle or trailer which makes an excessive noise due to the faulty packing or adjustment of the load.

It is provided that excessive noise due to some temporary or accidental cause which could not have been prevented by the exercise of due diligence and care shall not constitute an offence. It is also provided that where a person other than the driver is responsible for the maintenance of the vehicle or for its loading the driver shall not be held liable unless the noise could have been prevented by the exercise of reasonable diligence and care on his part.

The effect is given to a recommendation in the new regulations that it shall be an offence to sound a motor horn on a stationary vehicle except when an audible warning was necessary on grounds of safety.

Cross-Roads.

As regards the cross-road danger, the Minister has addressed a letter to all highway authorities

Traffic noise was becoming something of a problem in 1929 so the Government introduced new laws.

OUT OF THE VERY HEART OF ENGLAND
THE CAR THE PUBLIC WANTS IS HERE!

Out of the rich experience of twenty-eight years of continuous motor-car manufacture—out of thousands of pounds spent in research—out of the brains of the finest designers, the craftsmanship of famous engineers—*four new mechanical wonders have emerged* . . . A new series of cars built to meet the economic conditions of to-day . . . A new series of cars—high in comfort and performance, *yet sensationally low in price and running costs* . . . Surely no cars have ever been launched with greater confidence than these new Standard models! . . . For, are they not just what the public *wants*—what they have *waited* for ? . . . To a public educated by prosperity to demand the highest measure of luxury and performance in a car, Standard announce their 1932 models!

THE "STANDARD LITTLE NINE"

A car is made . . . to seat four grown-up people in roomy comfort . . . to give a comfortable maximum speed of 56 miles an hour . . . to hold the road with the steadiness of much larger cars . . . to run for over 40 miles on a single gallon of petrol. A car is made . . . all-British, constructed of the finest materials . . . powerful, yet light enough to reduce running costs to a minimum, sturdy enough to ensure the utmost reliability, small enough to be garaged easily and cared for by the owner. A car is made . . . luxuriously finished and lavishly equipped . . . with springing that is a positive revelation . . . for £155!

Coachbuilt Saloon £155 Ex works   Tourer £145 Ex works
(For full descriptions and road tests of all models see July 31 issue of the "Autocar.")

THE "STANDARD BIG NINE"

The "Big Nine" in its 1932 form! Even cheaper to buy, even cheaper to run. All coachbuilt bodies now . . . rear petrol tank . . . a four-speed gearbox, with really silent third . . . the new impressive radiator design . . . sliding roof as standard . . . Protecto-glass screen, Magna type wire wheels. A full-sized family or business car with all the economical advantages of light weight, low horsepower and small chassis dimensions.

Coachbuilt Saloon £205 Ex works
Tourer   - £195 Ex works

THE "STANDARD SIXTEEN"

A car with all the costly qualities of luxury, comfort and performance—yet at a revolutionary price! A sweet silent speed of 65 m.p.h. . . . easily operated controls . . . flexibility and acceleration suggestive of much larger cars. The famous Standard "Ensign" ready for, 1932—with even more luxury and comfort, even more lavish equipment, even more brilliant road capabilities!

Coachbuilt Saloon £235 Ex works   Tourer £225 Ex works

THE "STANDARD TWENTY"

A still more spacious model of the Standard "Envoy," with all its magnificent luxury—coachbuilt for £325! This model is built for the motorist who requires a really large car. Yet good looks have not been sacrificed to size; you have to look inside to realize the roominess of this great comfortable car. All models this year are upholstered in furniture hide, seats are deeply cushioned and a wealth of equipment and appointments supplied.

Coachbuilt Saloon £325 Ex works Coachbuilt Special Saloon £355 Ex works

STANDARD DEALERS IN EVERY TOWN ARE WAITING TO SHOW YOU THESE FOUR AMAZING CARS . . .

Write for a wonderful new catalogue to the Standard Motor Co. Ltd., Canley, Coventry.

the STANDARD
by which all other cars are judged

In Distributors for STANDARD CARS: ERNEST W. HATFIELD, Ltd

Four new "mechanical wonders" from 1931.

IF YOU

HIKE - BIKE

TRAMP - CAMP

BOAT OR - MOTOR

don't forget your

DIPLOMA

For meals out-of-doors, for food to carry with you—in your haversack, in the picnic basket, on your motor bicycle, in the car—Diploma Cheese is absolutely the thing . . . appetising, delicious, satisfying, this famous English cheese turns the wayside snack into a wholesome meal.

The English Crustless CHEESE

Whether you are hiking, biking, tramping, camping, boating or motoring...for goodness sake, DON'T forget your Diploma cheese! According to this 1932 advertisement from The Star, it turned a wayside snack into a wholesome meal.

Sheffield Corporation Transport Department has received the first two of the new double-deck buses on order. Here is one of the buses, which are the last word in design and comfort.

A new Sheffield Corporation bus in 1947 – "the last word in design and comfort."

Barges were an important form of commercial transport in the 1950s and this 1954 picture shows a bridge on Staniforth Road, Sheffield, being lifted to give more clearance to waterways traffic.

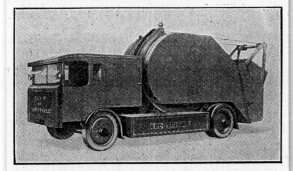

GRAPH AND STAR, SATURDAY EVENING,

THE LATEST IN DUST CARTS.

Sheffield the First Authority to Acquire New Dustless Type.

THE Sheffield Corporation is the first which is rests the door portion

A first for Sheffield in 1931 – the new dustless dustbin lorry.

SHEFFIELD'S first four traffic wardens went into action yesterday.

They were described as "ambassadors for the police force" by the Chief Constable, Mr. Edward Barker.

But the wardens are so far at half strength—the police have been able to recruit only four of the eight men needed to cover the city.

At the last meeting of the Watch Committee, the rates of pay for wardens were stepped up in an effort to encourage applicants.

Goodwill

Mr. Barker said yestardey: "I am not interested in numbers of convictions or prosecutions.

"The wardens main job is to be helpful and show goodwill towards the motorist — they are ambassadors for the police force."

The four men, who have spent the last fortnight in training, will be expected to cover the same area as the full complement of wardens, and will have some assistance from constables on normal duty.

Mr. Barker pointed out that they would also undertake some traffic survey duties

● Warden L. Bullas, on duty for the first time, notes down car numbers in a restricted waiting area.

INJURED TRAIN

Sheffield's first traffic wardens patrol the streets, March, 1966.

The city's first women traffic wardens, Mrs M.J.Watson (left) and Mrs M.Millward, start work in June,1966.

Set fair for a fair fare are these Rotherham taxi drivers pictured in 1971.

Brenda Cork, of Rotherham, made history in March, 1976, when she trained to become Sheffield's first woman bus driver.
She learned to drive a double decker in Nottingham and had also worked as a taxi driver and a driving instructor.

This 1974 futuristic traffic plan of a computer controlled mini-tram system designed to carry Sheffield shoppers on a "tramway" on stilts never got off the ground but it did bear an uncanny resemblance to the Supertram system which followed 20 years later.

The picture is an artist's impression of a mini-tram crossing Castle Square.

Sheffield's most famous train, The Master Cutler, had its inaugural run on October 6, 1947, from Sheffield Victoria to London Marylebone down the Great Central line which had opened for passenger traffic in 1899.

It was a very special day for the city. The train was officially named the Master Cutler by the then Master Cutler, the Hon. R.A.Balfour, who travelled on the footplate to London in a muffler, overalls and a train driver's cap.

The daily train became a prestigious Sheffield businessmen's special with Pullman coaches and upmarket dining facilities.

By 1962, the Master Cutler was diesel hauled as opposed to steam.

WHAT A PLAICE FOR A TRAIN CRASH

A railway accident on the Barnsley to Sheffield line just outside Ecclesfield Station 100 years ago gave locals an unexpected treat.

In the early hours of November 29, 1900, 30 wagons on an express goods train came off the track, blocking both lines and causing thousands of pounds worth of damage.

The train was carrying mostly beer from Tadcaster Brewery, fish, timber and dried fruit and when dawn came locals flocked to the scene of the crash and helped themselves to the ale and fish.

A report in the Sheffield Telegraph, The Star's sister paper, said: "The fish furnished an appetising breakfast at many of the cottages round about. As these provisions could otherwise have been wasted, no one interfered with those who were turning them to practical use."

No one was injured in the smash but the driver and fireman of the locomotive, which had stayed on the rails, were later hailed as heroes.

They "proceeded with all haste" on their engine to Wincobank and told the signalman there what had happened.

He put the signals on red in both directions to stop other trains smashing into the wreckage.

43066

November 2, 1993, and the Master Cutler is pulled by a sleek High Speed Train.

ROBERTS B... ...ERS
ROCKINGHAM HOU... THE MOOR   ...No. ...   TUESDAY, SEPTEMBER 14, 1954   A KEMSLE... ...EWSPAPER.   ...NE 25482

ELECTRIC TRAIN CLIF
TEN MINUTES

Service Opens To Manchester

AN electric train opened a service between Sheffield and Manchester today by making the 41-mile journey in record time—53 and a half minutes, ten minutes faster than the steam train schedule.

British Transport chairman Sir Brian Robertson blew the whistle which started the train from Sheffield.

After arriving at Manchester Sir Brian shook the hand of the train's driver, Mr. Frank Laming, of Elm Lane, Sheffield, and said: "Well done; very good run!"

Mr Laming said the average speed for the run was 45 m.p.h. Because he was running ahead of time he had had to cut his speed down from its peak of 60 m.p.h.

WORKMEN

Amid the galaxy of important railway, civic and industrial personalities making the trip was a group of men who, as much as anyone else, had helped to bring to fruition the £10,000,000 schem...

Drawn from... workshops, ...rmanent ...al boxe...

THE MEN—AND A TRAIN

ALL ready for the first trip—at Sheffield Victoria Station British Transport Commission Chairman, Sir Brian Robertson, talks to the Lord Mayor, Alderman J. H. Bingham. And on the left is the record-breaking Co-Co engine which hauled the train on its run to Manchester.

What's Wrong at Bramall Lane?

THIS is a dark hour for Sheffield United F.C. ...at ...their first four game... ...amall Lane this se... ...it is clear...

Cze...
F...
on ...

A CZECH... fired o... Army Bavarian-Cze... U.S. Army sa...

The Amer... return the rounds came f... weapon, but n... injured.

SECOND

There was ...property. Barnau is a... of Bayreuth. This is th... incident alon... recent days. On Thursda... patrol was fi... patrols in the ...tenberg.

Widow's ("Quit...

Mrs. Violet the Bromham who was atta... on Saturday... Devizes Hospi... had a comfor... condition wa... "quite good."

NATO CALLED TO

Sheffield is electrified by the speed of its new train service to Manchester on September 14, 1954. The new electric train makes the 41-mile journey from Sheffield Victoria in a record time of just over 53 minutes, ten minutes faster than the steam train it replaced.

The record breaker sets off from Sheffield Victoria on September 14, 1954, the first inter-city electrified service in the country.

The end of a railway era

LAST TRAIN TO CITY OVER WOODHEAD LINE

By a staff reporter

A PIECE of railway history ended in confusion at Sheffield early today.

What should have been a sentimental journey from Sheffield to Manchester in the last passenger train to travel along the Woodhead line turned into a fiasco.

It all began when a group of railway enthusists boarded the 7.30 p.m. train from Sheffield to Manchester last night in order to take one last look at the old line.

But, due to a derailment, the enthusists missed the train which was to have returned them to Sheffield.

Sit-in

After being told that they would have to wait four hours for the next train back to Sheffield the Hope Valley railway hungry train

The last train via Woodhead pulls into Sheffield

January 5, 1970, and the end of another era. The red light goes on for the electric passenger service from Sheffield Victoria over the Woodhead line to Manchester.

The last electric passenger train leaves Victoria and there's a sad wave to the driver from a fellow railway worker.

Back in 1944, one of the country's most powerful locomotives was in Sheffield for a special ceremony.

LMS Coronation class 6249, which spent most of its life hauling passenger traffic on the fast West Coast main line between London Euston and Glasgow, was chosen to carry the name City of Sheffield.

Steam buffs will appreciate the significance of this historic photograph taken by enthusiast John Naylor, who was then 17, at Sheffield Midland Station on the same day that the Lord Mayor, Coun Hartley Marshall, carried out the naming ceremony.

For it is believed to be the only time a Coronation class worked into the city.

The City of Sheffield nameplate is officially presented to the city in 1965.

Letting the train take the strain are these youngsters from Christ Church Youth Club, Attercliffe, about to leave on a Sheffield United special for the match against Arsenal in 1973. In charge of the flock is a smiling Rev John Smith.

These 1953 trainspotters would not have been allowed on to the platforms at Sheffield Midland Station so peering through the bars was their only option.

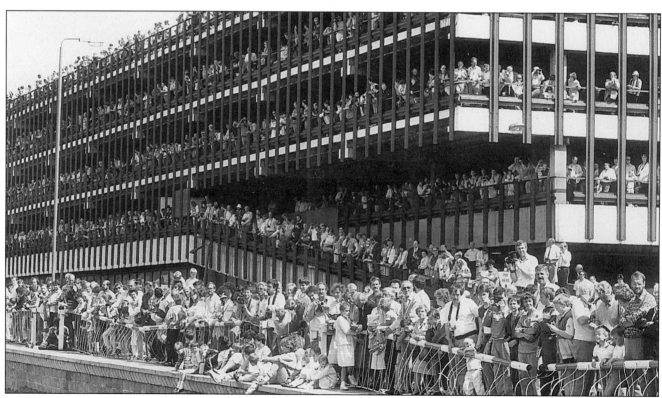

Just what are they all waiting for? One clue is that many of the huge crowd packing this car park at Doncaster are carrying cameras.

Here's the reason. Slipping into Doncaster station on July 3, 1988, is one of the world's best known steam locomotives, Mallard.

The pictures were taken exactly 50 years to the day since the A4 locomotive achieved an all-time record for steam traction, reaching 125mph between Grantham and Peterborough on July 3, 1938.

Mallard has been preserved and attracts huge crowds wherever she goes. It's a common sight to see camera and video-carrying bank managers, vicars and all kinds of enthusiasts hanging over railway bridges and popping up out of line-side cornfields.

The cream of Britain's locomotives have pulled steam specials into Sheffield Midland Station at some time or other and Duchess of Hamilton was a popular visitor in May, 1985.

All steamed up at the Midland in June, 1980 is the Flying Scotsman.

A gleaming Princess Margaret Rose glides in on March 18, 1994.

Sheffield Newspapers photographer Steve Ellis set off to look for newsy snow pictures in February, 1994, decided to pop into the Midland Station and came across this surprise visitor, 34027 Taw Valley.

The lure of steam! More than 50,000 were at Doncaster Plant Works in November, 1970, to see Valerie Singleton name an A2 locomotive after the Blue Peter children's television programme.

Oops! Police had to seal off part of Sheffield Parkway in December, 1978, after a Class 56 diesel locomotive overran the buffers and finished up protruding into the slow lane.

Four months later, in April, 1979, it happened again. This time the victim was a shunting engine.

UP, UP AND AWAY

EXCHANGE COMPANY LTD.

Free Delivery on First Payment.

136, BRAMALL LANE,
SHEFFIELD.

SHEFFIELD: TELEPHONE 22055 (FOURTEE

№. 13,601.

Spectacular Lan

EMPIRE'S EMPIRE DAY HEROINE.

TRIUMPH OF YORKSHIRE GIRL.

FEAT EQUALS DEEDS OF GREAT AIRMEN.

LAST 500 MILES OVER SEA WITHOUT ESCORT.

MISS AMY JOHNSON REACHED AUSTRALIA TO-DAY.

MISS JOHNSON left England 20 days ago "with the object of waking up England to the greater possibilities of aviation." In this she has succeeded She has raised British prestige throughout the world, and, in the words of a famous airman, has shown that women are as capable as men in the air.

She flew from England to India in record time, and while bad weather and accidents prevented her reaching Australia quicker than had been done before, she has the honour of being the first woman to fly solo to Australia.

Her last stage to-day was 500 miles over sea. She had a great reception after making a spectacular landing at Port Darwin.

HEROINE OF THE FLIGHT.

It was international news and the world paid tribute to Amy Johnson in May, 1930, when she became the first woman aviator to fly solo from England to Australia.

What may not be common knowledge is that the famous air pioneer studied at Sheffield University and had close links with the city. So when she made her historic flight, it was, quite naturally, all over The Star's front page.

The Editor of The Star, proud of Amy's associations with Sheffield, sent her a congratulatory telegram in Australia on behalf of readers.

Council to Protest Strongly at Minister's Decision

SHEFFIELD AIRPORT SCHEME REJECTED

The Queen and

SHEFFIELD'S plan to use land at Lodge Moor as an aerodrome has been turned down by the Minister of Housing and Local Government.

A letter containing this decision was considered by a special meeting of the Council's Parliamentary and General Purposes Committee this afternoon.

The Minister states that he would consider a renewed application from the city for permission to develop an aerodrome at Redmires Road — after three years.

A minute, moved by Ald. J. H. Bingham and seconded by Ald. H. W. Jackson, recommending the Council to protest most strongly against the decision of the Minister, was presented to the Council.

173 ACRES

It also recommended that the local M.P.s be asked to discuss the matter with the Committee and representatives of the Cutlers' Company, Sheffield Chamber of Commerce and Sheffield Trades and Labour Council

Sheffield was thinking about an airport in 1952 but a plan was turned down by the Minister of Housing and Local Government.

First passengers make airport history

Passenger Rebecca Cowen, of Totley, boarding her plane at Sheffield airport today en route to Vienna. Her flight was slightly delayed by high winds across Holland

We have lift-off! Sheffield Airport opens in 1998 with flights to Amsterdam. And it was not long before our new airport was spreading its wings with flights to several other destinations.

Royal Visits to Sheffield and South Yorkshire

A contemporary drawing
of the Town Hall.

A WELCOME FROM THE ROOFTOPS FOR QUEEN VICTORIA

The day Queen Victoria came to Sheffield to open the Town Hall was "the proudest page in the annals of our local life."

A "vast multitude" of people, some on rooftops, thronged the thoroughfares along the route from the Midland Station on May 21, 1897.

The Queen's visit, coming as it did at the start of her Diamond Jubilee celebrations, was a major coup for Sheffield and the city responded with a welcome that showed a "remarkable outburst of loyalty."

The Star said it was appropriate that the Queen should be visiting Sheffield at the start of her Diamond Jubilee festivities because the city had built for her Navy "that grim armour of steel" which guarded her Empire upon the seas.

The paper's leading article on the day of her visit continued: "She (Sheffield) has manufactured in countless numbers the weapons of war and the implements of peace.

"To Sheffielders, down to the tiniest tot whose recollection of the day may in future years be a hazy remembrance of crowds, and flags, and music, and cheers, the day must ever be of an especial red letter character.

"To have seen the Queen in her Diamond Jubilee year will remain a distinction of a lifetime."

After the official opening of the Town Hall, Queen Victoria moved on to Norfolk Park where 50,000 children waited to "greet her majesty in song."

Later, she visited the Cyclops Works of Charles Cammell and Company where she witnessed the rolling of an armour plate for HMS Ocean.

The following day, the Queen telegraphed from Balmoral to express her "great gratification at the very loyal and hearty reception I met with yesterday."

Her message added: "I also wish to say how much I admired the children's singing and the admirable way in which everything was arranged."

The Town Hall was thrown open for public inspection and on the same day the Mayor entertained nearly 10,000 old and poor people at 15 centres throughout Sheffield.

Y 21, 1897.

Evening Telegraph

AND STAR.

SHEFFIELD, FRIDAY, MAY 21, 1897.

OUR GRACIOUS GUEST.

Sheffield has found favour in royal eyes. With the exception, of course, of the Metropolis, probably no city or town in the United Kingdom can boast of a more extensive list of royal visitors. The visit of the Prince and Princess of Wales, though a quarter of a century has elapsed since it occurred, is still fresh in the memory of Sheffielders, while in more recent times we have had the honour and the gratification of welcoming the late Duke of Albany, the late Duke of Clarence, and the Duke and Duchess of York. Favoured thus by royalty, though we have been, it has been for years a common sentiment of regret that the cutlery capital had never welcomed as a guest within her borders the great Queen-mother of the Empire. That regret is dissipated to-day. At an age when exertion must of necessity be physically exhausting, and in a year in which peculiar demands will be made upon her strength, the Queen does Sheffield the signal honour of paying the city a visit. The Diamond Jubilee of Queen does Sheffield the signal honour of paying

The Star welcomes Queen Victoria in its leader column.

THE QUEEN'S VISIT.

TELEGRAM FROM BALMORAL.

HER MAJESTY'S GRATIFICATION.

THE DUKE OF NORFOLK'S REPLY.

The following telegram has been received from Her Majesty the Queen:—

"O.H.M.S.

"Balmoral, 10.20. Received in Sheffield, 10.31.

"To Duke of Norfolk,—

"Safely arrived here. I wish to express my great gratification at the very loyal and hearty reception I met with yesterday at Sheffield.

"I wish also to say how much I admired the children's singing, and the admirable way in which everything was arranged.

"V.R.I."

The Duke of Norfolk has forwarded the following reply:—

"To Her Majesty the Queen, Balmoral.

"Your Majesty's gracious message is received by Sheffield and myself with deep thankfulness for your appreciation of our efforts to show our love for the Queen and our loyalty to her throne. By none are your words welcomed with greater joy than by the children of whom your Majesty speaks so graciously. That your Majesty has not suffered from the fatigue entailed by your great goodness to us is the cause of heartfelt rejoicing to us all. With my humble duty,

"NORFOLK, Mayor."

ARRIVAL AT BALMORAL.

The Queen reached Ballater this morning, and drove to Balmoral. The Royal train only stopped at Perth five minutes, and the blinds of Her Majesty's saloon remained drawn.

Princess Beatrice passed through Perth by ordinary train.

Her Majesty looked quite fresh and well after her journey, and was apparently unaffected by the fatigue and

The Queen's telegram from Balmoral the day after her visit.

"To The Best of Queens", says the Royal arch in Barker's Pool, Sheffield, in 1897.

THE

"Sheffield Daily Telegraph" and the Queen's Visit.

THE ROYAL NUMBER.

20 PAGES—160 COLUMNS.

UNPARALLELED SUCCESS— UNABLE TO COPE WITH DEMAND.

RECORD SALE.

150,000 COPIES SOLD; MACHINES STILL RUNNING.

SHEFFIELD, Noon.

In consequence of the enormous demand for to-day's issue of the

"SHEFFIELD DAILY TELEGRAPH"

(20 PAGES, 160 COLUMNS),

we find it difficult, even with the great facilities afforded by our

TWO NEW THREE-DECKER HOE MACHINES,

to anything like approach satisfying the requirements that are

POURING IN FROM ALL PARTS

of the country. We, therefore, beg the indulgence of those who have not been able to secure copies, and assure them that

EVERY EFFORT POSSIBLE

will be made to meet their wishes. We shall keep the machines at work until

FOUR O'CLOCK THIS AFTERNOON,

beyond which time we do not feel justified in taxing further

THE ENDURANCE OF OUR PRINTING STAFF,

some of whom had at noon been on duty unceasingly for 27 hours. Should the demand not be satisfied to-day, which is exceedingly probable, we shall

RESUME PRINTING ON MONDAY

morning, and in the interim we have to ask news-agents to estimate carefully

WHAT SUPPLY THEY REQUIRE,

and forward written orders by to-night's post. As

AN ILLUSTRATION

of how

GREAT IS THE DEMAND

we may say that already

150,000 COPIES

have been disposed of. Should would-be purchasers be unable to obtain copies through the ordinary channels, application to these offices will ensure attention.

THIS ESTABLISHMENT CLOSES EVERY FRIDAY AT 5 p.m. AND RE-OPENS ON SATURDAY EVENING AT 6 O'CLOCK.

THE   QUEEN'S   VISIT

IT MAY RAIN.

BE PREPARED AND

DON'T GET WET.

COME AND BUY A MACINTOSH DIRECT

FROM THE MAKER.

LADIES' FROM .... 7s. 6d.

GENT'S FROM ... . 12s. 0d.

L. SMITH AND CO.,

(Opposite Bower Spring)   145, WESTBAR.

Just about the only Sheffielder not celebrating on May 21, 1897, was probably this advertiser! This notice was placed in The Star the day before the visit – and there wasn't a drop of rain in sight. The weather was perfect and the Queen's visit took place "under a blue heaven", said one report in The Star.

The Star's then sister morning paper, the Telegraph, published a special Royal Edition which was so popular that some of the printing staff worked non-stop for 27 hours to produce extra copies!

This advertisement said that they would keep the machines going until 4pm "beyond which time we do not feel justified in taxing further the endurance of our printing staff."

Spanish Embassy has called at Marlborough House. The Spanish flag at the Embassy is flying at half-mast.

THE NEWS IN SHEFFIELD.

Sheffield people can talk of nothing else this morning but the Queen's death. The newspapers are being eagerly bought, and every scrap of information allowed to leak out with regard to the last moments of Her Majesty is hungrily seized upon. Many men and women are dressed in mourning, and in thousands of cases, where the sterner sex have not gone to this extent, a black tie has been donned. There has been a considerable increase in the number of flags flying at half-mast; draped shutters have been put up at many of the shop windows, and every hour brings news of some public or private function having been abandoned or postponed. The U.S. Consulate flag is a prominent feature in High Street.

This morning the Master Cutler (Mr. R. Groves Holland) sent a telegraphic message on behalf of the Cutlers' Company, conveying the condolences of his ancient guild with the Royal Family in their loss. Later on he will no doubt receive a reply. It has been decided by Mr. Joseph Poole not to give an afternoon performance of his myriorama at the Albert Hall to-day, but the show will be open to-night. Up to the present nothing can be said definitely about the Empire. There has been a consultation in London this morning between those primarily responsible for the syndicate under which the various Empires are run, and a message is expected telling the manager of the Sheffield house what course is to be adopted.

SHEFFIELD MOURNS QUEEN'S DEATH

Queen Victoria died four years later and Sheffield, probably because her visit in 1897 had been so successful, felt the loss deeply.

Many shops boarded up their windows as Sheffield went into mourning. Among The Star's many articles was one fondly recalling the day the Queen came to open the Town Hall.

Sheffield is in mourning.

DEATH OF THE QUEEN.

A PEACEFUL ENDING

Scene at the Bedside.

The Family Assembled.

THE NATION'S GRIEF.

THE KING ARRIVES IN LONDON.

Meeting of the Privy Council.

THE KING'S NEW TITLE.

Edward VII.

The long, glorious, and beneficent reign of Queen Victoria came to a close at half-past six yesterday evening, and a quarter of an hour later the physicians in attendance upon Her Majesty at Osborne—Sir James Reid, Sir R. Douglas Powell, and Sir Thomas Barlow—issued the following announcement:—

Her Majesty the Queen breathed her last at 6.30 p.m., surrounded by her children and grandchildren.

At eleven o'clock last night a black-bordered "Gazette Extraordinary" was issued in London containing the foregoing announcement which had been received by Mr. Secretary Ritchie.

Of the last sad scene of all Sir Arthur Bigge

The Star announces Queen Victoria's death in 1901. A thick black border surrounds the article.

KING AND QUEEN IN SHEFFIELD.

AN ENTHUSIASTIC WELCOME.

THE UNIVERSITY OPENED.

BRILLIANT PAGEANTS AND PICTURESQUE CEREMONIES.

From an early hour this morning the eyes of hundreds of thousands of persons in Sheffield and district were expectantly turned to the skies, mutely inquiring whether the Fates would be propitious for the great and eagerly-anticipated day of the coming of the King and Queen. The day broke brilliantly, and though at times ominous-looking clouds gave rise to apprehension, while the sultriness suggested not far distant thunderstorms, there was happily not even a shower to damp the pleasure of the multitudes who thronged the streets.

Sheffielders were up betimes this morning. In very many cases parties had been arranged to make at an early hour a tour of the Royal route for the purpose of inspecting the decorations with the finishing touches added to them. Almost every vehicle in Sheffield appeared to have been chartered for the occasion, from the dignified open carriage with a couple of spanking horses, down to the costers' cart and coal waggon, specially fitted for the occasion with seats for the accommodation of occupants. The trams were also liberally patronised for the purpose of decoration gazing.

which arose outside gave signal to those assembled that the auspicious moment had arrived, and an upstanding gathering, waving handkerchiefs and lustily cheering, greeted the advent of the Sovereign and his Consort. The proceedings were brief, but impressive. The address read, the Duke of Norfolk, the most popular of those Sheffield recognises as her sons, made a statement in a well-known crisp, incisive manner, and then His Majesty, in clear tones heard throughout the hushed assembly, declared the institution open.

With little loss of time, the programme before their Majesties being still an extensive one, the procession was re-formed, and the Royal entourage swept out into the Park, the assembly crowding after in orderly fashion to witness the ceremony of presenting the Colours.

The scene the Park itself was one which baffles description Some thousands of guests had been invited by the University authorities to participate in the welcome to their Majesty and ground was one grand blaze of brilli

The big day has arrived.

KING EDWARD VII OPENS UNIVERSITY

When King Edward VII and Queen Alexandra came to Sheffield in 1905, hundreds of people had taken up vantage points outside the Midland Station even before the Royal train left London!

They were kept occupied during their long wait, said The Star, by watching the arrival of all the "notabilities" chosen to welcome the Royal party.

Ten thousand schoolchildren accompanied by 476 teachers, had to be in their places outside the station an hour before the King and Queen were due to arrive but "the time passed pleasantly enough".

The King and Queen, in Sheffield to officially open the University on Western Bank, were told by one of the speakers at the opening ceremony: "We cannot at first expect to hold an equal position with Universities of longer traditions or larger endowments but at least we must see to it that we do nothing to disgrace the great comity of learned bodies to which we have been admitted.

"We must maintain the fair fame of Sheffield by making our University a school of sound teaching, of high standards, and of research, and, as the years pass, and the patriotism of our fellow citizens constantly strengthens us, we must hope that the University of Sheffield will be counted as not the least of the Universities of the world."

The new University.

SCENE AT THE MIDLAND STATION.

GREAT ENTHUSIASM.

CHILDREN WELCOME THE KING AND QUEEN.

The greatest excitement and interest prevailed at the Midland Station for some time prior to the arrival of our Monarch and his gracious Consort and the coming of the notabilities who were to welcome the King and Queen to the centre of the cutlery industry kept the crowd of spectators

Hundreds were outside the Midland Station before the Royal train left London.

(Right) Flags fly on Fargate on the day of the Royal visit.

The crowds start to gather.

The King and Queen arrive at the University.

They even decorated the Cathedral spire to welcome the King and Queen.

FARGATE A BLAZE OF COLOUR

When the Prince of Wales, later King Edward VIII, opened the Town Hall extensions in 1923, he was following in the footsteps of his great grandmother, Queen Victoria, who opened the Town Hall itself in 1897.

The Star reported that Fargate was a blaze of colour with flags and bunting and excited crowds waving "favours" such as imitation silk handkerchiefs containing the Prince's portrait.

When the Royal visitor passed on his way to the Town Hall "the cheering of the crowd vied with the clanging of the Cathedral bells."

THRONGS ACCLAIM ROYAL VISITOR.

HIS ROYAL HIGHNESS'S CROWDED DAY IN THE CITY.

SCENES OF ENTHUSIASM.

VISITS TO EAST END WORKS, AND TALKS TO EX-SERVICE MEN.

H.R.H.'s SPEECH AT VICTORIA HALL.

THE PRINCE OF WALES, continuing his Yorkshire tour, devoted to-day to Sheffield, fulfilling a heavy programme of engagements spread over seven hours. His reception by the citizens was of the most enthusiastic description, many thousands of men, women and children assembling along the route of the Royal procession and giving His Royal Highness a typical Yorkshire welcome.

Leaving Wentworth at 9.50, the Prince reached Sheffield Town H...
...en The sun shone brilliantly as the Roy...

A "great continuous roar" emphasised the Prince's immense popularity.

The Prince leaves the Town Hall (top). Below, flag waving children greet the Royal visitor.

A DAY OF WONDER.

Invited Sheffield Boy's Fine Time in London.

GOOD VIEW OF WEDDING.

Tremendous Rush from Sight to Sight.

Charles Parker, of 131, Graham Road, Sheffield, the 17-year-old apprentice-engineer, who represented Sheffield at the Royal wedding, was back at his work this morning, feeling a little tired after the strenuous day in London yesterday, but with a proudly eating heart, exulting in the memories of one of the most wonderful and eventful days he is ever likely to experience.

He told a "Yorkshire Telegraph and Star" reporter, who talked to him at the Weedon Street Works of Messrs. Thomas Firth and Sons, to-day, that it was a tremendous rush from early morning till late in the evening, when he returned to Sheffield.

"Mr. Marshall, our welfare supervisor, saw me off at the station on Wednesday evening," he said. "I was strung up to the top pitch of excitement during the journey to St. Pancras, in anticipation of the thrilling day we were

Charles Parker.

going to have on the morrow, thinking about the luck I had had in being chosen to be present at the wedding, and also about London, for you see it was my first visit.

"At St. Pancras I was met and warmly welcomed by Mr. Rowntree, who rushed me off to the Hotel Bonnington, Southampton Row, where he introduced me to the other welfare lads, who came from all parts of the country, including Scotland, Birmingham, Hull, Port Sunlight, and many other towns up and down the country. They were an awfully nice lot of lads and although, as you can guess, we were all full of the wedding, we found time to talk about our works, and got to know a lot about our different

When the present Queen Mother married in 1923, a 17-year-old was chosen to represent Sheffield at the wedding.

Apprentice-engineer Charles Parker, who worked at Thomas Firth and Sons, Weedon Street, had a grandstand view of the ceremony at Westminster Abbey and told a Star reporter later that as he travelled to London for his big day, he had been "strung up to the top pitch of excitement."

Readers of The Star had their first glimpse of Princess Margaret in October, 1930.

First Photo. of Princess Margaret Rose.

Official photograph by Speaight Ltd. of the Duchess of York and the Princess Margaret Rose.

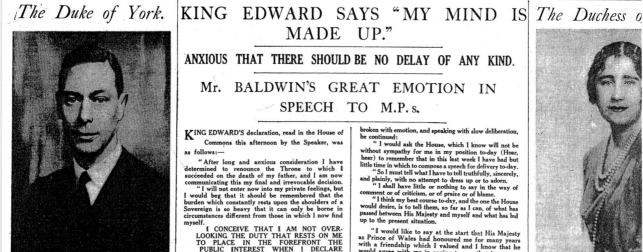

The Star's front page on December 10, 1936, when King Edward VIII abdicated, the shortest reign for 453 years.

HELLO, I'M THE QUEEN. DO YOU MIND IF I COME IN AND LOOK ROUND?

When a Shiregreen family living in a humble little Council house answered a knock on their door on October 21, 1937, the lady standing there asked if she could look round.

It was the Queen. And by her side, also wanting to come in, was King George VI.

The visit, near the end of a Yorkshire tour, was not in the official programme and The Star said it was a new indication of Royal interest in and anxiety for the welfare of ordinary citizens.

The family, Mr and Mrs George Leslie Damms and their 12-year-old daughter Dorothy, of Gregg House Road, were overwhelmed by the Royal couple's kindness.

The King and Queen looked at rooms both upstairs and downstairs and congratulated the family on their spotlessly clean home.

Mrs Damms, whose husband was unemployed, told The Star later: "The Queen was marvellously sweet. It was a great thrill to me to be standing talking, quite naturally, side by side with Her Majesty."

When a reporter from The Star called round next day for a follow-up story, Mr Damms had gone to collect his dole. His houseproud wife told the reporter that she wanted to refute a rumour that had marred an otherwise wonderful day.

"There have been wicked rumours that the Corporation lent me some furniture for the occasion", she said. "They are absolutely untrue. The King and Queen saw my home exactly as it always is."

The King and Queen Visit a Sheffield Unemployed Man's Home

This is the house at 100, Gregg House Road, Shiregreen, which was visited by the King and Queen this afternoon.

Above Mr. and Mrs. G. S. Damms and their daughter, Dorothy, photographed in their living room, and the smaller picture shows the honoured couple at the door of their home.

WHAT THEIR MAJESTIES SAW AT SHIREGREEN ESTATE

A SHEFFIELD unemployed man and his wife were honoured by a visit from Their Majesties. This incident—not in the official programme—was new indication of Royal interest in and anxiety for the welfare of ordinary citizens.

The couple, Mr. and Mrs. George Leslie Damms, of 100, Gregg House Road, Shiregreen, were complimented on their admirable little home, spotlessly clean and bright, and a great credit to them. Their only child, Dorothy (12), a pupil at Hartley Brook Council School, participated in her parents' thrill.

WAR SERVICE.

Mr. Damms is an ex-Serviceman who has met with much misfortune since his discharge from the Army. He served in the R.E. Signals attached to the Royal Naval Division in France, and subsequently in the Army of Occupation in Cologne. The General Service and the Victory Medals were awarded him. During his active service in France he had many narrow escapes from death, and although he escaped serious injury he still suffers a little from the effects of gas, and actually to-day the excitement of the occasion brought on some of the old trouble.

In conversation with a "Star"

Actually he devotes most of the garden to growing vegetables for consumption in his home, but he has had quite a nice display of sweet peas, carnations, and other flowers, and he was regretting to-day that Their Majesties had not seen them in bloom.

Mr. and Mrs. Damms attend Shiregreen Methodist Church at present, their daughter also attending the Sunday School. But Mr. Damms, who is an organist of ability, will be known to other churches, for he has acted as deputy organist at St. Luke's Church, and elsewhere.

TO BROADCAST.

Arrangements have been made by the B.B.C. for Mr. and Mrs. Damms to broadcast in the National programme about 9 o'clock to-night. They will describe how Their Majesties received them.

When Their Majesties arrived at the house of Mr. and Mrs. Damms, the Lord Mayor and Lady Mayoress and the Town Clerk were there to receive them, and to accompany them into the house. Large crowds of people had learned of Their Majesties' intentions, and had assembled in the road to give the King and Queen a very hearty reception.

THROUGH INSPECTION

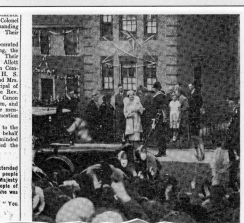

The Queen shaking hands with the Chief Constable of Sheffield (Major F. S. James) after leaving the home of Mr. and Mrs. Damms, at Shiregreen, this afternoon.

raph & Star

INCORPORATING "THE SHEFFIELD MAIL"

SHEFFIELD, THURSDAY, OCTOBER 21, 1937.   ONE PENNY.

s Love For King

Major and Secret Documents

SEQUEL TO ENTRY OF BUNGALOW

THREE CHARGES under the Official Secrets Act were brought against Wilfred

KING IS TOLD: 'DON'T WORRY, OWD LAD. WE'LL PULL YOU THROUGH'

One of the most emotional Royal visits to Sheffield came in January, 1941, when King George VI and Queen Elizabeth were here to see the bomb damage after the Blitz.

It inspired the city and lifted the spirits of its people.

The Star reported that at several points of their tour, the Royal couple left their car to talk to victims left homeless by the bombings.

It was a typically warm Sheffield welcome. Loud speakers blared out Elgar's "Pomp and Circumstance", children sang "God Save The King" and "There'll Always Be An England" and everybody cheered until they were hoarse.

There was lots of humour, too. Signs across streets of damaged houses said: "Our windows are out but we are in."

And one workman shouted to the King as he passed: "Don't worry, owd lad. We'll pull you through." The promise brought a smile to the Royal faces...

One workman who, with his wife and eight children, had been bombed out of his home, was asked by the Queen if his family had suffered.

"Not much. Anyway, he (Hitler) won't frighten us. Leave him to us, that's all."

The Queen replied regally: "That is the way. There is nothing like the British bulldog spirit."

The King and Queen talk to blind John Wilson who told them: "We can take all Hitler can give us. He won't break us."

Sheffield's Lord Mayor, Coun. Luther F.Milner, tells the King how homeless families are coping.

WATER, WATER, EVERYWHERE!

More than 30,000 were at Ladybower Reservoir when King George V1 and Queen Elizabeth arrived to open it on September 25, 1945.

After arriving at Sheffield Midland Station, the couple drove through the city centre at 5mph to give the huge crowd a chance to see them.

The King launched the £6 million project by manipulating a hydraulic valve to send water gushing into the Derwent Valley at the rate of 400m gallons per day.

The King opens a valve to send water gushing into the Derwent Valley.

A right Royal welcome from Sheffield.

February 6, 1952, and the new Queen, Elizabeth II, flies home from Kenya after the death of her father, King George VI.

The Star gives readers a detailed programme for the new Queen's Coronation in 1953.

THE STAR'S HOTLINE TO THE QUEEN

The young Queen came to South Yorkshire early in her reign, visiting Barnsley, Wombwell, Brampton Bierlow, Rotherham and Sheffield.

The 1954 tour was a triumph and the Queen and Duke seemed particularly impressed by a display given by schoolchildren at Hillsborough Football Ground.

And so that The Star can take its rightful place in history, it is important to record for posterity that the newspaper came to the Queen's rescue when she arrived at Hillsborough Football Ground.

Desperate to know the result of the Cambridgeshire, she passed an urgent message to the police. They didn't know so they sent a message to The Star's editorial department.

Fifteen seconds later, the result was being wirelessed back to Hillsborough.

Race pundits will recall that the winner was Minstrel, with Queen's Beeches in second place and Marshall Ney third.

We'll never know which horse the Queen backed. Bet it was Queen's Beeches!

THE QUEEN GOES UNDERGROUND

After her 1954 visit, it was 21 years before the Queen came to Sheffield again.

She opened the new South Yorkshire County Police Headquarters in Snig Hill in 1975 and also went 600 yards underground at Silverwood Colliery to watch work in progress at the coal face.

All smiles and no sign of pit dust. The Queen leaves the pithead after her underground tour.

The Queen 600 yards underground.

A "plush red carpet of welcome" for the Queen in 1975.

THE MOST SUCCESSFUL EVER?

The Queen's 1977 tour of South Yorkshire, which took in Barnsley, Doncaster and Sheffield, was hailed as one of the most successful ever.

Everywhere she and Prince Philip went, crowds turned out in their thousands and many Royal watchers were impressed with the relaxed atmosphere of the visit.

The front page of The Star's Royal Jubilee Visit souvenir.

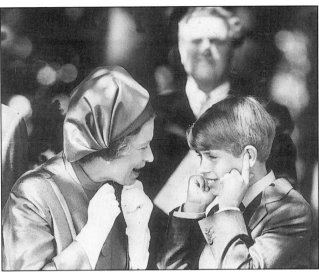

This picture, taken at RAF Finningley during the 1977 tour, won an award for Chris Lawton, then working as a Sheffield Newspapers photographer. He cleverly captioned it: "Don't listen with mother."

Cannon Hall, Barnsley, and miles of smile…

Even more smiles at Cannon Hall, Barnsley.

The Queen at Doncaster Racecourse.

This beautiful picture, touching in more ways than one, was taken at Maltby.

HRH The Prince of Wales opens the Royal Hallamshire Hospital in November 1979.

Charles and Diana marry in 1981.

1984 and it's all smiles for the Sheffield Newspapers cameraman.

The Star christens the Prince of Wales the Prince of Smiles when he went walkabout in Orchard Square in 1988.

December 9, 1992...and the end of a fairytale.

Charles and Diana at St Luke's Nursing Home in 1984.

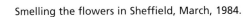

Smelling the flowers in Sheffield, March, 1984.

Sheffield's Wars – How Our Spirit Saw Us Through

HEARTBREAK BEHIND THE THUMBNAIL PHOTOGRAPHS

It is perhaps just as well that The Star was never really able to capture at the time the full horror of one of its biggest and most tragic stories.

In 1916, hundreds of brave lads, bursting with pride because they were fighting for their country, had left South Yorkshire in high spirits. They finished up being slaughtered like cattle on the battlefields of The Somme...

Back at home, The Star's coverage of the war was relatively upbeat and, initially at least, there was no general coverage of the dreadful losses we were suffering.

That was the way it had to be. Any published material that gave positive encouragement to the enemy was to be avoided.

But there were hints that the war was going awfully wrong. Photographs of local lads killed or wounded began to appear in The Star almost nightly and, 84 years on, it is difficult to imagine the heartbreak that lay behind those thumbnail pictures as mums, dads, brothers, sisters and girlfriends mourned the wasteful loss of a loved one.

The Star, in common with other regional newspapers, also published official casualty lists – in retrospect, cold, straightforward announcements that gave the soldier's name, rank, regiment and home address followed by a stark "wounded" or "killed".

Sometimes the words "twice wounded" would appear. The lists would also mention men with the same surname and from the same address. You had to assume they were brothers...

Grieving families would hardly have been comforted by the words of General O'Gowan who praised the York and Lancaster Regiment, which included the Sheffield and Barnsley Battalions, for the way they had "distinguished themselves by their coolness, dash and extraordinary behaviour" in the "great push" of July 1, 1916.

That was the day the Sheffield City Battalion was almost wiped out in less than an hour.

A typical casualty list published by The Star.

High Praise From a British General.

WHAT THE Y. AND L. MEN DID

More Sheffield Soldiers Killed and Wounded.

Many of the correspondents who have written on the "great push" of the 1st July have referred to the remarkable work done by York and Lancaster battalions and East Lancashire men. The former include hundreds of men from Sheffield and district, and unfortunately many have been killed and wounded. But General O'Gowan says "it was worth it." A letter from this distinguished military officer—General R. Wanless O'Gowan—was read by the Lord Mayor at the annual meeting of the Sheffield Y.M.C.A., at which the Princess Victoria Helena was present yesterday. The General wrote:—"I am certain you will be interested to know how well the York and Lancaster Brigade fought on Saturday last (July 1). All the battalions and many of the men of the East Lancashires distinguished themselves by their coolness, dash, and extraordinary bravery. Their advance in the face of a terrific bombardment was beyond all praise, and one of the finest performances ever accomplished by British soldiers. I am sure Yorkshire and Lancashire will appreciate the way the whole Division behaved."

Deep sympathy will be extended to Mr. Herbert Barber, of Oak Hurst, Manchester Road, Sheffield, ex-Master Cutler, who this morning received the sad news that his son Captain Herbert Graham Barber, of the York and Lancaster, has been killed. Captain Barber was 31 years of age, and was educated at Leighton Park School, Reading. He entered the firm of Messrs. Daniel Doncaster and Sons, in 1903, and became a director in 1909. He was awarded the Military

High praise from a British general...after thousands of our local lads had died.

IN THE GREAT DRIVE.

More Sheffield and District Soldiers.

THE KILLED AND WOUNDED.

The list of officers and men from Sheffield and district, who were killed or wounded in the advance which commenced on the morning of the 1st July, continues to grow, and each day brings new names and fresh photographs.

News of the July 1, 1916, carnage starts to filter through.

BATTLE OF THE SOMME

The Adventures of a Soldier Journalist.

WAITING FOR THE WORD.—I.

The following articles are written by a journalist on the editorial staff of the "Yorkshire Telegraph and Star," who for several months past has been serving as a private with the Army in France. His brigade was one of the first, if not the very first, to go "over the top" on July 1st, and set the Great Advance in motion. He was wounded early in the action, and now from the quiet of a hospital ward he describes his experiences on the battlefield and on the way back to "Blighty."

We knew for weeks before the Big Push began that it was coming off. We had spent a week near a pretty little town well behind the firing line. Those were very pleasant days, playing at war, knee deep in the long bush grass, moving up and down the sunlit fields like rows of chess board figures. We enjoyed the fun, though we knew that when it came to the real thing it would be a serious business.

Then, the training over, we went back to our billets on the fringe of the firing line. When we were not in the trenches as a battalion we were out on working parties, perhaps digging or repairing trenches, or more probably carrying ammunition or rations forward to the firing line.

And then came the eve of the great day. It was a quiet day in camp. Everything was ready. In the morning a famous General made a short speech to the troops. His words were plain and unmistakable. He told us what we would have to do. And he told us that ours would be no easy task. We gave him three rousing cheers at the finish.

The Star actually had one of its own journalists on the front line.

Joining the Army several months before the Battle of The Somme, W.C.Scott, a member of the paper's literary staff, found himself in one of the first brigades to go "over the top" on the day of the big push.

He was one of the lucky ones. Wounded early in the action, the young private was taken to hospital, from where he wrote a series of articles called "the adventures of a soldier journalist", for The Star.

His articles would presumably have been checked by the official censor whose job it was to strike out any sensitive information.

ANOTHER ZEPPELIN RAID.

Seven Airships Visit North Midland and other Districts.

DRIVEN OFF BY ANTI-AIRCRAFT GUNS.

Twenty-Nine Deaths : No Munition Works Damaged.

The Field Marshal Commanding-in-Chief the Home Forces reports as follows :—

TUESDAY, 12.10 p.m.

Seven airships carried out a raid on England last night and in the early hours of this morning.

The districts attacked were the South Coast, East Coast, North-East Coast, and the North Midlands.

The principal attack was aimed against the industrial centres in the last-mentioned area.

Up to the present no damage to factories or works of military importance has been reported. It is regretted, however, that a number of small houses and cottages were wrecked or damaged in some places, and 29 deaths have been reported.

No attempt was made to approach London.

The raiders were engaged by the anti-aircraft defences, and were successfully driven off from several large industrial centres.

Earlier communiques issued by the Field Marshal Commanding-in-Chief Home Forces were as follow :—

MONDAY, 11.45 p.m.

Several hostile airships crossed

IN THE DANGER ZONE.

Graphic Story by an Eye-Witness.

A member of a newspaper staff who lives within a couple of hundred yards of where the first bomb dropped, retired to rest about 12.15, and a few minutes later had a fine view of the awe-inspiring spectacle.

"Before I was nicely settled," he said, "I was startled by a vivid light blue glare followed immediately by a terrific reverberating roar. I jumped out of bed and went to the window, and was in time to see a second flash, and hear another explosion succeeded quickly by a third within a radius of a few hundred yards.

"The sound of the bombs dropping was like nothing so much as a clean shot from a gun which, preceded by a glare, seemed to indicate that the anti-aircraft guns had got to work. Each report was clear and well defined. I hastily dressed myself and joined my father, who had been an outside witness of the affair.

"The raid did not last more than four minutes. I saw no sign of raider or raiders. I heard eleven projectiles explode. To their credit folk seemed to take the business with characteristic British phlegm.

"A fire made its appearance on our left," he continued, "whilst another of larger dimensions sprung into life in front of us away. the first

The only really damaging raid on Sheffield during the Great War came on September 25, 1916. The next day, The Star reported that 29 people had been killed when a Zeppelin airship bombed a North Midlands town.

The North Midlands town was Sheffield but the paper wasn't allowed to say so.

The report also mentioned that the principal attack was aimed against the industrial centres of this North Midlands town. That was Sheffield's East End, which escaped relatively unscathed.

The Zeppelin dropped more than 30 bombs that night and among the dead were eight victims found in the cellar of a bombed house at Burngreave.

YORKSH

RAID VICTIMS.

Coroner's Comments at an Inquest.

THE INQUIRY ADJOURNED.

Inquests were held by a North Midland Coroner to-day on the bodies of the victims of the recent air raid. The majority of the bodies were those of women and children.

The Coroner expressed very sincere and deep sympathy with the relatives of the unfortunate persons who met with their deaths in the raid.

The course he had decided to adopt was to identify the unfortunate victims, hear short evidence as to their injuries and the cause of death, and then to adjourn the inquiry for possibly a fortnight. In the meantime he proposed to confer with the authorities to see whether, at the adjourned inquiry any statement or any evidence or any information could be put before the Court which might have the effect of reassuring the public.

The Coroner, continuing, said he was going to appeal to their common-sense not to come to such a conclusion as to return a verdict of "Wilful murder" against the Kaiser, as a jury had done in another part of the country. It was an absurd verdict, for there was no evidence to implicate the Kaiser, and their opinion and his opinion were, after all, worthless in Germany. Another jury had returned a verdict of "Murder" against the crew of a Zeppelin, but that was equally absurd. The soldiers, or sailors who manned the Zeppelin were bombing the towns on instructions.

Evidence was given by an institutional surgeon as to the injuries sustained by a woman and a boy who had died in hospital some hours after admission. The woman was suffering from a fracture of the right femur and extensive lacerated wounds on the right leg, and the boy was covered with contusions as though he had been crushed by something falling upon him.

Inquests begin on those killed in the air raid in September, 1916.

ELEGRAPH AND STAR FRID

BEFORE THE BENCH.

Tales Told to the Sheffield Magistrates To-day.

Too Much Light.

In the Second Court to-day, before Messrs. F. C. Wild and W. F. Osborn, the following were fined for exposing too much light at night time: Charles Markham, 334, Main Road, Darnall, 5s. Fanny Stevens, 22, Askern Street, 10s.; Edward Wadds, 81, Carbrook Street, 10s.; William Nowill, of 1 house, 15 court Portland Street, 10s.; Charles Moore, 6, Wood Street, 10s.; Jane Lister, 94, Cuthbert Bank Road, 7s. 6d.; Joseph Bramall, 78, Cuthbert Bank Road, 10s.; Albert Edward Jackson, 77, Bramwell Street, 10s.; Ernest Piersey, Victoria Hotel, Langsett Road, 20s.; Samuel Driffield Foster, 361, Langsett Road, 10s.; James Parker, 23, Burnaby Street, 10s.; Arthur Congreve, 117, Burnaby Street, 10s.; Herbert Hancock, 83, Greaves Street, 10s.; Beatrice Wood, 71, Sanderson Road, 10s.; Reuben Canter, 26, Tipton Street, 10s.; John Willis, 15, Bubwith Road, 10s.; Gertrude Parkin, 129, Meadow Hall Road, 15s.

Protecting the Specials.

A case heard in the West Riding Court against an Ecclesfield moulder named Heward Johnson, for using violent and abusive language emphasised the folly of person interfering with special con-

It was an offence to expose too much light at night time, as these defendants found to their cost.

A pneumatic trench gun for grenade firing, which is being introduced

Life in the trenches – a picture published in our sister paper, The Sheffield Daily Telegraph, in December, 1916.

EPTEMBER 29, 1916.

TOLL OF ADVANCE.

Local Casualties in the Great Push.

KILLED, WOUNDED, ETC.

Pte. T. CONROY, Y. and L. '24, Oborne St., Sheffield, killed.

Rifleman W. HENSMAN, King's Royal Rifles, 94, Nidd Rd., Sheffield, killed.

Pte. W. TRAYNOR, Y. '14, Reliance Place, Sheffield killed.

Pte. A. A. NEALE Lincolnshire Regt., 27, Longfield Road, Crookes, died from wounds.

Pte. F. GODBEHERE, Y. and L. 6, Norwich Street, Park, gassed and wounded in action, from which he died.

Lce.-Cpl W. V. SAVAGE, King's Royal Rifles, 2, Bulwith Road, Brightside, wounded.

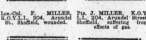

Lce.-Cpl. F. MILLER, K.O.Y.L.I., 204, Arundel St., Sheffield, wounded.

Pte. J. MILLER, K.O.Y. L.I., 204, Arundel Street, Sheffield, suffering from effects of gas.

Pte. H. BIRCH, Y. and L. 5, New Row, Lambert St., Sheffield, died from wounds.

Gunner J. SCOTT, R.F.A. 2, Bloor St., Walkley, ill in hospital.

Pte. H. DOWNS, K.O.Y. L.I. 83, Allen St., Sheffield, wounded.

Pte. J E. SHAW, Y. and L. 2, Hinchliffe Walk, Sheffield, wounded.

STAR, TUESDAY EVENING, MAY

SHEFFIELD HEROES.

Serre Memorial Unveiled Yesterday.

CITY'S SACRIFICE.

Splendid Episode of a Vain Daring.

The memory of the heroic deeds and terrible sacrifices of the Sheffield City Battalion in the attack on Serre on July 1st, 1916, will be perpetuated on the spot by a monument which was unveiled and dedicated at a solemn ceremony yesterday.

The memorial, which is in Villebois stone, has been erected on a slope before Serre, overlooking the field where within an hour the battalion suffered 600 casualties. On it is the inscription, in English and French:

To the memory of the officers and men of the 12th Battalion York and Lancaster Regiment (Sheffield City Battalion) who fell before Serre, 1916.

Above are four plaques, representative of Sheffield's coat of arms, those of Serre, and the regimental badge of the York and Lancasters. The large gathering yesterday included about a hundred people from Sheffield, who had specially journeyed out for the occasion. Among them were a company of survivors of the battalion, besides parents and friends, and citizens who occupied prominent positions during the war. Several old officers of the battalion, now living in other towns, also attended. A number of leading Frenchmen of the district were present, together with an assembly of the peasantry. The unveiling ceremony was per-

The "terrible sacrifices" of the Sheffield City Battalion were marked in May, 1923, with a special memorial, erected on a slope in the French village of Serre, overlooking the field where the battalion suffered 600 casualties in an hour. A party of 100 went from Sheffield.

September 29, 1916…and still the casualty lists appear.

A First World War welcome home party in Stovin Road, Sheffield, in 1917.

Sheffield City Battalion on a road smoothing exercise.

4   YORKSHIRE TELEGRAPH AND STAR. MONDAY EVENING, NOVEMBER 11, 1918.

THE WORLD WAR AT AN END.

Armistice with Germany Signed at Five O'Clock This Morning.

THE TERMS: EVACUATION—RETURN OF PRISONERS AT ONCE—SURRENDER OF ALL SUBMARINES—WARSHIPS DISARMED.

"Hostilities Will Cease on the Whole Front as from 11 a.m."— MARSHAL FOCH.

THE PRIME MINISTER MAKES THE FOLLOWING ANNOUNCEMENT:—

THE ARMISTICE WAS SIGNED AT 5 A.M. THIS MORNING, AND HOSTILITIES ARE TO CEASE ON ALL FRONTS AT ELEVEN A.M. TO-DAY.

MARSHAL FOCH TO COMMANDERS-IN-CHIEF,—

HOSTILITIES WILL CEASE ON THE WHOLE FRONT AS FROM NOVEMBER 11 AT 11 O'CLOCK (FRENCH TIME). THE ALLIED TROOPS WILL NOT UNTIL A FURTHER ORDER GO BEYOND THE LINE REACHED ON THAT DATE AND AT THAT HOUR.   (SIGNED) MARSHAL FOCH.

GERMAN PLENIPOTENTIARIES TO GERMAN HIGH COMMAND.
TO BE COMMUNICATED TO ALL THE AUTHORITIES INTERESTED.
RADIO 3084 AND G.H.Q., 2 NUMBER 11,386 RECEIVED.
ARMISTICE WAS SIGNED AT 5 O'CLOCK IN THE MORNING (FRENCH TIME). IT COMES INTO FORCE AT 11 O'CLOCK IN THE MORNING (FRENCH TIME). DELAY FOR EVACUATION PROLONGED BY 24 HOURS FOR THE LEFT BANK OF THE RHINE, BESIDES THE FIVE DAYS, THEREFORE 31 DAYS IN ALL. MODIFICATIONS OF THE TEXT COMPARED WITH THAT BROUGHT BY HELLDORF WILL BE TRANSMITTED BY RADIO.   (SIGNED) ERZBERGER.—Admiralty, per Wireless Press.

SIR DOUGLAS HAIG REPORTS TO-DAY AS FOLLOWS:—
MONDAY, 10.19 A.M.—SHORTLY BEFORE DAWN THIS MORNING CANADIAN TROOPS OF THE FIRST ARMY (GENERAL HORNE) CAPTURED MONS.

AMERICAN OFFICIAL REPORT, MONDAY:—
IN ACCORDANCE WITH THE TERMS OF THE ARMISTICE HOSTILITIES ON THE FRONTS OF THE AMERICAN ARMIES WERE SUSPENDED AT 11 O'CLOCK THIS MORNING.

THE TERMS OF THE ARMISTICE.

Immediate Evacuation of Belgium and Alsace-Lorraine.

PRISONERS TO COME HOME AT ONCE.

All Submarines to be Handed Over and Warships Disarmed.

RIGHT TO OCCUPY HELIGOLAND RESERVED.

Duration of the Armistice 36 Days.

The following are the points of the armistice conditions as announced in the House of Commons by the Prime Minister this afternoon:—

Immediate evacuation of Belgium, Alsace-Lorraine, and Luxembourg.
Evacuation by the enemy of Rhine lands completed within 16 days.
The railways of Alsace-Lorraine to be handed over.
Immediate repatriation, without repatriation of Germans, of Allied and United States prisoners.
All German troops in Russia, Rumania and elsewhere to be withdrawn.
Complete abandonment of the treaties of Bucharest and Brest-Litovsk.
Immediate cessation of all hostilities at sea.
Handing over to the Allies and the United States of all submarines.
To be disarmed, six battle cruisers, ten battleships, eight light cruisers, fifty destroyers, and other services.
Allies reserve the right to occupy Heligoland to enable them to enforce the terms of the armistice.
Duration of the Armistice is to be 36 days.
The Prime Minister added that the terms included the surrender of 5,000 locomotives, 5,000 guns—2,500 heavy, 2,500 field—and 30,000 machine-guns.

THE TERMS.

Premier's Statement in the Commons.

THE U-BOATS.

Duration of the Armistice 36 Days.

RETURN OF PRISONERS.
(BY OUR PRIVATE WIRE)

On Mr. Lloyd George's entry into the House of Commons this afternoon, he was received with loud and rousing cheers, the members standing and waving their hats, while others waved the order papers by the day.

The Prime Minister immediately rose and said that the armistice, as had already been announced to the Press, was signed this morning at 5 o'clock, after a discussion, which was prolonged all night.

He would read to the House the conditions of the armistice, in so far as they had reached them up to the present. He ought to warn the House and the public that they had only received such portions as were rendered necessary by the new conditions. These corrections had only been received by telephone, and there was a possibility that there might be a few mistakes, but substantially the terms represented the conditions which Germany had accepted relative to the Western front cessation of operations by land and in the air six hours after the signatures to the armistice.

The armistice was signed at 5 o'clock this morning, and the war ceased at eleven o'clock this morning.

Immediate evacuation of invaded countries, Belgium, France, Alsace-Lorraine, Luxembourg ... to be completed within 14 days from the signatures of the armistice. German troops, which had not left the abovementioned territory would become prisoners of war.

HINDENBURG

Places Himself at Disposal of New Government

WITH THE ARMY.

The German Chancellor's Proclamation.

EMPIRE IN MELTING POT.

Copenhagen, Sunday (received to-day).—The Chancellor Ebert has issued the following proclamation:—

The new Government has taken charge of the Administration in order to preserve the German people from civil war and famine, and to fulfil their legitimate claim for autonomy. The Government can only solve this problem if all officials in town and country help. I know that it will be difficult for many people to work together with the new men who have taken charge of the Empire, but I appeal to their love of our people.

To omit to organise would, in this serious time, mean anarchy for Germany, and would involve the country in untold misery. Therefore, help the Fatherland with a peaceable and indefatigable work for the sake of the future. Everyone to his post until relief is forthcoming.—Reuter.

Copenhagen, Monday.—A semi-official Berlin telegram states:—Hindenburg has placed himself and the army at the disposal of the new Government in order to avoid chaos.—Reuter.
[The report on Page 3 that Hindenburg had fled with the Kaiser to Holland is refuted by the above message.]

Copenhagen, Sunday (received to-day).—The Wolff Bureau of Berlin, which is now in Socialist hands, states that numerous Workmen's and Soldiers' Councils have been established generally throughout Germany without bloodshed or disturbances. Such councils have been formed at Frankfort-on-Main, Osnabruck, Magdeburg, and Darmstadt, Hesse-Darmstadt has been proclaimed a Socialist Republic until a German Republic is established. In Dresden, the garrison since yesterday afternoon is in the hands of a Provisional Workmen's and Soldiers' Council. Civil officials are co-operating with the councils.—Reuter.

Copenhagen, Sunday (received to-day).—A Berlin semi-official telegram says the Soldiers' Council which has been established there has issued a proclamation announcing that it has taken over the military administration, and that its orders must be obeyed.
"Comrades," continues the proclamation, "we have stood together in the field and bled together in the battle. United we will lead Germany towards a happy future. Be absolutely true to our people and its aim. We work in union with workmen and their Government. You will shortly regularly receive orders from our Council."—Reuter.

Copenhagen, Sunday (received to-day).—A Stuttgart telegram states that the King of Wurtemberg and Cabinet have issued a proclamation which says the new Cabinet will summon the Constituent National Convention, which will be elected by equal, direct, and secret suffrage. Its aim, the proclamation declares, will be to give the State a new democratic constitution in accordance with the needs of the new time. The King declares that his personal wish will never be a hindrance to the development desired by his people.

CEASE FIRE.

Sheffield Enthusiastic Over the News.

FLAGS, CHEERS, & BUZZERS.

How the People Received "Star's" Intimation.

"Armistice Signed : Official."

The words appeared on the front of the "Sheffield Telegraph" offices in High Street just before half-past ten.

The news spread like wildfire. In a few moments the unfurling over the "Telegraph" building of a string of bright flags—flags representing all those brave nations which have been allied with Great Britain during the great war which has just ended in a magnificent victory—was the signal for a mighty cheer, for in this brief space of time thousands of people had gathered and the crowd grew each moment until it assumed huge dimensions, and the car service was continued with the greatest difficulty.

The procession of striking workmen from the "Gesellschaft Fuer Draphose Telegraphic" reached the front of the Reichstag at 1.30. A detachment of Chasseurs occupied the outside staircase before which the crowd had assembled. Deputy Scheidemann made a speech: "The Kaiser and the Crown Prince have abdicated. The dynasty is overthrown. A splendid victory for the German people. Herr Ebert has been charged to form the new Government, in which all shades of the Social Democratic Party are to participate. Only an order of the Government bearing Herr Ebert's signature have validity, and only orders of the Minister for War bearing the counter-signature of a Social Democrat, acting as an assistant to an official."

CEASE FIRE.

Bale, Monday.—A telegram from Darmstadt announces that a Republic has been proclaimed in Hesse.—Exchange.

Copenhagen, Sunday (received to-day).—A revolutionary movement broke out in Leipsig on Friday afternoon without bloodshed, after a general strike had been proclaimed in the morning. The military headquarters surrendered and officers and policemen were disarmed in the streets. A Workmen's and Soldiers' Council was established, and seized the munition depots. The town administration was taken over by the Council, which posted troops in all the main streets to preserve order.—Reuter.

Paris, Monday.—A telegram from Bale says the King of Wurtemberg abdicated on Friday night.—Exchange.

Paris, Monday.—A telegram from Berne reports that the King of Wurtemberg, fearing manifestations at Stuttgart and the hostile attitude of the people, has left the town for an unknown destination.—Exchange.

At the Cathedral the Archdeacon immediately arranged for special prayer at frequent intervals right through the afternoon—a popular service of thanksgiving will be held at three o'clock this afternoon. A special service will also be held to-morrow.

LIGHTS UP.

Gloom Officially Abolished.

RESTRICTIONS RELAXED.

The Home Office has telegraphed to police authorities the following instructions with regard to the relaxation of the lighting restrictions and use of fireworks, bonfires, etc.:—

The masking of street lamps may be removed, but in view of the coal shortage the lamps may be withdrawn, but the prohibition of lights in shop-windows and of advertisement lights must be maintained on account of the coal shortage, except for to-night when the use of lights in shop windows will be allowed. The military authorities will give permission for a display of fireworks and bonfires subject to approval of the arrangements by the police and the sale of fireworks for authorised displays is permitted. But the general use of fireworks by the public is not permitted at present.

IN THE POLICE COURTS.

New Lord Mayor Announces the Armistice.

In Sheffield Fire Police Court, to-day, the Lord Mayor of Sheffield (Alderman William Irons) presided, and with him were Mr. Harry Flather, Mr. T. W. Ward, Councillor E. Holmshaw, and Mr. W. W. Chisholm.

ARMISTICE ITEMS.

Special Services at the Cathedral.

At the Cathedral of Sheffield, on getting the news of the conclusion of hostilities, arranged special services of prayer in the Cathedral, and many people availed themselves of this opportunity of quietly and reverently returning thanks to God. The civic service will be held to-morrow afternoon at 3 o'clock the Bishop will give the address, and the Lord Mayor and Corporation will attend.

AT SHEERNESS.

Joy Bells Rung and Warships Beflagged.

Joybells were ringing and sirens sounding on the warships at Sheerness to celebrate the armistice. Troops were cheered as they were proceeding through the streets. Schools are closed and the whole port liberally beflagged.

NOTE.

All Recruiting Suspended.
All Calling-up Notices Cancelled.
Lighting Restrictions Relaxed.
(Official.)

A FIGHT FOR "STARS."

Remarkable Rush for Historic News.

The demand for copies of the "Yorkshire Telegraph and Star," containing the Prime Minister's historic message, was unprecedented.

The Star announces the end of the First World War on November 11, 1918.

SHEFFIELD...CITY OF STEEL

That was always our proud boast and the main reason we took such a merciless battering in the Second World War.

Our region's immensely significant contribution to the country's war effort, in the form of materials for planes, ships, trains, bombs, ammunition and fighting equipment generally, was no secret to anyone, including the enemy.

It made us extremely vulnerable but also more aware of our wartime responsibilities, such as strict adherence to black-out regulations and other safety precautions.

In terms of passing vital information to readers, The Star and our sister paper The Sheffield Telegraph were invaluable.

Advice on how to stay safe regularly featured in our columns and the public were constantly being warned against any careless talk that could give encouragement or help to the enemy.

But no amount of advice could have prepared Sheffield's people for the night of December 12, 1940.

The German bombers arrived at just after 7pm and the all clear sirens went at 4.17am. It was the longest, most terrifying night in the city's history.

When daylight dawned on December 13, the city centre had been devastated.

Three hundred German planes had ripped Sheffield's guts out.

But, as someone said later, if our city reached the height of suffering that night, it also reached the heights of greatness because of the way everyone, emergency workers and ordinary people, came together in a unifying spirit of courage and comradeship.

There were no strangers that night. It was neighbour helping neighbour.

But for the brave rescue workers who worked tirelessly, many of them for 16 hours and longer without a break, it paid not to think too much about what was going on around you.

One fireman told The Star later: "Scared? We were all scared. There were times when you didn't look down because a dead man might be there. Wherever you turned, there were flames and ruins, and, if a man stopped to think about it, he'd have gone out of his mind."

On Sunday, December 15, the bombers were back again, this time wreaking their havoc on Sheffield's industrial east end where several major steelworks were badly damaged.

Not generally known at the time was that Sheffield had Britain's most precious piece of war machinery. A giant 200 ton drop hammer in the Vickers works of the English Steel Corporation was the only one in the country, certainly for the first 18 months of the war, with the capability to forge crankshafts for the Spitfires which eventually won the Battle of Britain.

On the night of December 15, parts of the Vickers works were damaged but the drop hammer survived.

UNBELIEVABLE DEVASTATION

Official figures released later told the story of the Sheffield Blitz better than any colourful prose.

❋ Nearly 700 people killed, 589 seriously injured and 1,228 slightly injured;

❋ A total of 77,624 homes damaged, including 2,849 completely wrecked;

❋ More than 200 water mains fractured, depriving 30,000 people of water;

❋ Eight gas holders bombed;

❋ Eight of the city's 154 schools destroyed and 106 damaged;

❋ Eighteen churches and chapels wiped out and 90 damaged;

❋ A total of 1,218 business and commercial premises destroyed;

❋ More than 30 trams and 22 buses wrecked.

It's just a piece of paper containing the names of cities and some dates. But one of the cities was Sheffield, the date alongside was December 12 and the piece of paper is a German bomber pilot's flight log on the night of the Blitz.

SIVES CHARGE | AIR RAID SHELTERS
UNDER CAR PARK

OLD CELLARS BENEATH THE CAR PARK IN NORFOLK STREET, SHEFFIELD, HAVE BEEN OPENED AND COVERED WITH SAND BAGS TO PROVIDE PUBLIC AIR RAID SHELTERS. PICTURE SHOWS MEN FINISHING ONE OF THE ENTRANCES.

TERVAL | Territorial | CUPID GETS BUSY

Underground cellars beneath a car park on Norfolk Street, Sheffield, were converted into public air raid shelters in August, 1939.

SHEFFIELD HAS MADE ARRANGEMENTS TO EVACUATE 30,000 SCHOLARS, BUT THE NUMBER REGISTERED IS ONLY 20,000 OUT OF A POSSIBLE 60,000, SO THAT THERE REMAIN PLACES FOR ANOTHER 10,000.

"Evacuation, which will take several days to complete, is being undertaken as a precautionary measure in view of the prolongation of the period of tension," says the statement. "The Government is fully assured that the attitude of quiet confidence which the public have been displaying will continue."

It hopes that no unnecessary movements which would interfere with the smooth operation of the transport arrangement will take place, and that all concerned in the receiving areas will entirely put aside every consideration of personal interest and convenience and do everything possible to contribute to the success of a great national undertaking.

In order to help people who are desirous of leaving London by road as rapidly as possible, nine routes will be operated as "one-way streets" in an outward-bound direction as from 7 a.m. to-morrow.

CONTINUED ON BACK PAGE

Sheffield makes arrangements to evacuate 30,000 children in August, 1939.

Leaving City For Safety | *Wonderful Cal:*

A Sheffield scene to-day when the general evacuation began.

BABIES IN MANY HOSPITAL TRANSFERS

Proud Father Carries Away A Newly-born

Several London hospitals were involved in the evacuation scheme, and there again the scenes were marked by a remarkable display of calmness.

MEDICAL students in shirt-sleeves acted as stretcher bearers when ...

The first children start to leave on September 1, 1939.

REMOVAL OF CITY HOSPITAL PATIENTS

PATIENTS, including children, will be transferred to-morrow morning from the casualty hospitals in Sheffield to outer hospitals.

Instructions were received late this afternoon to do this.

Most of the patients that can be moved will be transferred from the City General Hospital, Royal Hospital, Royal Infirmary, Jessop Hospital, and Children's Hospital (Western Bank), mostly to Nether Edge Hospital.

MANY SENT HOME

A large number of patients, "The Star" was told this afternoon, were sent home when the crisis began.

There are now vacant beds in all the casualty hospitals in the city.

Hospital patients are evacuated on August 31, 1939.

SHEFFIELD'S FIRST ISSUE OF PETROL RATIONS

"... er ... I think I'll take my No. 3 iron to this, caddy."

SHEFFIELD motorists may now obtain their petrol ration books from the General Post Office or the Local Taxation Department at the Town Hall.

Distribution commenced yesterday.

Upon production of a motor-car registration book motorists receive ration books, containing units varying with the horse-power of the vehicle.

The first issue consists of two books which cover the period September 16th-October 15th and October 16th to November 15th.

A large number of motorists have already obtained their books.

The amounts available in the respective books are as follow:—

Horse-Power.	Gallons a month.
Up to 7	4
8—9	5
10—12	6
13—15	7
16—19	8
20 and over	10
Motor cycles	2

Emergency Powers in Australia. — A ... Security Bill providing for

Petrol rationing starts in Sheffield, September, 1939.

FEW GAS MASKS LOST

SHEFFIELD people are looking well after their gas masks. Since Sunday, when citizens started carrying their masks, only a dozen have been lost, "The Star" was told to-day.

"We have had only nine left on trams and 'buses since Sunday," said an official of Sheffield Transport Department.

"Half-a-dozen of those have already been claimed.

"I think it is very good for a city of half a million people."

Only about three lost masks have been taken to the police lost property office in Water Lane and of these two had been claimed.

Most people have put their names and addresses either on the mask or the container.

Half a million people – and only 12 gas masks lost.

RUSH TO BUY BLACK-OUT PAPER

Salesman with rolls of black-out paper attracted one of the biggest crowds of shoppers in Sheffield to-day.

Black-out paper street salesmen were quick off the mark in September, 1939.

MR. F. HOWARTH, the Football League secretary, revealed to-day that the League is setting up a war-time committee, and that an early meeting will be called to review the situation.

The problem was how to go about the task of putting the game on a war-time basis should the ban on competitive football be removed.

"With football prohibited in the big cities the League competition must be off, but it would be possible," said Mr. Howarth, "to arrange various competitions on a sectionalised basis under the jurisdiction of the League.

"That would take time, perhaps a week or two, as various matters, including remuneration to players, would have to be discussed."

Wartime football programme reviewed.

CHURCH SERVICES IN DAYLIGHT

MANY Sheffield churches will to-morrow hold their "evening" services in the afternoon to comply with lighting restrictions, and to give worshippers time to get home in daylight.

At the Cathedral the evening prayer and sermon will be at 3 p.m., though there will be devotions and compline from 6.30 to 7 p.m.

Most Baptist Churches will hold services in the morning and at 6 p.m. Among Unitarian Churches, Upper Chapel will meet at 6 p.m., and Unity Church at 3 p.m.

Many other churches are to hold their services as usual, closing a little earlier in the evening.

VICARAGE CELLAR REFUGE

At Holy Trinity Church, the Wicker, evensong will be at 3 p.m., but there will be service in the Church Hall at 7 p.m.

The Vicar, the Rev. S. Price, told "The Star" to-day that the Church Hall could be darkened easily·

In case of emergency, the Vicarage cellars could accommodate about 100 or more people.

Gatherings had been held in the Church Hall every night this week, and they had been well attended. Children had come with their gas masks for a play hour, followed by adult meetings and sing-songs, ending with intercession.

Church services brought forward.

"Mark the Ball" —and Stop Worrying

Much has been written during the past few days regarding the importance of maintaining the morale of the public in wartime.

Cinemas, theatres and organised sport are all accepted as valuable assets on the "home front," and as soon as possible they will all be functioning again under conditions as similar to those in peace-time as is consistent with public safety.

But few, it seems, have paused to consider the part played by newspaper competitions in taking people's minds off the war.

When it is realised what a tremendous regular following many of these competitions have it will be understood why a contest such as "Mark the Ball," for example, is to be retained each Saturday night in "The Star."

Thousands of people enter each week. With many of them it is a regular Saturday evening pastime.

League football has stopped and nobody knows how long we shall be without soccer of this class. "Mark the Ball" is a football competition which can in some measure replace even the game itself for the enthusiast.

Turn to page 3 and enter for "Mark the Ball." There is £20 to be won.

"Mark The Ball" competition is good for morale, says The Star.

"STAY INSIDE CINEMAS"

What to Do in Case of Air Raid

The Sheffield Emergency Committee says the safest place for cinema audiences in an air raid is inside the cinema itself unless one's home can be reached within five minutes.

"At their last meeting the Emergency Committee were informed that at one particular place of entertainment there was exhibited a notice informing the public of the position of the various Public Air Raid Shelters in the vicinity, says a statement issued to-day by the Committee.

They were also informed that a notice had appeared relating to another place of entertainment in which it was stated that there was opposite to such place of entertainment a commodious air-raid shelter.

"These notices are misleading and, in fact, dangerous because the audiences at these two places of entertainment would be largely in excess of the accommodation provided in the air-raid shelters referred to, and in case of an air-raid it would be impossible for all the members of the audiences to find shelter —in fact, an attempt to do so would probably lead to a catastrophe.

"The object of the public air-raid shelter is to find accommodation for the person who happens to be in the street during an air-raid and it is not intended to find accommodation for those who may be at a place of entertainment.

"Those persons who visit a place of entertainment ought to do so on the understanding that should there be an air-raid the safest place for them is to

Air raid advice to cinemagoers, September, 1939.

(Continued on Back Page.)

More 'Toddlers'' Masks Soon

Nearly 6,000 gaily coloured respirators for children between two and three years old have been distributed in Sheffield, and it is expected that a further supply, to complete the issue in the city, will be available shortly.

These "toddlers'" respirators were made originally for all children between two and four, but it was found that many children approaching four were able to wear the small size civilian respirator. Consequently, these have been issued to the older children, except where a "toddler's" respirator was essential.

Distribution of the babies' protective helmet, which has bellows operated by the person carrying the baby, has been completed.

INTELLIGENCE

Gas masks for toddlers in January, 1940.

How You Can Avoid Helping the Enemy

SHEFFIELD is to have an anti-rumour and anti-gossip week soon. It is being organised by the Information Committee. It will follow largely the methods successfully employed in other places, where there were special speeches, slogans, streamers across streets, the placing of slips in customers' parcels at shops, and the display of notices in buses and trams.

It is probable that in Sheffield a loud-speaker van will also be used.

The Information Committee feel that their most urgent duty is to engender the people's confidence, to counteract the pernicious effect of rumours, and to discourage unwise talk about military and other matters.

LESSON OF FRANCE

The proposal is enthusiastically supported by the Rev. George Needham, who as a psychologist and vicar of a city parish (St. Philip's) knows more than most people the trouble which can be caused by gossip and rumour.

"Nothing undermines a people's morale quicker and more effectively than rumour. Hence it is of prime importance to the enemy to have people who can spread dreadful stories or alarmist news," he said in an interview.

"I am told that in the defeat of the French Army rumour was the next deadliest weapon to the tank. Among the horde of refugees were those who whispered fearful views about the destruction of the French. A sense of defeatism spread like a prairie fire throughout the people of France.

HELPING THE ENEMY

"There are folk in this country who are helping the enemy to win by this means. Many do not know that they are enemy agents. Yet every time someone says to you: you must admit that Hitler has

anything to hamper their country's defence. Any harm they have done has been unwitting. Yet if you consider some of the following points you will realise how easy it is, even for honest and conscientious citizens, to spread rumour.

"If three people witness a motor accident there will be three different accounts given. Each claims to be an eye-witness and all are honest, but their reports are inaccurate nevertheless.

"Have you played a party game where one person whispers a message to another, and so on? The version at the end is vastly different from the one given at the beginning.

UNCONSCIOUS FACTORS

"You may say that that is explicable, because people in fun deliberately alter the whispered message to make it silly, or applicable to somebody in the room. This is true but unconscious factors have the same result.

"Take a newspaper report of any political event. Go to representatives of the various political parties. You know that you will get a different version from each. We all tend to read in what we wish to find. Everybody can see the cloven hoof in his opponent's gestures!

"There is a natural tendency on our part to believe the worst

July 6, 1940…and dangerous talk can cost lives.

MORE PANS, MORE PLANES

THE GROWING PILE of aluminium pans salvaged by housewives at the W.V.S. headquarters in Church Street, Sheffield. Anything made of aluminium is urgently wanted to make planes.

OUT OF THE FRYING PAN INTO THE SPITFIRE

Give Up Your BEST Aluminium

WE want every ounce of aluminium we can get. No matter where it is or in what form, let us have it. This is the slogan of the aluminium campaign.

The real idea behind the voluntary contribution scheme initiated by Lord Beaverbrook, Minister of Aircraft Production, is to create an abnormal supply of high-quality aluminium found in domestic utensils.

There is no question of the ordinary channels being neglected.

Every normal source of production is being employed.

The drive aims at providing the R.A.F. with more and more fighting machines by unorthodox means. Peace-time commercial practices do not rule.

Original methods are commended; originality and enterprise are behind the aluminium speed-up.

CALL FOR SACRIFICES

Every little contribution by the housewife adds one more essential piece to the fighting strength of our air arm.

There may be hundreds of tons of aluminium on the scrap metal heaps throughout the country, but much of this scrap aluminium is below the standard required for aircraft production.

It cannot reach the high content of the material used for pots, pans and kettles. In these is the best material for the immediate purpose.

That is why the Ministry is appealing for unselfish sacrifice and the donation of kitchen vessels that still in good condition.

shops when required so urgently can buy the articles and give them as a national contribution.

Many of the aluminium pans taken to the W.V.S. headquarters in Church Street, Sheffield, yesterday were brand new. At least one still had the price label on it.

This is evidence of the enthusiasm with which women of the city are responding to the call for aluminium.

It is estimated that already they have supplied sufficient to use in the manufacture of a Spitfire.

In the morning and from 2 to 3 p.m. from Monday to Friday, July 15th to 19th, householders will be able to take their gifts to the nearest school.

Other depots are already in use besides Church Street. Every Corporation department or depot from the Town Hall to the swimming baths will receive contributions. Only hospitals are excluded.

CONTINUOUS STREAM

Throughout yesterday there was an almost continuous stream at the Rotherham W.V.S. headquarters in Fred ck Street. The collec had s assumed suffi

Give us your pans – and help make an aeroplane.

GOT HIS FISH AND CHIPS!

AFTER five and a half years away from England, a Sheffield sergeant has arrived back home, and the first thing he made a dash for on disembarking from the boat was "a good helping of fish and chips and a pint of beer."

"Both tasted like the best things in the world," Sergt. Leonard Gregory told "The

Great to be back in Sheffield!

No. 16,885   SHEFFI

SHOWERS OF H.E. SHEFFIELD, CI

CASUALTIES NOT UNDULY HEAVY

—*Ministry communique*

SHEFFIELD BORE THE BRUNT OF LAST NIGHT'S AIR ATTACKS ON BRITAIN, AND BOMBS OF THE HEAVIEST CALIBRE WERE DROPPED AND EXTENSIVE FIRES WERE STARTED, CLAIMED OFFICIALS IN BERLIN TO-DAY.

is claimed that armament works were the chief targets of the Nazi raiders which, according to Berlin, took off in waves from aerodromes i Belgium.

o-day's Air Ministry communique announced that two German bombers had been brought down during the night.

escribing how the Lufttwaffe developed its attack on an industrial region in the North of England, the communique added: " The principal damage was done in one town, where a number of buildings were destroyed and roads damaged or temporarily blocked.

arge numbers of incendiary bo we el, employed, but the fire

The Sheffield Blitz. The Star of December 13, 1940, reports that Sheffield bore the brunt of last night's air attacks on Britain but the headline says that casualties were not unduly heavy…

Dawn on December 13, 1940, revealed the extent of the damage.

A sorry sight…Angel Street after the Blitz.

HOUSING ESTATE, AND CINEMA AP

INCENDIARY bombs caused extensive outbreaks of fire during last night's raid on Sheffield and the Sheffield area. A church was burnt out and shops and showrooms were extensively damaged. The church, situated in a residential suburb, was left with only the shell of the building and the spire standing.

While a large furniture showroom was burning patrons of a theatre adjoining and in the same block had to leave.

An announcement that the theatre would have to be cleared on police instructions was made from the stage. The house was full and as the audience left they were ushered in directions away from the fire to the nearest shelters.

Although the furniture premises on a corner position were extensively damaged, the efforts of the fire brigade and the A.F.S. to prevent the blaze from spreading to the theatre and other property in the block were successful.

The top floor of the property was

Ran over a fire bomb

A MOTORIST stopped his car to draw attention to an incendiary bomb hanging from the roof of a building during last night's raid in the Sheffield area.

As he continued on his way he ran over an incendiary in the roadway.

One fire bomb fell on a public house. The licensee told his customers of what had happened and they left for public shelters. The bomb was quickly extinguished and little damage caused.

mainly involved. The flames were tackled from the theatre roof as well as from the streets below, and the fire was well under control in a very short time.

An incendiary bomb which fell in a thoroughfare of the town was put out by soldiers who were passing at the time.

A tramcar was hit by an incendiary bomb, but nobody was injured. Gas and water mains in a street in the neighbourhood were damaged.

Early details of the blitz bombing.

Blitz City Keeps the Flags Flying

SHEFFIELD'S spirit in facing the "blitz" and its after-effects is exemplified by the flags that are appearing from wrecked shops and shattered windows.

THE UNION JACK HANGS AT HALF-MAST FROM THE CITY WAR MEMORIAL, AS A TRIBUTE TO THOSE WHO DIED IN THE RAID.

Wreaths from the base of the memorial were blown about the roadway.

"Everybody is working like bricks," said Mr. E. B. Gibson, Town Clerk of Sheffield and Chief A.R.P. Controller, to a reporter of *The Star* to-day.

MR. GIBSON, speaking of the Civil Defence services and the W.V.S., of which his wife is chief organiser, said: "I have never seen a finer exhibition of self-sacrificing work, not only among the civilians, who volunteer, but among the paid

out on duty during the raid.

Not long after they found their own houses, which lie alongside each other, had been wrecked and the contents destroyed. They carried on with their duty.

They have since been offered hospitality by brother wardens.

City centre wrecked – but not Sheffield's spirit.

The Star

LATE FINAL

INCORPORATING THE "EVENING TELEGRAPH" AND "SHEFFIELD MAIL"
No. 16,887 SHEFFIELD, MONDAY, DECEMBER 16, 1940 THREE HALFPENCE

– Radio: Page 5

TWO, OR THREE, RAIDERS BELIEVED SHOT DOWN IN SHEFFIELD AREA

H.G.s Hunt Nazis Said To Have Baled Out

ALTHOUGH THERE IS AT PRESENT NO OFFICIAL CONFIRMATION, IT IS BELIEVED THAT TWO, AND POSSIBLY THREE, GERMAN BOMBERS WHICH WERE TAKING PART IN THE ATTACK ON THE SHEFFIELD AREA LAST NIGHT WERE DESTROYED.

Although there is no official confirmation, five German airmen are said to have baled out at Penistone and two more a few miles away. Others are reported to have come down near Doncaster. Home Guards took part in a search.

PLANES CAME OVER IN CONTINUOUS WAVES AND MANY FIRES WERE STARTED. CASUALTIES WERE NOT HEAVY, CONSIDERING THE INTENSITY OF THE RAID.

Congested residential areas were among the raiders' targets. Large numbers of people were evacuated to schools and emergency feeding arrangements were put into operation. A number of incendiary bombs fell on another town in the North-east, but these were quickly dealt with.

CONSTABLE'S HEROIC RESCUE BID

IN addition to house property, shops were damaged. The whole of one district in a North-east town is talking of the heroic rescue attempts of a so far unnamed police-constable.

When the re-inforced cellar in which 11 people were killed received a hit, the constable tried time after time to get through to the people without success.

A warden's post which claimed several casualties was near a church. A bomb fell near and the concrete roof caved in.

Once again the services worked magnificently, particularly the regular and auxiliary fire services. The numerous blazes were quickly under control.

Wonderful Barrage

A large number of incendiaries were dropped in a second North of England industrial town, which had a raid lasting some hours, but all were very quickly dealt with, and no fires were allowed to develop. No high explosive bombs fell.

A resident told a reporter: "Planes came over every few minutes, but the A.A. barrage was wonderful. The guns nearly blew me out of my house."

Two large calibre bombs which fell in an urban district of the East Midlands last night set fire to a school, which was gutted, and caused considerable damage to residential and business premises. A number of people had to be evacuated to a local dance hall.

There were, however, only three minor casualties, one a woman warden struck on the head by debris and taken to hospital, and two others treated at a local first-aid post.

Many fire bombs, flares and high explosives were dropped on the East of the town, but the attack bore no resemblance to the earlier severe raids on provincial centres.

Over the Midlands activity was generally slight, and most of the raiders appeared to pass to the North-east.

Post Gunned

Another town had some incendiaries dropped on it, but damage was slight.

Six incendiary bombs were dropped in another North of England town nearby, and an A.F.S. post was machine-gunned. The bombs did little damage.

When the A.F.S. post was machine-gunned the firemen took cover and there were no casualties.

A stick of incendiary bombs was dropped near to the town but they were quickly put out by miners.

Waves of Raiders

Either a bomb or an A.A. shell fell into a house near by and hit the fireplace. There were no casualties.

Waves of raiders which passed over a West Midlands town met intense A.A. fire. Four high explosives fell in open country.

After having enjoyed some days' respite a South-West town was visited by an enemy raider which dropped a trail of fire bombs.

A few fires were started, but they were put out within five minutes. The enemy plane dropped a flare, and left after being over the town for a few minutes.

No reports of heavy attacks were received from the North-west, and the general early ending of the night's raids was possibly due to heavy mist in France.

Guns Open Fire

A.A. guns in a south-east coast area opened fire on enemy planes which crossed the Kent coast in bright moonlight. There were reports of brisk activity from other areas.

In the London area only a few planes were heard in most districts. High explosives were dropped in one borough. These resulted in a number of persons being trapped.

A heavy bomb fell in Parkland It shook neighbouring buildings, but caused no damage.

People Trapped

Seven persons were trapped in the debris of houses wrecked by a high explosive bomb on the outskirts of London

Rescue parties found two children who were dead. The others were suffering from injuries. Another bomb damaged a school in an adjacent area.

A small bomb which fell in one London district burst in the roadway outside an emergency feeding centre. All the windows were blown in but nobody was hurt.

GAVE LIFE TO SAVE MAN WOUNDED IN RAID

ONE of the most courageous acts during the recent Sheffield blitz was that of Mr. Thomas Parramore (35), of Ringinglow Road, a first-aid driver, who sacrificed his life while protecting a wounded man.

Called to the wounded man, Mr. Parramore rendered first-aid, and finding that he could not get him into his own car to take him to hospital, sent for an ambulance. Before the ambulance arrived, a bomb was dropped and Mr. Parramore sacrificed his life by protecting the injured man with his body. The man, who later was taken to hospital, is still alive. He owes his life to the heroism of Mr. Parramore.

Mr. Parramore was well-known in the city, being a leather merchant with premises in Spital Hill. He leaves a widow and a seven-year-old daughter.

Full Communique

The full Air Ministry and Ministry of Home Security communique is as follows:—

"Yesterday evening enemy bombers attacked an industrial region in the North of England, where damage was caused to houses and other property. Reports so far received indicate, however, that casualties were not very heavy. In one town particularly a number of fires were started, but the fire services dealt with them promptly, and they were all soon under control.

"A small-scale attack was made on parts of the London area, but bombs were also dropped in some other parts of the country. The damage caused was slight, and the number of casualties was extremely small."

Dayflight Raid

A town in East Anglia was machine-gunned by a German plane this morning. The only casualty was a man who was struck by a glancing blow from a bullet, and was taken to hospital with head injuries. It is understood that his condition is not serious.

The plane came down to about 70ft., and made about nine runs over the area, dropping nine bombs in the vicinity. All of them fell in open ground, causing slight damage.

One of the bombs set fire to a barn.

PRIVATE BURIALS

Relatives of people who died in the air raid are now, in many instances, arranging private burial for them.

Those not claimed by the relatives will, it was stated by the Town Clerk of Sheffield (Mr. E. B. Gibson), to-day, be buried at the city's expense, either at Abbey Lane or at City Road. The date of the burials has not yet been fixed.

ITALIAN CROWN PRINCE INTERNED?

While Italian Fascism after 18 years stands grimly at bay, shaken by military disasters, rumours of internal troubles which lack confirmation continue to reach the other world.

An Athens dispatch says that Italian non-commissioned officers surrendering in Albania yesterday alluded to a belief that Crown Prince Umberto is interned somewhere in North Italy.

According to another report received from the Yugoslav-Albanian frontier Italian prisoners say that there are great food and ammunition shortages; that they have heard of peace propaganda in Italy, and that the German Army is on the way there.

They are also reported to have said that they were astounded that the R.A.F. did not attack Italian towns more violently because the population was already demoralised. One heavy blow, they asserted would have very serious effects.

Meanwhile in Italy the blackshirt "bosses" are taking stock of the position. At a conference at Forli yesterday the Fascist Party secretaries of the province of Northern Italy met in conference.

According to the official Italian News Agency the reports made by the secretaries emphasised the calm and absolute faith in victory with which the Italian people and the Fascist Party are watching the course of the war.

These reports, it is added, show complete contempt for recent enemy propaganda to the contrary.

According to the Ankara radio a secret wireless station in Rome is reported to be operating.

HITLER'S WAR

471st Day.

BLACK-OUT & LIGHTING-UP TIMES:

5.17 p.m. to 8.47 a.m. to-morrow.

DEFIANT!

Britain Accused of Sabotage

"The British Intelligence Service has carried out new acts of sabotage in the Rumanian oil-fields," the German radio announced last night.

"The railway line from Ploesti to Bucharest was struck by an explosion which damaged a bridge. Traffic on the line will be interrupted for several days. Dynamite is said to have been found at the place of the explosion.

"Only a few days ago two large oil tanks were destroyed by fire and another mysterious fire occurred in the timber depot in the oil region.

"This indicates renewed and intensive activity of the Intelligence Service."

BRITONS IN TURKEY GIVE £16,000

The British colony in Turkey has subscribed £16,000 to the Spitfire Fund opened by the British Ambassador, Sir Hugh Knatchbull-Hugessen.

The question of opening a second fund is being considered.—Reuter.

MORE ALARMS IN MALTA

Further air raid alarms in Malta are announced in the following communique:—

"During the night several air raid alarms were sounded when enemy aircraft flew over Malta at intervals.

"Several bombs were dropped, but little damage resulted and no casualties.

"This morning an alarm was sounded when enemy aircraft approached the island. None crossed the coast."

TORPEDOED LINER

The Canadian Naval Defence Department has issued the following statement, which is understood to refer to the torpedoed liner Western Prince.

"No announcement can be made until the ship or, in the case of its sinking, until the survivors have reached harbour."

Mr. C. D. Howe, the Canadian Minister of Munitions and Supply

TIRELESS GREEKS PUSH ON

THE fall of Tepelini, the Italian base between Argyrokastro and Valona, the only seaports left to the Italians south of Durazzo, is imminent, according to the latest reports of the fighting in Albania.

Tepelini has been completely evacuated, according to a Turkish Radio broadcast, and its occupation by the Greeks is expected soon.

Meanwhile the Greeks appear to have encircled the town, and have cut the road northwards to Valona, according to reports reaching Struga, on the Yugoslav frontier.

The road was cut by the occupation of the village of Dukaj after the Greeks had attacked with bayonets. They are now continuing to advance.

BATTERED BY R.A.F.

At the same time, states the Ankara radio, Greek cavalry units are now within striking distance of Himara, the main objective between the Greeks and Valona in their coastal drive towards the port.

Other Greek forces are already reported to have cut round Himara and driven northwards along the coast.

Meanwhile the R.A.F. have again delivered a battering attack on Valona, scoring direct hits in daylight on harbour installations and wharves, says a British United Press correspondent.

The British bombers also attacked the coast south of Valona.

These raids added not only to the confusion caused by previous raids on Valona, but also to the retreating Italian troops, who are being driven back along the coast towards Valona, in the face of the tireless Greek infantry and cavalry advance.

HEAVY FIGHTING

No details of the fighting are announced in the Greek war communique issued in Athens last night, which merely states:—

"Successful local actions on the front. We have taken two more heights, a number of prisoners, and an important number of machine-guns and trench mortars."

The Greeks are also only about a mile from Klisura, on the Premeti-Durazzo road, according to reports reaching Struga.

Heavy fighting, say these reports, is taking place in this area.

Mystery of Laval's Dismissal

BY OUR DIPLOMATIC CORRESPONDENT

BRITISH diplomatic quarters take the view that it is too early as yet to appraise the effect of the Laval sensation on French relations with this country.

There is still great mystery about the circumstances which led to the downfall of this "double crosser," and it is not expected that this will be dissipated for some time to come.

A fortnight ago I mentioned that Berlin was exhibiting some uneasiness about the Vichy Government's backwardness in operating the "Loyal Collaboration" with the Nazis to set up the "new order" in France.

Vichy, too, was suspicious that Laval was attempting a coup d'etat with the object of replacing Petain and usurping his position as head of the Government.

SECRET OF VITAL QUESTIONS

Another factor which certainly played against Laval was the collapse of Italy. Part of his policy had been the re-institution of a Latin block in the Mediterranean, but his Vichy colleagues saw more profitable chances in the possibility of France succeeding Italy as the "white-headed boy" of the Nazis.

When these deductions are assembled it will be seen that the dubiety in British quarters about whether the change will be ultimately beneficial to us has some foundation.

A veil of impenetrable secrecy remains drawn over the vital questions of whether the Nazi demands for passage through France of German troops, the cession of French naval forces to them, and facilities at the Mediterranean ports are included in the "loyal collaboration" which eht new consultative committee will have to decide.

Laval Arrest Said to be Confirmed

A Vichy correspondent of a Geneva newspaper claims to be able to confirm that M. Laval has been arrested.

The correspondent says that the French ex-deputy Premier and Foreign Minister, is obliged to remain on his property at Chateldon Auvergne under a police guard.—Reuter.

R.A.F. BOMBS ON BERLIN'S UNDERGROUND

Bombers of the R.A.F. last night made what is described in London as a prolonged attack on targets in the Berlin area.

An admission that part of the district railway line and the underground in Berlin were hit in last night's R.A.F. raid is made by the official German News Agency to-day.

"BRITISH planes over Berlin last night caused only slight damage," the agency adds.

"Apart from some roof fires which were soon put out, hits were registered on part of the district railway line and the underground.

"Some dwelling houses were damaged. Two persons were killed and five injured.

The R.A.F.'s last visit to Berlin was on the night of November 26th-27th, when they bombed railway stations near the centre of the city.

The sirens in Berlin went early in the evening, report neutral journalists.

Owing to the fact that there had been no alarms in the city for more than a fortnight, tens of thousands of people, not expecting a raid under present weather conditions, were caught.

A tremendous traffic jam of buses, trams, and underground trains resulted after the "all clear" had gone.

"It was officially announced later by the Germans that a few British planes had succeeded in reaching the city."

MAJOR F. S. JAMES, Chief Constable of Sheffield, says: "You must keep away from the bombed areas."—See story on Back Page.

ITALIAN PLANES IN BELGIUM

The presence of hundreds of Italian planes and pilots in Belgium is reported by a neutral observer who has just returned from a tour of the country.

The observer revealed to the British United Press in Istanbul the main points of a confidential report he has made to his Government, adding that he could personally vouch for all of them.

"I have seen hundreds of Italian pilots, planes, and a great number of Italian lorries in and around Brussels," said this observer.

"It was impossible to obtain any check on the actual number there, but they are much in evidence. When I left Brussels for Berlin a squadron of Italian planes 'convoyed' our train to the Belgian frontier.

FORCES WITHDRAWN

"The British Air Force have been so successful in their raids that the Germans have withdrawn their forces some 12 miles inland," the observer also said.

"In Antwerp practically all the docks have been destroyed and hundreds of barges and small boats which the Germans brought to the harbour have been sunk or destroyed.

"There have been few civilian casualties in Antwerp. Brussels itself is hardly ever bombed, but railway centres and the industrial districts around it are often visited by British planes.

"Many factories working for the Germans have been destroyed, including the General Motors factory.

"Air-raid shelter facilities in Brussels are extremely poor. The Germans are making some attempt to protect the town, but no batteries are vikible during the day as they are removed to camouflaged sheds outside the city each morning."

FRENCH STEAMER'S SUGAR CARGO

The French steamer Quercy (3,100 tons) arrived at Virginia last evening with passengers from Guadeloupe.

She is bound for Casablanca, Morocco, with a cargo of sugar.—Reuter.

Siam Blamed For Renewal of Hostilities

A hundred bombs were dropped in eight air raids on four towns in Indo-China during the week-end, while both Indo-China and Siam were suggesting that a settlement of the dispute might be possible.

Many houses were destroyed, and there were three French casualties in the raids on Indo-China, says the British United Press correspondent at Hanoi.

Admiral Decoux, Governor of French Indo-China, declared that Indo-China was ready at any moment to renew normal relations with Bangkok.

He blamed Siam for the renewal of hostilities, and said Indo-China must retaliate.

This statement follows the suggestion made by the Siam Government that a French mission should go to Bangkok to discuss the question of Indo-China territories which Siam has demanded.

MEXICO BRITONS JOINING UP

Fifteen of the best type of youths from the British colony in Mexico City have left by train for the port of Vera Cruz where they will sail later to-day for New York as war volunteers. They do not know what their destination will be after they have arrived in New York, and no official statement is yet available on the matter.

It is thought in Mexico that they may be sent to Canada for their training, although it is possible that they may cross direct to England.

Almost the entire British colony turned out at the station to bid them farewell. Their departure was a mixture of sadness on the part of parents and enthusiasm from hundreds of young friends.

Italians Admit British Advance Proceeds Unabated

British troops, one week after they began their victorious drive against Mussolini's forces in Northern Africa, are battling in a raging sandstorm on Libyan territory. Reports reaching Rome from Benghazi, admitted that the British attacks were unabating, and that battles were in progress for Fort Capuzzo, inside Libya, and Bardia.

INTO these battles, the Italian report claimed the British were throwing thousands of fresh Australian and New Zealand troops.

The whole action for Sidi Barrani was fought by British troops, who were outnumbered by four to one.

All the officers engaged in it give warm praise to the suport given, by the Royal Air Force Only two dive-bombing attacks were made on the British troops throughout the battle for this hamlet—and they were ineffective

At a given word the Highlanders and other infantry, with fixed bayonets, charged straight at the enemy in a number of places at once.

SCARED BY BAYONETS

There was little fighting among the actual houses of Sidi Barrani.

"Once we began to get close in with our bayonets the Italians

"Those who fled westwards were mopped up by armoured forces operating on Buk Buk.

"It was an exciting show," was the Major's verdict.

"The Italians fought pretty well and on the whole they stuck to their guns against our tanks."

FALL OF BIBEIWA

Further details of the capture of Bibeiwa, the great encampment established by General Maletti as an invasion base show that the General and his officers were just sitting down to their breakfast coffee when from out of the distance came the muffled roar of many engines.

Within a few minutes dozens of British tanks charged into the centre of the camp from the rear, all their guns blazing, and their tractors sending up fresh clouds of sand, creating a thick fog over the camp.

Some of the Italian tank officers never even had time to run

braving the minefields, some of which blew up.

"It was the nearest thing to hell I have ever seen," was an Italian doctor's subsequent description of the scene that followed.

GENERAL KILLED

Gunners operating field guns swung them into the centre of the camp [illegible] to stop the British tanks. Their shells, however, [illegible]

Many Italian officers and men seized machine-guns and blazed away for a short time.

Then General Maletti got a bullet through his lung, and died while he was being carried to his tent.

The other officers and men realised the hopelessness of the battle and surrendered. Only a handful escaped.

Throughout the battle mules ran madly round the camp, adding to the general confusion.

Immediately the surrender of

LATE NEWS

('Phone No. 23055)

German Agency says aerodrome hit in Berlin raid. Houses were set on fire. Two hospitals damaged. In Hurfurth church was destroyed. Fire caused in Central Germany works soon put out. Production not disturbed

LODGE MOOR HOSPITAL BULLETIN

Doctor wishes to speak on telephone to 2026 2842 1686 2096.

RAIDERS IN N. WEST

Enemy planes believed in vicinity of two North-West of England inland towns this afternoon.

German planes shot down in December 15, 1940, raid.

Hawksley Avenue, Hillsborough, after the Blitz.

And this family still found time to say "thank you"...

The Salvation Army were there to provide food as well as spiritual sustenance during the dark days of the war.

The Church Army's mobile canteen is no longer mobile.

Thumbs up from Sheffielders as a sympathetic King George VI and Queen Elizabeth are warmly welcomed during a visit to the city three weeks after the Blitz in January, 1941.

Sheffield had less than two weeks to recover from the Blitz before Christmas 1940 arrived...but still managed to pick itself up and raise a smile.

Blitz or no blitz, bath times goes on at St Ann's, Heeley, Rest Centre.

A year on from the Blitz and an anniversary service is held on the site of a warden's post in Coleford Road, Sheffield, where ten people died.

Growing your own veg was a major contribution to the war effort and this Sheffield allotment holder received some help from the Navy.

Sheffield Newspapers set up a war fund and used this display of bombs to promote it. The notice says: "These bombs have been made harmless by the bomb disposal squad. Help them and your own Sheffield boys by subscribing to the Sheffield Newspapers War Fund."

In 1945, Sheffield Girl Guides and Boy Scouts staged a "Help The Housewife" campaign to raise money for a new joint headquarters to be built after the war. It was a forerunner to Bob A Job Week and tasks included looking after the children while mum had a break, gardening, washing up and, as this picture shows, pegging out the washing.

Sheffield Had a Silent New Year's Eve

Sheffield streets were deserted and silent last night, and the usual New Year's Eve scenes were absent.

It was in striking contrast to pre-war days when queues of cars waited outside dance halls and hotels in a blaze of lights, and revellers kissed in the ballrooms on the stroke of midnight, while clouds of balloons were released to float down over their heads.

The Hogmanay Ball, for which there were sometimes 1,000 applications for tickets—though the ball was limited to 400—was not held, for Sheffield "Went to it" as usual, and halls and hotels once used for revelry were given over to offices and businesses for war production.

No one sang "Auld Lang Syne" in the city streets, and no Watch-Night services were held in the churches.

Neighbours stole out in the dark to tap on one another's door, and to devise impromptu little ceremonies.

"You come to our house and we'll drink a toast at midnight."

"No, you come here!"

In the end there were many neighbours who made little tours of greeting in their own group of houses.

1941 comes in quietly.

Bombs to Save
THEN GUARDED OFFICE SAFE

How some Corporation employees, assisted by four civilians, saved a number of buses during the night of one of the Sheffield air raids, was told to "The Star" to-day by one of the men.

An employee was on duty at one of the Corporation garages when a large number of incendiaries were falling in the district, and with the help of other drivers several bombs were dealt with.

As soon as the high explosive bombs began to fall the party went to a nearby shelter, treating two casualties they found on the way.

The garage received a direct hit and with a church blazing close by the men decided to make an attempt to take the buses out of the garage.

CIVILIANS HELPED

Four civilians from a nearby house offered their assistance and a conductor, whose tramcar had stopped some distance away, also helped.

Several buses were removed from the garage and parked in neighbouring streets.

Later they found that several of the vehicles in the streets had caught fire from sparks from burning houses, and the buses were removed to other streets and the fires extinguished.

The day's takings were in the office safe, but they were unable to get it to headquarters, and the men stood guard over the safe.

The men then turned their attention to injured people in the district, and gave great help to the casualty service.

Tribute was paid to the excellent work accomplished by the men, and the Corporation employees spoke highly of the assistance received from the civilians.

to Double of Airmen

5,000 More City

Stories of great bravery and courage started to emerge in The Star a few days after the Blitz.

A selection of gramophone records available for the Sheffield public in January, 1941.

The ★ Star

Saturday, January 4, 1941

DON'T WASTE FOOD

IN the present circumstances it is nothing short of a crime to waste food.

It is only slightly less venial to be extravagant in the use of food.

Many people eat too much. Some of us would be better in health and temper if we would bring ourselves to the stage where we eat to live rather than live to eat.

Others are still too exacting in demanding certain kinds of food simply because it is the particular kind to which they have become accustomed.

How many of us consider in regard to a specific food as to whether or not it has taken up valuable cargo space in a ship needed for urgent war purposes?

Let us begin to be more economical in the consumption of bread.

That extra slice which is not wanted and thus allowed to get too dry to eat should not have been cut.

Bread means wheat and wheat means shipping.

If we eat more potatoes and less bread we ease the shipping position. In the last war potatoes were scarce. By the perversity of human nature this led to many people who previously ate very few potatoes, developing a sudden passion for them. This winter potatoes are plentiful. Let them take the place of bread to some extent.

GROW MORE

We must grow more food in this country. With all that has been done and all that is going to be done we shall grow not more than a tithe of what we could grow. In our own City of Sheffield there are acres and acres of land growing nothing but rough grass which has not even food value for cattle.

Some are over-run with docks and thistles, seed from which is blown over land patiently cultivated by the more energetic section of the population working allotments.

Don't waste food, says The Star in its leader column of January 4, 1941.

ANNOUNCE THAT OWING TO THE CITY HALL BEING TEMPORARILY CLOSED FOR DANCING, DOES INVITE OUT OF SHEFFIELD INQUIRIES. COMS, 9, CARTER KNOWLE ROAD. 'PHONE 52058 AND 72147.

NORTON HOTEL BALLROOM.
EVERY SATURDAY.
MARJORIE FIELDS' SELECT DANCE.
7.30 to 11. Jack Crich and his Band. Ad. 1/6. Dancing Every Monday, 7.30 to 11. Ad. 1/-.

ABBEYDALE PICTURE HOUSE.
COLLINSON'S TEA DANCES.
Every MONDAY & TUESDAY AFTERNOON.
2.30 to 5.30 p.m. Tickets 1/3.
BERNARD TAYLOR'S BAND.
A really enjoyable time assured.

CAVENDISH SCHOOL OF DANCING,
218, WEST ST. 'Phone 24984.
TO-NIGHT
PRACTICE DANCE, 7.30-11.0, 2/-
CAVENDISH COLLEGIANS BAND.

LEARN TO DANCE NOW AT COLLINSON'S LEARNERS CLASSES.
Every MON., TUES., THURS., & FRIDAY
From 7.30 to 10 p.m. 1/6 Thorough Tuition. Studio, 71, Wilkinson St. (off Glossop Rd.). Private lessons daily from 10 a.m.

CARLTON SALON, Rotherham.
Acc. 400 Dancing every Sat., Tues., Fri., 7 p.m. Thurs. & Sat. Afternoon, 3.

PUBLIC NOTICES

STEVE'S SHOOTING SALOON,
18, CAMBRIDGE STREET.

The R.A.F. dropped 20,000 fire bombs on Bremen!

Smuts says we shall be invaded ! !

You MUST be prepared! Learn to shoot at Steve's.

Open daily, including Sunday, till black-out.

Learn to shoot at Steve's! A January, 1941, advertisement in The Star.

Letters to the Editor

CALL TO STOP TRAMS DURING "ALERTS"

WE in Sheffield ought to pass a resolution of heartfelt thanks to our tramway men for declining to run tramcars during an "alert."

These men know the danger to which they subject the city if they allow the trolleys to splutter and flash and give out lights which obviously must be visible to any airman passing overhead.

The lights may not be of any "navigational assistance" to airmen, as the big wigs at Leeds said, but they certainly do indicate the presence of a town.

Let us stop this foolish running of trams in "alerts."—**Would-Walk.**

SHEFFIELD people will have noted with interest, no doubt, that the German military authorities have stopped all trams from running after dark at The Hague. They state that the sparks from the trams act as a guide for the R.A.F.—**Common Sense.**

THEATRES	CINEMAS

Letters published in The Star in January, 1941, not long after the Blitz.

GREYSTONES BALLROOM
(ECCLESALL ROAD),

"THE HOTSHOTS"
(A Riot of Musical Tempo)

20ft. Underground; 8 Emergency Exits.

7 p.m. till 11 p.m. Adm. 2/- inc. (limited)

Ecclesall trams. 'Phone 61115.

Entertainment wartime style – 20 feet underground!

v this People minus over bus

net by ch do e way.

at we . We some going the n of

THE MOON IS NEWS

Light Nights Next Week

Beginning of week

End of week.

DURING the coming week the moon will be of more use to people in the black-out than it has been in the past week. The first-quarter occurs to-morrow and it will gradually get brighter and brighter until it is at full on Monday week.

The times during the coming week of rising and setting are:—

	Rises.	Sets.
Saturday	12.11 p.m.	12.56 a.m.
Sunday	12.32 p.m.	1.58 a.m.
Monday	12.54 p.m.	3. 3 a.m.
Tuesday	1.20 p.m.	4. 7 a.m.
Wednesday	1.49 p.m.	5. 8 a.m.
Thursday	2.14 p.m.	6. 9 a.m.
Friday	2.53 p.m.	7. 5 a.m.

is on te shows change still Ir

What German they ge elemen appear dreamer as well volcano Eire.

Notice Are Bla another well ver Open T

Our "Three not be the air one."

To-nig At a c ing one called to explained there. H "Have asked the "No," volun

Full moon helps in the black-out.

Be warned. Rats are doing Hitler's work.

Survivor Praises Victims Trapped in Hotel Cellar

A graphic story of the wrecked Marples Hotel on the night of a Sheffield air raid was told to "The Star" to-day by one of the seven men rescued alive from the cellar beneath the hotel.

HE is Mr. Edward Riley, a cellarman, living at the Banner Cross Hotel, Sheffield. How he came to be one of the seven rescued alive he does not remember.

Mr. Riley lapsed into unconsciousness in the cellar, and woke up in hospital more than a week later.

As reported on Page 3, 70 people were killed in the hotel, which suffered a direct hit.

On the night of the raid Mr. Riley was having a night off from duty and had arranged to meet a friend in the hotel. Then came the raid.

"In the main passage of the hotel there were several people in front of me making their way out when the building received a hit, and I was blown back to the top glass, but as I was at the back of the party I got off the lightest.

ENTRANCE BLOCKED

"I made my way down the steps to one of the lower bars and later moved to a still lower bar, where some first-aid men attended to our cuts and injuries.

"I saw the manager, Mr. A. Burgess, assisted by another man, shepherding staff and others below to the basement, and Mr. Burgess then went upstairs again. He came back shortly to say the entrance was blocked.

"He went up later, but I did not see him again.

"I went into the cellar with other people.

"'There were a number of them in the cellar and also some of the staff. Everyone was behaving splendidly.

"'They were all won...

Seventy people enjoying themselves in the city centre Marples Hotel were killed when the building took a direct hit on the night of the Blitz. It was the worst single tragedy of that dreadful night.

Seven were rescued alive, including Edward Riley whose miracle survival story made front page news in The Star.

Comforting the injured after the Marples Hotel blast.

Escapes with Few Bruises

A 16-year-old Sheffield boy had an almost miraculous escape when a bomb hit a cellar, killing the other occupants—his parents, brother, and two neighbours.

HE is Geoffrey Hulley, of Sheffield, who, although trapped for two days and nights, escaped with only a few bruises apart from the shock which followed. He is now in Sheffield Royal Hospital.

Geoffrey went to the pictures on the night of the "blitz" on the city and when the raid started made his way from shelter to shelter until he reached home.

There he went down into the cellar with his father, mother, brother. and two neighbours.

TERRIFIC BUMP

"I had not been in there more than a quarter of an hour," he said. "when there was a terrific bump and everything fell around and on top of us.

"I called out, but got no reply from anyone. I could tell that I was not seriously injured, for I could move about a little, though I felt sore in one or two places.

"I could still hear the bumps overhead and started to crawl about in the small space at my disposal.

"I had been sitting on the bottom of the cellar steps, but the others were at the far end of the cellar. There was a lot of stone and rubble between myself and the other side, and I started to move what I could, at the same time shouting for all I was worth. hoping I should be heard.

LOST COUNT OF TIME

"I lost count of time altogether, but continued to move what loose stuff I could.

"After that I lay quiet, reserving my strength, but keeping up my shouts for help every so often. After what seemed days I heard faint sounds, and came to the conclusion that a rescue party was at work. and I shouted with renewed vigour.

'After another dreary wait I saw a thin shaft of light at the far end of the cellar, and tried to get across to it, but there was too much debris in the way.

"I told the people outside that I could not get across to that part, and they said they would try another way. They kept talking to me, and I knew that it was only a question of time before I should be rescued.

PASSED HOT MILK

"While they were trying to get through at another angle

Boy rescued after two days and nights but parents and brother die.

CONSTABLE HERO OF CITY RAID

How a Sheffield policeman worked five hours under burning debris to rescue a youth trapped during an air raid was related to "The Star" to-day.

HE was Police-constable Radford, who later the same evening helped to bring out a man alive from a block of houses which had been hit.

During the raid eight members of Mr. Alfred Greenwood's family went into the cellar of his daughter's house. but the row of houses was demolished by a bomb.

Thanks to the foresight of the daughter a small emergency exit had been made from the cellar, and all the family scrambled out except one son. Joseph Greenwood, aged 19, who was trapped by fallen debris at the other side of the cellar

Police-constable (545) Radford, on being told the youth was underneath started rescue operations the help of the boy's father.

and has been treated at home by his mother, the family's own house having escaped damage.

He has now recovered, and started work to-day.

Police-constable Radford, hearing some houses had been hit in the next road, went straight there and carried on with rescue work through the night.

SIX HOUSES DEMOLISHED

Here six houses had been demolished and it was known the occupants were buried. Clearing debris away as fast as he could he, with the help of Police-constable Thorpe, brought out a man, who though he was rescued alive, died in hospital the next day.

Everyone in the district highly

UNOFFICIAL WORKERS SAVED OVER 29 IN RAID

Trapped by Bomb, She Aided Rescue

Tired after a hard day's work, Mr. Samuel Douglas Hutchinson, now staying with friends in Deerlands Avenue, Sheffield, was among the first to go out on duty during a recent raid on the city, but before he left home he made sure that his wife and two young children and members of his wife's family were in the cellar.

BUT within a short time the house was wrecked, only two of the ten occupants escaping.

They were his wife and her brother, Rhondda Simpson, both of whom were rushed to hospital. They have since been discharged. The victims were Mr. Hutchinson, Patricia, aged 8.

Although my wife and I lost all—our children were killed and we haven't a stick left—we are determined to see this thing through so that there might be a better world," Mr. Hutchinson told a reporter of "The Star."

"With another warden, I was patrolling quite near to my home

NEW POST FOR K.C.?

Heroism Under Debris

How two self-appointed patrolmen assisted by a young man and a member of the R.A.F. saved over 29 lives during a raid on Sheffield was related to "The Star" to-day.

THE rescues took place on the Flower Estate, and the story is one of heroic and continued hard work height

THE STAR

THE QUEEN TALKED TO BOY HERO

Saved

Wonder Deeds in Night of Terror

The proudest boy in Sheffield is Eric Alsopp (16), an A.R.P. messenger. It has just been divulged that at a private ceremony at the Sheffield Town Hall he was presented to the King and Queen in recognition of the wonderful work he did on the night of a Sheffield air raid.

DURING that night, among other things, he was blown off his cycle by a bomb, but he carried on and did wonderful work.

He was at his depot when the raid started, and at once went to a warden's post for help and equipment to fight incendiary bombs. With a stirrup pump numerous incendiaries were extinguished, and he returned to his depot only to be told that his home had been demolished.

After phoning to a report centre he started to go to his house to see what had happened.

Before he had gone far bombs began to fall and about, and Alsopp

broke into flames, and with the help of a warden, he managed to keep the fire from spreading to adjoining houses.

Alsopp and the warden kept a stirrup pump going for three hours, and their action saved at least two houses from catching fire.

Alsopp stayed there until the all-clear was sounded.

Asked about the presentation to the King and Queen, Eric said he knew nothing about it until just before it took place.

He had been told to report "spick and span" to his depot, where he was rigged up with a new uniform and Town Hall

ERIC AL

Boy hero meets King and Queen at Sheffield Town Hall.

MODEST HERO OF DUNKIRK

At the invitation of Lance-Corporal Alfred Shaw, a Sheffielder, his wife and father will attend at Buckingham Palace, next month, to see him presented with the Military Medal, awarded for gallantry at Dunkirk.

LANCE-CORPORAL SHAW was one of the first to volunteer when men were wanted to bring in the wounded from the Dunkirk beaches.

He rendered valuable service under machine-gun fire and bombardment and escaped un-

Lance-corporal A. Shaw

Sheffield lance-corporal Alfred Shaw honoured for bringing in wounded soldiers from the Dunkirk beaches.

A message to the Public about TENNANT'S BEERS in wartime

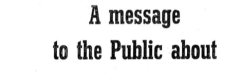

There may not be as much variety because of the war – but the beer's still as strong.

Penistone's War Weapons Week makes Hitler sweat!

CRAVEN 'A'

These are the cigarettes I like – always the same and they never affect my throat!

10 FOR 9d
20 FOR 1s6

C.A.907   Carreras Ltd, 150 Years Reputation for Quality

A wartime cigarette advertisement.

The Star

No. 17,962   Radio: Page 3   SHEFFIELD, TUESDAY, JUNE 6, 1944   Threehalfpence

INVASION TANKS ADVANCE FOR MILES

Slashing Inland From Allied Beachheads

Allied tanks have penetrated several miles to the south between Caen and Isigny in Normandy, says to-day's German official news agency.

THE Allies have established beachheads in Northern France, and are slashing inland, according to photo reconnaissance pilots back from the landings, says a Reuter message.

This was the latest news of progress following General Eisenhower's communique stating that Allied naval forces, supported by strong air forces, began landing Allied armies in Northern France this morning.

Landings took place in Normandy between 6 a.m. and 8.15 a.m. Airborne landings were carried out. The naval bombardment went "in manner planned."

First reports are, therefore, good. U.S. battleships took part in the bombardment.

Montgomery in Charge

General Montgomery is in charge of the Army group carrying out the assault. This Army group includes British, Canadian, and U.S. Forces.

Allied bombers, roaring over London at dawn, gave Londoners the first hint that big events were under way.

The machines passed over the capital in constant procession heading south, and almost simultaneously the B.B.C.'s French transmissions began to warn French people to get away from coastal areas, to avoid roads, railways, and bridges.

First news of the invasion came from German sources, indicating land, sea, and air attacks from Havre to Cherbourg.

Thousands of Paratroops

"A strong wind is blowing and heavy rain is falling," said Oslo radio to-day, quoting Berlin's latest invasion report.

"Tens of thousands of paratroops were dropped in the area of the mouth of the Seine in a rather small area in order to capture important aerodromes," said the broadcast.

"The coast of Normandy is simply swamped with invasion barges and strong enemy naval forces are engaged in a bitter fight with German naval units.

"The paratroops were dropped in a continuous stream in the Le Havre area. They are trying hard to capture the aerodrome in the neighbourhood of the coast in order to land their gigantic air formations.

Landings Reinforced

"At the present time the focal point of the invasion battle is in the area of Caen (Normandy). German forces are engaged in bitter fighting with the invasion troops.

"Invasion troops which have been landed on the mouth of the Seine are being reinforced."

The German Overseas News Agency now gives these points as the centre of the Allied airborne attacks:

HARFLEUR, north-eastern tip of the Cherbourg peninsula;

CARENTAN, on the Orne estuary.

Turn to Back Page, Cols. 5 & 6

The King will broadcast to the world at 9 p.m.

On Radio To-night

Chief Calls to Europe

GENERAL EISENHOWER, in an order of the day to the Allied Expeditionary Force, said:

"Your task will not be an easy one.

"I have full confidence in your courage, devotion to duty, and skill in battle.

"We will accept nothing less than full victory."

Broadcasting to Europe, General Eisenhower said: "Wait until I give you the signal to rise and strike the enemy."

To France he said: "In the course of this campaign you may sustain further loss and damage.

"Great battles lie ahead. I call upon all who love freedom to stand by us."

. See Reports on Pages 5 and 8

Works of Wisdom.
DREAD not, neither be afraid of them. The Lord, your God which goeth before you, he shall fight for you.—Deut. I, 29, 30.

Armada of Over 4,000 Ships

AN armada of upwards of 4,000 ships, with several thousand smaller craft, and backed by over 11,000 first-line aircraft, are taking part in the invasion.

This was announced in the Commons to-day by Mr. Churchill, who said that landings on the beaches are proceeding at various points, and that the fire of shore batteries had been largely quelled.

"There are already hopes that actual tactical surprise has been attained, and we hope to furnish the enemy with a succession of surprises during the course of the fighting," the Prime Minister continued. "The battle will grow constantly in scale and in intensity for many weeks to come, and I shall not attempt to speculate upon its course."

"But this I may say, complete unity prevails throughout the Allied armies. (Cheers.) There is a brotherhood in arms between us and our friends in the U.S. There is complete confidence in the Supreme Commander, General Eisenhower, and in his lieutenants, and also in the Commander of the Expeditionary Force, General Montgomery.

Landings Behind Enemy

"Mass airborne landings have been successfully effected behind the enemy's lines. (Cheers.)

"The ardour and spirit of the troops as I saw for myself when they were embarking in these last few days was splendid to witness.

"Nothing that equipment, science or forethought can do has been neglected, and the whole process of the opening of this great new front will be pursued with the utmost resolution, both by the commanders and by the United States and British Governments, whom they serve."

Mr. Churchill said the obstacles which were constructed in the sea have not proved to be as difficult as was apprehended.

Mr. Greenwood, Leader of the Labour opposition, Mr. Churchill said that certainly in the early part of the battle he would endeavour to keep the House fully informed. "It may be," he added, "that I shall ask their indulgence to press myself upon them before we rise to-night."

"So far, the commanders who are engaged report that everything is proceeding according to plan, he said—and what a plan. This vast operation is undoubtedly the most complicated and difficult which has ever occurred.

CHANNEL ISLES LANDING

ALLIED paratroops have landed on the Channel Islands of Jersey and Guernsey, says a German overseas news agency.

The Agency claims that the paratroops were immediately engaged in battle.

The Channel Islands, says Reuter, have been occupied by the Germans for four years—since June, 1940. They lie 15 to 30 miles off the Cherbourg peninsula.

75 SQ. MILES

The Channel Islands were the only British territory to be occupied by the Nazis.

There are five main islands in the group—Jersey, Guernsey, Alderney, Sark, and Herm, of which Jersey and Guernsey are the biggest.

The total area of the islands is but 75 square miles. The population before the war was about 100,000.

Dover Area Shelled

Big guns on the French coast opened fire across the Strait of Dover a few minutes after mid-day to-day. A salvo of four shells was seen to explode. Shellfire warning was sounded in the Dover area.

A little later Allied aircraft flew out over the Channel towards the French coast.

MR. CHURCHILL AT THE PALACE

The King received the Prime Minister in audience at Buckingham Palace to-day, and Mr. Churchill remained for lunch.

The Star's front page on D-Day, June 6, 1944.

Britain's Blitz Babies To-day — No. 1

BORN IN HEAVY RAID

JEREMY was born in London, September 1, 1940, during a heavy raid. "I had to be removed to the shelter," his mother said. "Jeremy was a wonderful baby. To look at him now, no one would think he was born in that dreadful period. I am sure that the regular drinking of Rowntree's Cocoa plays a great part in keeping him robust."

How right Jeremy's mother is! You see, so many mealtime drinks contain no nourishment at all. But Rowntree's Cocoa contains protein (body-building food); fat; carbohydrate, which gives energy (in the way *sugar* does); and iron for the blood. Besides, Rowntree's Cocoa aids digestion. Make it *your* family's meal-time drink.

His favourite drink is

ROWNTREE'S COCOA

Full marks to Rowntree's for this 1944 advertisement.

THURSDAY, JUNE 8, 1944   Threehalfpence

Bravest, Most Tenacious Men I've Known

By LEONARD MOSLEY, "The Star's" Own Correspondent With the Paratroops

LEONARD MOSLEY, the only British newspaper man to drop by parachute behind the German "Western Wall."

THIS is one of those stories that will have to write itself, because I am too exhausted, excited and exhilarated to have any control over what goes down on his typewriter.

I parachuted into Europe at two minutes past one this morning—D-Day—six-and-a...

What a scoop! The Star had their own man parachuting into Europe on D-Day.

The ✡ Star

No: 18,247   1½d.   SHEFFIELD, TUESDAY, MAY 8, 1945   A KEMSLEY NEWSPAPER

EUROPE WAR ENDS AT MIDNIGHT

Pilgrimage With Thankful Hearts

Channel Isles Free To-day

NOW FOR JAPAN, SAYS THE PREMIER

Here are Sheffield people making their way to the Cathedral to attend one of the many services of thanksgiving for the ending of the war in Europe.

MR. CHURCHILL, broadcasting this afternoon, said: Yesterday at 2.41 a.m., at General Eisenhower's headquarters, General Jodl, representative of the German High Command and of Grand Admiral Doenitz, designated head of the German State, signed an act of unconditional surrender of all German land, sea, and air forces in Europe to the Allied Expeditionary Forces and simultaneously to the Soviet High Command.

To-day this agreement will be ratified and confirmed at Berlin, where Air Chief Marshal Tedder, Deputy Supreme Commander of the Allied Expeditionary Force, and General Tassigny will sign on behalf of General Eisenhower.

General Zhukov will sign on behalf of the Soviet High Command.

The German representatives will be Field Marshal Keitel, Chief of the High Command, and commanders-in-chief of the German Army, Navy, and Air Forces.

Hostilities will end officially at one minute after midnight to-night, Tuesday, 8th May, but in the interests of saving lives the cease fire began yesterday to be sounded all along the front and our dear Channel Islands are also to be freed to-day.

Germans Still Resisting in Places

The Germans are still, in places, resisting the Russian troops, but should they continue to do so after midnight they will, of course, deprive themselves of the protection of the laws of war and will be attacked from all quarters by the Allied troops.

IT IS NOT SURPRISING THAT ON SUCH LONG FRONTS AS IN THE EXISTING DISORDER OF THE ENEMY THE COMMANDS OF THE GERMAN HIGH COMMAND SHOULD NOT IN EVERY CASE BE OBEYED IMMEDIATELY.

This does not, in our opinion, with the best military advice at our disposal, constitute any reason for withholding from the nations the facts communicated to us by General Eisenhower of the unconditional surrender already signed at Rheims, nor should it prevent us from celebrating to-day and to-morrow Wednesday as Victory in Europe days.

To-day, perhaps, we shall think mostly of ourselves. To-morrow we shall pay a particular tribute to our Russian comrades, whose prowess in the field has been one of the grand contributions to the general victory.

Japan with all her treachery and greed remains unsubdued. The injury she has inflicted on Great Britain, the United States, and other countries, and her detestable cruelties call for justice and retribution.

We must now devote all our strength and resources to the completion of our task both at home and abroad. Advance Britannia. Long live the cause of freedom. God save the King.

"Solemn, Glorious Hour"

A SIMULTANEOUS statement was made in Washington by President Truman.

"This is a solemn but glorious hour," he said. "My only wish is that Franklin D. Roosevelt had lived to witness this day.

"General Eisenhower informs me that the forces of Germany have . . . . to the United Nations.

"The flags of fre. . . . .

More Rain is Expected

WITH the end of the war in Europe, an old friend returns to the newspaper columns — the weather forecast.

It says:—

N. Midlands: Light or moderate winds mainly between South and East. Very variable cloud.

Sporadic outbreaks of rain, with local thunder storms, more especially in the South.

Local fog or low cloud near the coasts, especially to-night.

Warm or rather warm.

WEATHER IS NEWS AGAIN!

FOR the first time since the war began it is possible to tell the world what weather Britain is having while it is having it, and to forecast what kind of weather is coming.

All restrictions were removed to-day by the censors, and the Strait of Dover's exclusive priority in up-to-date weather news was ended.

In London early this afternoon the sky was clouded. There was a fresh breeze, but it was not cold.

Early the sun shone brightly after the night's storm, but later clouds shut out the sun, and for a time there was a slight drizzle.

Rain fell persistently in Sheffield, and the sky was very cloudy.

'Nazi Party Gone' —Doenitz

"**T**HE Nazi Party has disappeared. There is no longer unity between State and Party," said Admiral Doenitz in a broadcast to the German people to-day.

"The foundations on which the German Reich was built are a thing of the past. The unity of State and Party no longer exists," he continued.

The Party has disappeared from the scene of its former activity. With the occupation of Germany, power has passed into the hands of the occupation forces.

The Basis For a Future Life

"It depends on them whether I and the Reich Government formed by me will be able to continue in office or not.

"If I can be of assistance to the Fatherland by continuing in office I shall do so until the German people have a chance to express their will by appointing a head of the State, or until the Occupation Powers make it impossible for me to continue in office.

"We must be inspired by the will to do our best in work and achievements without which there can be no basis for a future life.

"We want to march along this road in unity and justice without which we cannot survive the hardships of the times to come.

ON OTHER PAGES

It's all over. The celebrations begin...and hundreds of people make their way to church for thanksgiving services.

LATE NIGHT FINAL

The ✡ Star

No. 18,680   TUESDAY, OCTOBER 1, 1946   A KEMSLEY NEWSPAPER   1½d.

DEATH WILL END THEIR CAREERS OF CRIME AGAINST HUMANITY

GOERING   RIBBENTROP   KEITEL   JODL   KALTENBRUNNER   ROSENBERG   FRANK   FRICK

12 NAZI LEADERS ARE TO HANG

TWELVE of the Nazi leaders were today sentenced to death by hanging, three to imprisonment for life, two to 20 years, one to 15, and one to 10 years. Three were acquitted.

SENTENCED TO DEATH BY HANGING

HERMANN WILHELM GOERING, former Luftwaffe chief and successor-designate to Hitler—guilty on all four counts.

JOACHIM VON RIBBENTROP, Hitler's Foreign Minister from 1938 until the Nazi collapse—guilty on all four counts.

WILHELM KEITEL, former Chief of German High Command—guilty on all four counts.

ERNST KALTENBRUNNER, Chief of Security Police and Himmler's deputy—innocent on one count, guilty on counts three and four.

ALFRED ROSENBERG, intellectual high priest of Nazi "master race," and head of the Nazi department for foreign policy and ideology—guilty on all four counts.

HANS FRANK, former Governor-General of occupied Poland—guilty on counts three and four.

WILHELM FRICK, Minister of Interior from 1933-43, founded concentration camps—innocent on count one, guilty on counts two, three, and four.

FRITZ SAUCKEL, Nazi Labour Chief from 1942 till Germany's collapse—innocent on counts one and two, guilty on counts three and four.

JULIUS STREICHER, Jew-baiter No. 1—innocent on count one, guilty on count four.

ALFRED JODL, former Nazi Chief of Staff—guilty on all four counts.

ARTHUR SEYSS-INQUART, Governor of Austria after anschluss—innocent on count one, guilty on counts two, three, and four.

MARTIN BORMANN, Hitler's deputy in succession to Hess, reported killed on day of Hitler's death—innocent on count one, guilty on counts three and four.

IMPRISONMENT FOR LIFE

RUDOLF HESS, Hitler's former deputy, who flew to Scotland in 1941 to propose peace terms—guilty on counts one and two, innocent on counts three and four.

ERICH RAEDER, Grand Admiral, C.-in-C. German Navy—guilty on counts one, two, and three.

WALTER FUNK, President of Reichsbank 1939 to 1945—innocent on count one, guilty on counts two, three, and four.

SENTENCED TO TWENTY YEARS

BALDUR VON SCHIRACH, former Hitler Youth leader, and Governor of Austria—innocent on count one, guilty on count four.

ALBERT SPEER, built fortifications and was Hitler's armaments Minister—innocent on counts one and two, guilty on counts three and four.

SENTENCED TO FIFTEEN YEARS

CONSTANTINE VON NEURATH, applied anti-Jewish measures as protector of Moravia—guilty on all four counts.

SENTENCED TO TEN YEARS

KARL DOENITZ, successor to Raeder and previously commanded the U-boats. Hitler's successor in final days of war—innocent on count one, guilty on two and three.

COMPLETELY ACQUITTED

FRANZ VON PAPEN, Nazi ace diplomat who played prominent part in bringing Hitler to power—fully acquitted.

HANS FRITSCHE, Goebbels' right-hand man at Propaganda Ministry—acquitted.

HJALMAR SCHACHT, Hitler's financial wizard—completely acquitted.

FOR JUDGES' FINAL COMMENT SEE PAGE 2

These Nazis Escaped the Gallows

HESS   FUNK   RAEDER   SPEER

4 COUNTS OF INDICTMENT

THESE are the four main counts of the indictment at the Nuremberg trial:—

1 **The Common Plan or Conspiracy.** — To commit crimes against peace, war crimes, and crimes against humanity.

2 **Crimes Against Peace.** —Planning and waging of wars of aggression against Poland, Britain, France, Russia, the United States, and other countries.

3 **War Crimes.**—Murder and ill-treatment of civilians and prisoners of war, deportation of civilians for slave labour, killing of hostages, plunder of property, wanton destruction and Germanisation of occupied territory.

4 **Crimes Against Humanity.** — Murder, Extermination, enslavement, deportation and other inhumane acts committed against civilian populations before and during the war, political, racial and religious persecution.

How They Heard the Sentences

LORD JUSTICE LAWRENCE did not wear the black cap when pronouncing sentence. He had started to read the sentence on Goering when there was a delay, caused by a defect in Goering's earphones.

He apparently could not hear the sentence and the proceedings were halted while his head-pieces were changed. With a final flick of his finger Goering adjusted his new earphones and stood erect and motionless to hear sentence.

Hess was next to enter. He looked very downcast, and when a military policeman tried to hand him the earphones he made repeated grabs at them, mumbling something to himself.

Hess kept the earphones at his side as Lord Justice Lawrence declared sentence of life imprisonment.

Keitel stood stiffly, with his shoulders back, and with not the slightest flicker of emotion in his face.

NOT CHEWING

Streicher, for the first time in two days, was not chewing gum as he entered the dock.

He grimaced and nodded his head slightly as sentence was pronounced, then left the Court.

Schirach stood in the dock with his hands crossed at the waist. He was stern, and looked angry as he heard the sentence.

Words of Wisdom.

THE secret of the Lord is with them that fear him.—Ps. XXV., 14.

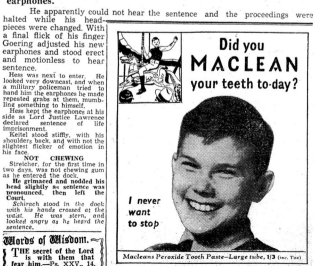
Day of reckoning for Nazi leaders on October 1, 1946. Goering was to commit suicide two weeks later, shortly before he was due to hang.

The Falklands War came close to home on May 5, 1982, when the city mourned the loss of its adopted destroyer HMS Sheffield. Twenty of its crew lost their lives.

The Duke of York, a helicopter pilot during the war, unveiled a memorial to their memory in Sheffield Cathedral in January, 2000.

Start of the Gulf War on January 17, 1991. The Star's readers responded magnificently to the newspaper's appeal for home comforts to send to our local boys and girls involved in the action.

Tragedies – and the Broken Hearts They Left Behind

SIXTEEN CHILDREN DIE IN CINEMA

The youngest was just four years old and the oldest nine. Sixteen children were crushed to death at a Saturday afternoon film show in Barnsley in January, 1908, and it was one of the saddest tragedies our area has known.

It happened on stairs leading up to the gallery of the public hall on Eldon Street, in the same block where the Civic Hall now stands, when a crowd of excited children climbing the stairs was told to go back because the gallery was full.

They came rushing back down and met other children who hadn't heard the instruction and were still coming up. The resulting crush had horrific consequences.

A Star reporter wrote at the time: "There is always a peculiar pathos about a catastrophe involving the loss of child life. In this Barnsley disaster, the pathos is all the more poignant because it was joyousness which was so dramatically turned to death and injury."

Another report in The Star said: "The little ones had looked forward with delight to the afternoon show. They had braved the cold and stood outside the hall for a long time, only to be killed, maimed or bruised in the terrible crush which followed."

BARNSLEY CATASTROPHE.

AWFUL SACRIFICE OF CHILD LIFE.

STAMPEDE TO DEATH.

SIXTEEN CHILDREN TRAMPLED AND SUFFOCATED.

TRAGEDY OF A GALLERY STAIRCASE.

SCENES AND INCIDENTS IN A TERRIBLE CRUSH.

The full story of Saturday's awful calamity at Barnsley makes this terrible sacrifice of child life one of the most poignant tragedies of modern times.

There is always a peculiar pathos about a catastrophe involving the life of child life. In this Barnsley disaster the pathos is all the more poignant because it was joyousness which was so dramatically turned to death and injury.

The sixteen tiny victims, and thirty others who just managed to escape with their lives, were overwhelmed at the foot of the gallery staircase in the Harvey Institute, whither a great number of young folk had repaired for a cinematograph entertainment.

The gallery was soon overcrowded. The children still pouring up the staircase were ordered back. The little ones lower down, owing to the joyous noise of the merry tribe and the construction of the staircase, could not hear the order. The result was a collision, in which the mites at the bottom of the staircase were overwhelmed, fell, and were either trampled to death or suffocated. The scene was heartrending in the extreme. For a time men were almost as helpless as the little children themselves, so overcome were they at the awfulness of the disaster and its appalling swiftness.

But there were many heroic rescues.

1908.

INQUEST OPENED.

SAD SCENES BEFORE THE CORONER.

GRIEF-STRICKEN PARENTS.

PATHETIC STORIES OF IDENTIFICATION.

The inquest on the sixteen little victims of the staircase disaster was opened this morning at the Town Hall before Mr. P. Maitland, district

.PORTRAITS OF BARNSLEY VICTIMS.

TOP ROW: MARY STOTT, HARDY STOTT, BEATRICE CARTWRIGHT AND JOHN CHARLES GRAHAM. SECOND ROW: JOHN CHARLES HIBBERT, WILLIAM P. GOODALL AND HARRY WILLIAMS.

TOP ROW: CHARLOTTE NORTON AND ALICE MARSHALL. CENTRE: ANNIE JOHNSON. BOTTOM ROW: MARY LEE AND WINNIE COUSIN.

HEARTRENDING SCENE.

AGONISED PARENTS' TERRIBLE DISTRESS.

The news of the calamity spread as only bad news can spread. Like a flash of lightning the whole town knew of the disaster. And then another wild rush set in—tortured mothers and other relatives making for the hall for information

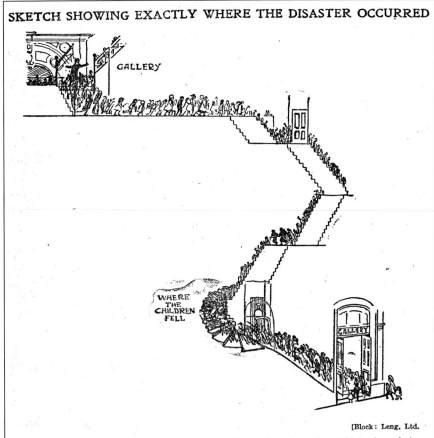

SKETCH SHOWING EXACTLY WHERE THE DISASTER OCCURRED

GALLERY

WHERE THE CHILDREN FELL

GALLERY

[Block: Leng, Ltd.]

The above sketch, drawn by one of our artists, shows where the children lost their lives, and also illustrates the difficulty of controlling a crowd of little people without a helper on each of the landings. A man at the top of the stair is unable to see what is going on below; and a man by the doorway cannot see what is happening beyond the first bend in the stair, where the pay-box is placed. It was just round the corner, above the pay-box, where the children fell.

BARNSLEY VICTIMS.

TWO LITTLE ONES BURIED.

PUBLIC SYMPATHY.

PATHETIC SCENES.

A MAYORAL WREATH.

The funerals of two of the little victims of the staircase tragedy on Saturday afternoon at Barnsley, which took place to-day, were sufficient to show at once the deep-rooted effect of the tragedy upon the minds of the rest of Barnsley's population. There were on all sides evidences of this—young children, youths, and persons of mature years being all deeply affected by the immensity and swiftness of the catastrophe, and this after-rcon, when the first two of the little victims were placed in their last earthly abode, the demonstration of grief which the ceremonies drew forth was as remarkable as it was earnest. Barnsley is still staggering under the blow it has just received.

To-day's funerals were those of Florence May Smith, aged 9, who resided with her adopted father, Henry Watson, at 35, Tower Street; and John Charles Hibbert, aged 6, son of Albert Hibbert, printer's cutter, who lives in the same street only a few doors away.

A SAD SCENE.

Tower Street is one of the incomplete streets which leads from Park Road at the rear of Locke Park. The street itself is only a comparatively short one, but a big work'ng class population lives close by, and when the two sad processions started from the homes, as they did almost simultaneously, a large crowd of mourners and sympathising friends gathered to bid farewell to the little innocents as they commenced the last long journey. Women wept, children sobbed, and in the eyes of many strong men there were seen tears, in the faint rays of the winter sun, which seer'' to hrow over

THE CADEBY COLLIERY DISASTER OF 1912

THE DAY QUEEN MARY CRIED

The tragedy of Cadeby Colliery, Conisborough, which killed 87 men in July, 1912, made a Queen cry with sadness.

Two separate explosions had rocked the pit, bringing deadly gas and roof falls in their trail.

After being told about the disaster, King George V and Queen Mary, who were on an official visit to South Yorkshire at the time, visited Cadeby at the first opportunity.

A colliery official took them into an office and explained how the men had met their deaths and it reduced the Queen to tears.

Despite the tragedy, the King went ahead with a scheduled visit to Elsecar Colliery, Barnsley, and chatted to miners at the pit bottom.

The disaster robbed our area of one of its best-known mining experts, William Pickering, HM Inspector of Mines.

He went into Cadeby pit with rescue parties after the first blasts and was killed in a subsequent explosion.

It was a cruel twist of fate. Mr Pickering had been chosen as the man to escort the King during his visit to Elsecar Colliery two days later and also have lunch with him.

TERRIBLE DISASTER

A Series of Six Explosions.

HEAVY DEATH ROLL.

Rescue Party Reported Overwhelmed.

THE KING'S SYMPATHY.

His Majesty's Message to Bereaved Families.

Gloom has been cast over the South Yorkshire coalfield by a series of terrible explosions which occurred to-day at the Cadeby Pit of the Denaby and Cadeby Colliery Company at Conisborough.

The pit is situated under the shadow of Conisborough Castle, where the King and Queen were so heartily received last night, and right upon the top of the scenes of loyalty and rejoicings comes grim tragedy —men underground hurled to death without a moment's warning, and anxious relatives with grief-stricken faces waiting on the surface, never giving up hope until the last moment that loved ones might be safe.

The death roll from the first two explosions ... would have been ...

DEATH'S TOLL AT C

Eighty-Seven Men Lose Their Lives.

KILLING THE GOB FIRE.

Burning Part of the Pit Now Safely Sealed.

RESCUERS' VIVID STORIES.

The toll of death at Cadeby Main is now fixed at 87. This is three less than at one time feared. Up to this morning seventy-one bodies had been brought to the surface. The others dead still remain in the mine. The work of bringing up the bodies went on all through yesterday. And sadder still was the work of identification.

Hour by hour silent men and women, some in twos, others alone, but all bowed by the crush of grief, walked to the improvised mortuaries to identify the dead. It was a heart-breaking sight. But the scenes inside the buildings where the victims lay were worse. And so the day dragged on—a long day of sadness beyond the power of description.

It is now generally believed that a gob fire was the main cause of the disaster. This is the view expressed by experts. Of course, nothing definite has been established on the point yet. The whole lamentable calamity will be the subject of a full inquiry later on. But at present a gob fire is blamed. So the management yesterday decided to take drastic steps. They determined to seal that portion of the pit where the gob fire is. That is the only way to stop the spread of these insidious conflagrations. Shut off the air supplies and you kill the fire. To seal a pit it is necessary to build a barrier of brickwork, woven so close that no air can pass beyond to fan the faltering flames. This work was begun and completed yesterday at Cadeby. Skilled men laboured speedily, undeterred in the face of danger. Once a puff of gas— small

The Star's artist captures the Royal grief.

King George V and Queen Mary during their industrial tour, pictured at Silverwood Colliery, Rotherham.

ROYAL SYMPATHY.

Telegram from the King and Queen.

The following telegram has been received at Cadeby by Mr. W. H. Chambers, managing director of the Colliery Company, from Lord Stamfordham :—

The King and Queen are shocked to hear of the terrible accident at your colliery, and perhaps that Their Majesties were near to the scene in the midst of so much rejoicing when they visited Conisborough yesterday, brings home to them still more the sorrow and sadness which now prevails amongst you.

I am desired to express Their Majesties' sympathy with the families of those who have perished and with the sufferers in their grievous calamity.

DISASTER STORIES.

Explosion which was Heard Two Miles Away.

Telephoning news of the disaster early this morning, one of our reporters stated that there ~e t~~ explosions, and fire follow~ the ex-

CADEBY COLLIERY. 1912

In the midst of great rejoicing, to welcome both our King and Queen
Came a blow of stinging sharpness, changing all that joyful scene.
Came the news. 'A Mine explosion'! men are missing!'-then the cry
Of the noble rescue party - we are here to do or die!

Came the news, a little later, shocking news and sad to tell-
The rescue party, noble heroes, had perished-how our hearts do swell
When we think of all their dear ones left to sorrow midst the joy.
Sorrow for their Father, Husband, lover or an only boy.

Sympathy throughout the Kingdom flows alike from high and low,
Royal hearts and hearts of Miners bow their heads in deepest woe.

A memorial card produced after the disaster.

Thousands turned out for the funeral of William Pickering, who died a hero.

THE MALTBY COLLIERY DISASTER OF 1923

STAR AND TELEGRAPH SET UP DISASTER FUND

The Star and the Sheffield Telegraph, its sister morning paper at the time, were quick to set up a disaster fund after an explosion killed 27 men at Maltby Colliery in July, 1923.

Miners at the pit had been withdrawn some weeks before because of a gob fire and a team was sent down to fight the fire and seal off the danger zones. So well had the work progressed that the pit was just about ready to re-open for coal getting when the tragic explosion happened.

It was the worst disaster in the South Yorkshire coalfield since Cadeby.

Pictured above are families of the dead men and union officials.

ELEGRAPH AND STAR.

"STAR" FUND.

The Thirty Thousand Shilling Mark Topped.

A FINE RECORD.

The "Star" Shilling Fund for the Maltby widows and children this afternoon topped 30,000 shillings. Thanks! But still more is needed. Now for the 40,000!

BRIDLINGTON BLAZE.

Garage and Dwelling-house Wrecked.

A fire broke out this morning in a garage in Midina Avenue, 50 yards from Lloyd's Hospital. Two motor-lorries, the garage, and an adjoining dwellinghouse are in flames, and likely to be burned out. The hospital was in no danger. The occupants of the house were safely got out.

FEARED LOSS OF 28 LIVES.

'GOB FIRE FIGHTERS CUT OFF: OVER 100 MEN IN THE PIT.

DESPERATE RESCUE WORK.

HEARTRENDING SCENES AT THE PIT-HEAD.

MALTBY MAIN Colliery, situated in the Rotherham area, was devastated, in part, this morning by a terrible explosion which has resulted, it is feared, in the loss of no fewer than 28 lives.

As reported in the "Yorkshire Telegraph and Star" a gob fire has been burning in the mine for some week, and, owing to the difficulties arising, the management, with wise discretion, decided to close down the pit as a working proposition until the threat had been removed.

With the main body of the men away, however, a number of workers, over 100 it is said, have been kept on to deal with the burning portion and these have been gallantly endeavouring to gain control.

Good progress was reported and it was stated that the mine would probably be re-opened next week. It was in these circumstances that the calamity occurred and it is a distressing fact that the terrible loss of life is among the men who have been so arduously engaged in the interests of their comrades.

So far as is at present known:
THE EXPLOSION TOOK PLACE AT 11 o'clock.
TWENTYEIGHT MEN HAVE BEEN CUT OFF AND, IT IS FEARED ARE DEAD.

Rescue parties have gone into the mine and intensive operations are being carried on by the colliery managers and other officials.

Immediately the fact of the explosion was made known there was a rush to the colliery for the purpose of first hand details and scenes of poignant anxiety and distress became accentuated as time advanced.

The first body was brought to the surface at three o'clock. The fact that it was unrecognisable intimated the awful nature of the explosion and added to the fears of the throng of waiting relatives.

Mr. Tom Smith, of Darnall, M.P. for Pontefract, left Sheffield this afternoon, prepared to take part in the rescue work.

The disaster is the worst in South Yorkshire since the Cadeby explosion in 1912—on the very day of the King's visit to the district—and on that occasion the death roll reached a total of 86.

"STAR" APPEAL.

Help for Sufferers in the Maltby Disaster.

SHILLING FUND FOR THE DISTRESSED.

A Splendid Start.

THE Proprietors of the "Yorkshire Telegraph and Star" have always been ready and anxious to assist those who have been left destitute by such a disaster as that which has occurred at Maltby.

They now open the columns of both the "Sheffield Daily Telegraph" and the "Yorkshire Telegraph and Star" for an appeal on behalf of the sufferers by the Maltby explosion, and in calling upon the generosity of readers they do so with the knowledge that they have never asked their readers in vain to support a good cause, and there never was a more deserving one, surely, than this.

The Proprietors of the "Sheffield Telegraph" are contributing 2,000 Shillings, and those of the "Yorkshire Telegraph and Star" a similar sum, a total of 4,000 Shillings, wherewith to start our Subscription List.

Subscriptions may be sent us by post or handed in at our main office in High Street, or they will be received at our Branch Offices, 1 Midland Street,

THE MARKHAM COLLIERY DISASTER OF 1938

Telegraph and Star

No. 16,076   SHEFFIELD, TUESDAY, MAY 10, 1938.   ONE PENNY.

80 FEARED DEAD IN PIT DISASTER

60 Entombed and 40 in Hospital

30 BODIES BROUGHT TO PITHEAD

IT IS FEARED THAT NEARLY MEN...

A GENERAL SCENE AT THE PITHEAD

RELIEF FUND: £250 START

The "Telegraph" and the "Star" and associated Sheffield journals have opened a relief fund for the dependents of the Duckmanton pit disaster with a donation of £250.

WHEN they have recovered somewhat from the feelings of shock and horror aroused by the terrible disaster, the first reaction of people throughout the country will be to turn their thoughts to the survivors — the wives and daughters, sisters and brothers who were in the sobbing crowds at the pit head to-day.

Sympathy with the bereaved will be deep and widespread. But sympathy alone is insufficient.

DEEP SYMPATHY

Undoubtedly sympathisers throughout the kingdom will wish to translate their feelings into cash contributions.

Particularly in the district of which Sheffield is the centre will there be this desire to help.

Chesterfield and the surrounding areas may regard the disaster as a sorrow of special application to the local residents, but the whole of Derbyshire, South Yorkshire, Notts, Lincolnshire and the wide area in which...

The Star and Sheffield Telegraph were again to the fore with a relief fund after the Markham Colliery, Duckmanton, Chesterfield, tragedy in May 1938.

Telegraph and Star

No. 16,077   SHEFFIELD, WEDNESDAY, MAY 11, 1938.   LATE FINAL   ONE PENNY.

THE VILLAGE OF GRIEF

DUCKMANTON, which, in common with a wide area in and around Chesterfield, is stricken with grief as a result of the pit disaster.

Sorrowful Scenes At Pit Identification Parade

ANOTHER MAN DIES

Expert Says End Came Immediately

THE total death roll in the disaster at Markham No. 1a Black Shale Pit of the Staveley Coal and Iron Company, at Duckmanton, was confirmed to-day as being 79, one man having died early to-day.

Among those in hospital are seven in a serious condition. The remainder, who are recovering, were stated to be "fairly comfortable."

Poignant scenes were witnessed at Markham pit to-day when relatives gathered to identify the bodies of victims. Sympathetic onlookers gathered in the vicinity.

Pit Disaster Relief Fund

HAVE YOU SENT A DONATION?

FASCIST REVOLT IN BRAZIL FAILS

The Brazilian Chief of Police broadcast over the radio to-day that the police and army easily overcame the revolt, according to a Rio de Janiero message.

The Star

No. 19,916   TUESDAY, SEPTEMBER 26, 1950   A KEMSLEY NEWSPAPER.   1½d.

80 DEAD IN CRESWELL PIT BLAZE

Area Sealed When Rescue Hope Abandoned

GREY morning scene at the pithead at Creswell today as news of the disaster spreads.

"BEVIN BOYS'" TRAINING PIT

THE pit is four or five miles from Markham Colliery, where 79 men were killed in an explosion in 1938.

The top hard seam at Creswell was reached in 1896 at a depth of 445 yards.

"Bevin boys" were trained at the pit during the war.

There are 1,444 underground and 355 surface employees at the colliery, which produces 623,000 tons of coal a year.

EIGHTY MINERS LOST THEIR LIVES IN A FIRE AT CRESWELL COLLIERY, DERBYSHIRE, TODAY.

By Reporters of 'The Star'

THREE bodies were brought out before rescue bids to reach 77 men trapped behind a wall of flame were abandoned and the affected area of the pit sealed off.

The trapped men, who are 1,000 feet down, three and a half miles from the pit-head, were among a night shift of between 200 and 300.

Many who escaped fought their way through choking fumes from the burning rubber of a conveyor belt, which caused the fire.

Some of the men crawled the last yards to safety on their hands and knees.

Desperate efforts we?...de to stem the ?...bu?... the m?...

NAMES OF ...

THE OFFICIAL STATEMENT

'N?...

September, 1950, and another mining community, at Creswell, Derbyshire, is in deep mourning. The pit was only four miles from Markham Colliery, scene of the 1938 tragedy.

The Star

No. 19,917   WEDNESDAY, SEPTEMBER 27, 1950   A KEMSLEY NEWSPAPER.   1½d.

47 BODIES RECOVERED

Fund Tops the £1,000 Mark

WITH canaries and breathing apparatus, miners who have just come up from Creswell pit after testing air conditions talk with Lord Hyndley, Chairman of the N.C.B., and Sir Philip Noel-Baker, Minister of Fuel and Power.

GENEROUS support was quickly given to the fund launched by "The Star" and the "Sheffield Telegraph" for the dependants of the 80 miners who died in the Creswell Colliery disaster.

The £1,000 mark was topped by mid-day and contributions continued to reach Kemsley House throughout this afternoon. The donations are:—

	£ s. d.		£ s. d.
Directors of The Sheffield Telegraph & Star Ltd.	250 0 0	Mr. L. Brocklehurst, managing director of Brocklehurst Motors, Chesterfield	105 0 0
Neepsend Steel and Tool Corporation Ltd.	200 0 0	Thos. Black Ltd., Sheffield	50 0 0
Morgan Fairest Ltd.	105 0 0	Joseph H. Downing Ltd.	25 0 0
Lt.-Col. Maurice W. Batchelor	52 10 0	I. E. & J. Graham	10 10 0
Leo's Car Mart	25 0 0	Mr. K. E. Crickmore	10 10 0
Mr. J. H. Bramah, Norfolk Road, Sheffield	10 10 0	L. Thorne	5 0 0
Ald. Keeble Hawson, Lord Mayor of Sheffield	10 10 0	W. J. R. Earnshaw	3 3 0
Maytime Ice-Cream Co.	10 10 0	Mr. R. G. Mason, on behalf of members of Sheffield branch of the Society of Cinema Managers	2 2 0
Master Cutler, Mr. W. R. S. Stephenson	10 10 0	Mrs. H. W. Lawton	2 2 0
Mr. & Mrs. F. Hahn	1 1 0	Miss G. H. Sissons	1 0 0
"With Sympathy"	1 0 0	Ebenezer Methodist Youth Club, Shalesmoor	10 0
C.H., Ridgway Drive	10 0		
Mrs. I. M. Brown	2 6		
Hayden-Nilos Ltd., Darnall Road, Sheffield	210 0 0	Total	£1,1?? 0 6

Fuel Chief Orders

The Star

No. 21,531 — SATURDAY, DECEMBER 10, 1955 — A KEMSLEY NEWSPAPER. 2d.

HOSPITAL HAVOC WHEN PLANE HIT WARDS

End of a Dive at 300-m.p.h.

THE graphic picture from Lodge Moor Hospital, Sheffield, today that epitomises the thoughts of everyone: it is miraculous that wide-scale tragedy was averted.

From the appalling destruction of the plane—pilotless it came down at 300 m.p.h. and hit two wards—there is a grim scene behind;

* * More Pictures on Page 4.

Pilot Unaware Woman Had Been Killed

MRS. ELSIE MURDOCH, the mother killed in the crash.

PILOT of the Thunderstreak jet which crashed on Lodge Moor Hospital, Lieut. Roy G. Evans, aged 24, left Burtonwood (Lancs.) air base for his home base at Sculthorpe (Norfolk) to day unaware that a 46-year-old woman had been killed.

Daylight revealed damage even more extensive than at first realised.

Wings of the plane had struck the roof of a ward, ploughed through a connecting corridor, demolishing it, and then tore through another ward carrying away one of the empty beds.

Wreckage littered the grounds. The damaged part of the hospital was a newly-built section.

In a telegram to the hospital today Major-General Roscoe C. Wilson, Commander headquarters, U.S. Third Air Force, said:

Staff Praised

"On behalf of the United States Air Force I extend deepest regret and sympathies in the tragedy of Friday night.

"U.S.A.F. hospital doctors and other medical assistance that can be rendered are available to you if needed."

From Sheffield went the reply: "Many thanks. Position under control."

Chairman of the Hospital Committee, Coun. J. S. Worrall, paid tribute to the staff and

others who went to rescue the injured.

"They did a wonderful job. Many of them were off duty and rushed back to risk their own safety from bullets, flying debris and fire."

Sheffield Fire Brigade tackled the blaze as exploding ammunition burst around them.

In the two wards involved were 28 people. Both wards have been evacuated.

An American Air Force chief explained to "The Star" today what had happened.

Flame-out

Lt. Roy G. Evans, who hails from Polaski, Tennessee, had taken off on a training flight from the Norfolk airfield.

Over Derbyshire he sent an urgent radio message to base: "I have flame—out . . leaving aircraft."

Releasing his cockpit canopy, (TURN TO PAGE 7)

HERE FOR PROBE

COL. E. SALISBURY, an investigator from the U.S. Third Air Force, arrived at Lodge Moor Hospital, this afternoon to probe the jet crash.

A spokesman at the headquarters of the Third United States Air Force said today representatives of the U.S. Air Force authorities would be calling on the relatives of the woman who was killed and the relatives of the injured to advise on the correct procedure for filing claims for compensation.

An inquest on Mrs. Murdock will probably be held on Monday—the day she was due for discharge from the hospital.

A pilotless United States Air Force Thunderstreak jet hit Lodge Moor Hospital at 300mph in December, 1955, killing Mrs Elsie Murdoch, a patient due for discharge two days later. The pilot had bailed out.

The ☆ Star

No. 22,199   THURSDAY, FEBRUARY 6, 1958   A KEMSLEY NEWSPAPER.   2½d.

Team, officials & famous writers in plane disaster—death toll may rise

MANCHESTER UNITED CRASH — 17 KILLED

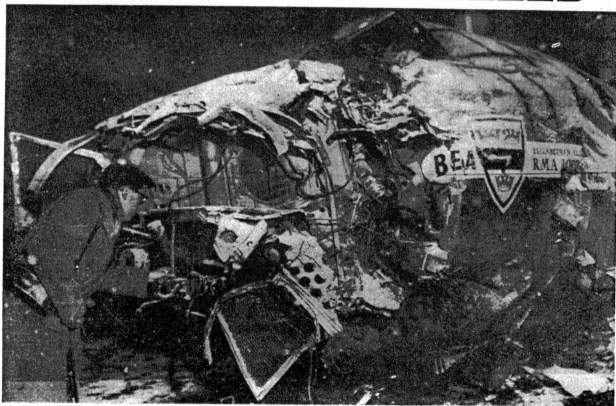

A DRAMATIC PICTURE SHOWING THE BOWS OF THE CRASHED PLANE

Gregg, Charlton and Foulkes among survivors: baby safe

THE STAR-STUDDED MANCHESTER UNITED FOOTBALL TEAM WERE AMONG 44 PEOPLE ABOARD A BRITISH EUROPEAN AIRWAYS ELIZABETHAN AIRLINER WHICH CRASHED SHORTLY AFTER TAKING OFF AT MUNICH AIRPORT THIS AFTERNOON.

It is believed that there were 16 survivors including ex-Doncaster goalkeeper Harry Gregg Bobby Charlton, in-side-right, and Billy Foulkes, right back.

The "soccer special" was bringing the team, club officials, sports journalists and others home after yesterday's drawn game at Belgrade against Yugoslavia's Red Star.

The plane — called Lord Burghley, with 9,000 flying hours behind it—had just taken off when disaster overtook it.

The airliner took off in a snowstorm. It was due in Manchester at 5 p.m.

STRUCK HOUSE

A customs official at the airport said that one of the two engines appeared to catch fire as the airliner made its take-off run.

The airliner struck a house as it crashed from about 60 feet. Rescue teams pulled 12 people from the wreckage.

At the airport, a police officer said the Elizabethan had just taken on petrol in Munich. He said: "It went up in a big blaze when it hit the ground."

Munich police said later that 118 bodies had been counted so far.

The "Hospital by the Isar" in Munich said by telephone that more than 15 men had been taken there.

WOMAN HURT

The Perler Hospital said it had received an Englishwoman and her three or four-year-old daughter, and both were in extremely critical condition. No names were released by the hospitals.

Police said that there might also be some dead in houses hit by the plane when it crashed on a village a few miles from the airport.

News of the crash came as a tremendous shock to Manchester, where the Lord Mayor described it as a "terrible tragedy."

He said Manchester regarded the news as "a disaster to their city."

Aboard the plane when it left England on Monday were:— MATT BUSBY, manager, WALTER CRICKMER, secretary, coach BERT WHALLEY, GREGG and WOOD (goalkeepers). FOULKES, BYRNE and BENT (backs), COLMAN, JONES, BLANCHFLOWER, EDWARDS (half-backs) MORGANS, BERRY, CHARLTON, WHELAN, TAYLOR, VIOLLET, SCANLON and PEGG (forwards).

CAPTAIN HERO

All crew members are believed to have escaped and an eye-witness said: "The captain of the aircraft struggled from the mass of wreckage and worked like a demon to try to get people out.

Two other survivors are Mr.

(TURN TO BACK PAGE)

The Manchester United plane crash of 1958 left the country in a state of shock and disbelief. Tommy Taylor, from Monk Bretton, Barnsley, a former Barnsley player whose great talent had taken him to Old Trafford, was one of several victims with local connections.

In the 1955-56 season, Tommy's 25 goals had helped Manchester United win the Division One championship.

GUEST SPOT

read what the sporting personalities say about their own world of sport in tonight's **Green 'Un**

The Star

No. 23,958   SHEFFIELD, SATURDAY, NOVEMBER 23, 1963   4d.

NIGHT FINAL

No evidence anyone else involved—police

KENNEDY MURDER —MAN IS CHARGED

Duke of Edinburgh will fly to memorial service

A SHARED SORROW

LEE HARVEY OSWALD, 24 - YEAR - OLD Ex-MARINE SHARPSHOOTER, WAS TODAY CHARGED WITH THE MURDER OF PRESIDENT JOHN KENNEDY.

Dallas District Attorney Mr. Henry Wade said: "Oswald appears to be sane. There was no evidence that anyone was behind Oswald or associated with him."

Oswald, during 10 hours of interrogation, denied the assassination. He also denied the murder of a Dallas policeman in the street shortly after the President was killed.

Described by an acquaintance as "a nice young man who did not seem ... have many ... ds." Or ... ... before the kill ... ... Gr ... next at ...

Latest   Ring News Desk Sheffield 22055

60 OLD FOLK DIE IN BLAZE

Sixty people died today when fire razed an old people's home at Norwalk, Ohio. More than 20 escaped after being trapped in the wreckage.

RESULTS

SHEFF WED 5	WOLVES	0
FULHAM .. 3	SHEFF UTD.	1
PRESTON .. 2	ROTH'HAM	2
CHESTERF'D 3	TRANMERE	1
DONCAST'R 3	HALIFAX	1
CREWE ... 1	BARNSLEY	2
BURNLEY .. 2	ASTON V.	0
LEYTON O. 0	LEEDS U. ..	2
CELTIC .. 5	KILM'NOCK	0
MOTH'WLL 3	FALKIRK	0
DUNDEE U. 4	T. LANARK	1
OXFORD U. 3	GILL'GHAM	1
HEARTS ... 1	DUNDEE ...	3
PARTICK T 2	ST JOHNSN	1
LEICESTER . 2	CHELSEA	3
IPSWICH .. 2	TOTT'NH'M	3
ARSENAL .. 5	BLACKPOOL	3
LUTON ... 4	Q.P.R. ...	4
MANSFIELD 1	OLDHAM	1
BRISTOL C. 2	WATFORD	0
W. BROM . 1	BLACKB'RN	3
GRIMSBY .. 2	PO'TSM'TH	3
ROCHDALE 2	LINCOLN C	2
EVERTON .. 2	STOKE C. .	0

N'WC'STLE 3	MAN CITY	1
R'ADING .. 2	W'G'HAM	1
HUDD'RS'D 5	SW'ND'N	0
MIDDL'BRO 2	BURY	0
DERBY C. . 2	CARDIFF	1
WALSALL . 0	BOURNM'TH	2
BOLTON ... 1	WEST HAM	1
BRADFORD 4	DARL'GTON	1
D'BARTON 1	BRECHIN	1
CHARLTON 0	SCUNTH'PE	1
WORK'TON 2	SOUTHP'RT	1
STOCKPORT 1	HARTLEPLS	0
QUEEN O'S. 2	ABERDEEN	3
YORK 1	ALDERSH'T	2
QUEENS P. 0	COWDENB.	1
ST MIRREN 1	HIBERNIAN	1
EAST 'IFE 6	'ERWICK	0

The Kennedy assassination.

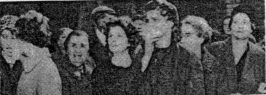

Walsh's

NYLON RUGS
For Hearth or Bedside.
LESS THAN HALF PRICE!
Finely textured, hard wearing.
Choice of plain colours.
54 x 27in. Usually 80/-.
NOW 29/6

The Star

No. 24,860   SHEFFIELD, FRIDAY, OCTOBER 21, 1966   4d.

DEFIANT

23in. TV from 8/11 weekly
19in. TV from 7/11 weekly
Reducing Rentals.
BRIGHTSIDE & CARBROOK
Castle House, Angel Street.

1,000 PITMEN STOP WORK TO AID RESCUE

Anxious mothers wait to hear news of their children.

MANY PERISH IN SCHOOL HORROR

Landslide deaths may reach 150

SEVENTEEN BODIES — 15 of children — were recovered, today, after an avalanche of coal slurry from a tip engulfed a South Wales school and homes.

Police ... 100 children are missing as well ...

Miners dig for survivors.

Latest   Ring News Desk Sheffield 78505
Personal Notices, Want Ads 26393

DEATH CRASH —MAN BAILED

A man accused of causing the death of a 19-year-old student by dangerous driving was allowed bail by city magistrates today.

The case against Barney Doherty, 22, of Princess Road, Edgbaston, charged with causing the death of Margaret Irene May Stimpson, of Fulwood Road, on October 7, was adjourned until November 4.

He was allowed bail in his own recognisance of £50 and a surety of £100 by his parents. He was also ordered to report daily to the police.

Opposing bail, Insp. Peter Grattan said: "He left the scene of the accident and it was only through very active police work that we were able to detain this man in Birmingham."

QUEEN'S MESSAGE

The Queen has sent the following message to the Secretary of State for Wales, Mr. Cledwyn Hughes:

"I am shocked and distressed to learn of the terrible disaster which has taken place at Aberfan.

"Please convey a message of heartfelt sympathy from my husband and myself to the children's parents and to the families of those who have lost their lives."

ACTOR AND WIFE AGREE OVER CHILDREN

Actor Richard Harris consented in the Divorce Court today to his wife, Elizabeth, daughter of Lord Ogmore, having interim custody of their three children.

Mr. Harris is to have reasonable access until he leaves the country again on November 10. The children are aged seven, five and 3. Mrs. Harris, of Bedford Gardens, Kensington, W., has started divorce proceedings.

Freeze: Rebel MPs put own formula

By Gerard H. Corr, our Parliamentary Correspondent

LABOUR'S Left wing, growing increasingly restless over the Government's economic policy, this afternoon put forward their own programme for dealing with the situation. It cam ... Comm ...

CAR MEN BOO GUNTER

MERTHYR DISASTER: 28 BODIES FOUND
Police estimated later that ...

The Aberfan tragedy of October, 1966. A total of 116 children and 28 adults died after tons of slurry from a coal tip slid on to the village school.

Sheffield people were among those killed and injured when a fun centre caught fire on the Isle of Man in August, 1973.

John Lennon gunned down in December, 1980.

When a big local story breaks, off-duty reporters don't wait for an invitation from the News Editor before rushing to the office. That was certainly so at The Star on Sunday, January 4, 1981, when the Yorkshire Ripper was arrested in Sheffield.

It was the end of a five-year police hunt and the fact that the Ripper, Peter Sutcliffe, was caught in Sheffield made it a sensational story.

Tragedy always seems starker when it happens on days of family happiness and Sheffield was stunned by the murder of a Sheffield solicitor and his wife and son after a wedding party at Dore in October, 1983.

Bradford Football Club horror blaze death toll may reach 70

SMOKE BOMBS WERE THROWN BEFORE FIRE

Ricky Eales, young fan helping out

SMOKE bombs were thrown at Bradford City Football Ground before its main stand burst into flames killing 52, people, police said today.

West Yorkshire's Assistant Chief Constable, John Domaille, said that similar bombs had also been used on previous Saturdays at the Valley Parade ground.

But Mr. Domaille would not say whether the smoke bombs had caused Saturday's tragedy. "I will not speculate with regards to the cause of the fire," he said.

He did say, however, that it was known that the blaze started in the stand's G block and police now knew the precise origin of the fire. He would neither confirm nor deny that police had traced any of the people who threw devices on Saturday.

Police had traced about 50 of the 100 people in that section of the stand. At least 2,000 people have so far been questioned.

POLICE SEARCHING DEBRIS

Police searching debris fear the final death toll could be nearer 70 because a number of people reported missing have still not been accounted for.

Mr. Domaille today appealed for anyone at the game who had not yet come forward to do so. He also made a special appeal to Lincoln City supporters at the match to get in touch with their local police.

A ... search of the ... d was ... ing carried out ... ding an auth ...

★ **GLORY DAY ENDED IN TRAGEDY:** P3
★ **PLAYER'S FAMILY ESCAPE INFERNO:** P3
★ **FORERUNNERS OF HORROR:** P3
★ **NEWSMAN FLED SCENE:** P3
★ **SEE VULCAN:** P6
★ **HOW SAFE ARE OUR GROUNDS:** P7

being prepared to deal with an expected 150 out-patients treated at the time of the fire and discharged.

At the ground today, about 30 police officers, wearing protective clothes, helmets and knee pads, were systematically crawling along each row of the wrecked main stand seeking any human remains or items of jewellery or other possessions which might help in identifying victims.

Each spot where a body had been found was being marked and photographed and rows of plastic dustbins were filled with debris and taken away for analysis.

Manager Trevor Cherry, a former Leeds United player, looked grim faced as he went into the administrative offices beside what remains of the 77-year-old timber stand.

Chairman Stafford Heginbotham, who declined to comment on the tragedy, was understood to be making a statement later today.

Fire officers at the ground today would not talk about the row over whether recommendations on safety were passed on to the club.

West Yorkshire's chief fire officer, Graham Karran, claimed yesterday that the club had been warned in a letter that improvements were needed — a claim rejected by Mr. Heginbotham.

United and Owls aid the fund plea

SHEFFIELD soccer clubs have lost no time in aiding the funds for tragedy-hit Bradford.

Both Sheffield United and their supporters' club today launched appeals, with a benefit cabaret and disco already planned for the Executive Suite at Bramall Lane next Monday evening.

Even if fans cannot get to the night, United are asking them to send in the price of the admission — one pound — to the fund.

Money won by Sheffield Wednesday fans in a national good behaviour competition is to be sent to Bradford.

The Owls received a £500 Top of the Kops award, and some of it w... be donated.

Yor...

The Bradford City Football Ground fire in May, 1985. Fifty-five died.

The Star

CITY LATE NIGHT FINAL

Celebrations Continue....
SEE OUR AD. ON PAGE 4
SORWIN HOUSE, MOORFOOT, SHEFFIELD.

No. 30,638 · Sheffield, Thursday, August 22, 1985 · 17p

54 KILLED IN HOLIDAY JET CRASH DISASTER

By Colin Clark, John Murphy and David Kavanagh

Horror for Sheffield families

Engine failure caused blaze tragedy

BRITISH Airways today confirmed that an uncontained failure of the turbine in the port engine caused the fire disaster in the Boeing 737 at Manchester.

The turbine is a large rapidly spinning unit within the jet engine near the combustion chamber where fuel and air are mixed to produce power.

Any part of this unit breaking out of the engine casing could have ruptured fuel lines or tanks causing fuel to leak around the structure and ignite, most ... from the hot ...

FIFTY-FOUR people died today in the blazing wreckage of a Boeing 737 jet on the runway at Manchester Airport.

The plane burst into flames as it roared down the runway at 100 knots preparing for take off to Corfu carrying 131 passengers and six crew.

This afternoon a Sheffield father and son were known to have escaped the crash but seven people from the city are still unaccounted for.

In addition Chesterfield man Roy Metcalfe was another of the 83 people who managed to survive the disaster.

The tragedy came when the British Airtours flight KT 328 was travelling down the runway. Fire broke out in the port engine and, as the pilot abandoned take-off, rapidly spread through the plane.

The aircraft careered off the runway and became a mass of flames and smoke before it broke in two.

Of the nine Sheffield people known to have been on the flight only John Lawrence and his 13-year-old son Chris are this afternoon known to have ...

... mother Rit... Law...

Families from our area were involved in the Manchester Airport plane crash which killed 54 in August, 1985.

The steel tomb of the Herald of Free Enterprise lies semi-submerged in the harbour this afternoon.

SIGNS OF LIFE IN THE STEEL TOMB

THE worst Channel ferry disaster since the war took a dramatic new turn this afternoon.

Divers, who had given up hope of finding more survivors, rushed back to the wreck of the Townsend Thoresen ferry Herald of Free Enterprise, which sank off Zeebrugge in Belgium, when heat-seeking helicopters found warm spots in the hull.

At least 139 people, mostly British, are dead or missing in the tragedy.

Divers searching for passengers who may have found pockets of air in the decks of the giant ferry had already found three survivors who had been trapped for seven hours.

There were tales of heroism, of courage, of miraculous escapes. One man carried a baby to safety in his teeth.

Latest official figures from Townsend Thoresen say 49 bodies have been recovered 90 people are missing and 405 have survived. But some reports say the final toll could be 200.

The tragedy was baffling shipping experts. The ship had not hit anything, they said.

But the bow doors had opened, sending a wall of water cascading through the vehicle deck which turned the vessel over and sank within a minute.

March, 1987, brought 292 deaths in the Herald of Free Enterprise disaster off Zeebrugge, Belgium.

Sixteen children and two adults die as crazed gunman goes on rampage

SLAUGHTER OF CLASS ONE

By Martin Smith, Charles Smith and Rob Hollingworth

SIXTEEN primary school children and one teacher were murdered in cold blood today after a maniac gunman walked into a school and opened fire.

All the children mown down by the hail of gunshot at Dunblane Primary School, Perthshire, Scotland were aged four, five and six.

Another adult - believed to be the gunman - is also dead.

Nine other children and a woman teacher were being treated in Falkirk hospital, 16 miles away.

The primary Year One youngsters were shot in their school gym hall before the man turned the gun on himself.

Some reports suggested the killer was an unmarried youth club leader.

Prime Minister John Major, attending an anti-terrorist conference in Cairo, immediately condemned the killings as mad and evil.

He said: "It's beyond belief that so many young lives could be ended in this brutal way. My heart goes out to teachers, parents of loved ones."

One MP called it "a slaughter of innocents."

At one stage of the drama, a hostage was thought to be involved.

All aircraft except for air ambulances were banned from the skies over the area.

In the aftermath a dozen ambulances and an air ambulance were sent to Dunblane.
■ **Continued on Page 3**

■ MASSACRE OF THE INNOCENTS ■ TEARS FOR MY VILLAGE ■ SPECIAL REPORT SEE PAGES 2 AND 3

Grief at the school gates ... frantic mothers wait to see if any of their children were among the victims of the horror shooting

Innocent children are mown down by a gunman at a primary school in Dunblane in March, 1996.

CITY GIRLS DIE

The huge crater across a busy main road, caused by the stricken bomba

The Lockerbie disaster happened just a few days before Christmas, 1988, bringing heartache to local families. A total of 281 died.

M1 AIR DISASTER

Picture special: Pages 3, 6, 7

The Boeing 737 M1 plane crash near East Midlands Airport in January, 1989, came only three weeks after Lockerbie.

SPECIAL SUNDAY EDITION — HILLSBOROUGH FOOTBALL DISASTER

GATEWAY TO HELL
93 crushed to death, 170 hurt

How? Why? Millions of words have been used to analyse the Hillsborough disaster of April 15, 1989, the worst of its type this country has known. It is still difficult to grasp not only that it happened, with 95 Liverpool supporters dying, but that it happened on our own doorstep.

The Star

City Final

SHEFFIELD Monday, September 1, 1997 ★ 28p   YORKSHIRE'S BEST-READ NEWSPAPER

DIANA, Princess of Wales 1961-1997
- Her dream was to quit the spotlight: P2-3
- A shining light has gone out: P4
- Love and betrayal: P5
- So much love: P6-7
- Sport faces shutdown: Back Page

A people's service for our Princess

11am
Westminster Abbey Saturday, September 6

'Unique funeral for a unique person'

THE funeral of Diana, Princess of Wales will take place on Saturday at Westminster Abbey.

It will be a "unique funeral for a unique person" Buckingham Palace announced today.

She will then be buried at the Spencer family home at Northants.

Her coffin was moved today to the Chapel Royal at St James's Palace where mourners are being invited to sign a book of condolence.

A similar book-signing was going on at Sheffield town hall today as South Yorkshire joined every other county in paying its own tribute. There will be no lying in state, Buckingham Palace said.

At the request of the Royal Family and the Spencers the coffin will lie privately in front of the altar of the Chapel Royal until the funeral which will start at 11am.

The coffin will be carried in procession from the Chapel Royal to Westminster Abbey on the morning of the funeral.

At the Abbey, a catafalque – a temporary tomb-like structure – will be constructed under the lantern, and on this the coffin will be placed for the service.

Following the service in the Abbey, the coffin will travel by road to the Spencer family home at Althorp for private burial.

The Palace spokesman said: "We are taking into account the wishes of the family and the need to allow people to express publicly their grief and their affection for the Princess.

"The funeral will contain the usual elements of a royal funeral and in particular elements to reflect the affection with which the Princess was held."

It was expected that members of both families would visit the Chapel Royal to see the light wood coffin. Invitations would go out to about 2,000 people for the Abbey service, which will be televised.

It the first time a condolence book has been opened at a royal palace in recent times. The book will remain open round the clock until midnight on Friday.

Family mourning will be observed by members of the Royal Family and by their households up to and including the day of the funeral.

Those in uniform will wear mourning bands. Those in civilian clothing will wear black ties and dark colours.

Flags will be flown at half-mast up to and including the day of the funeral.

Diana, Princess of Wales, had visited our area so many times that her loss somehow seemed personal to all of us.

Advertisements Over The Years

We can re-cover your umbrella in 17 and three quarter minutes!

That was the proud and very precise boast of one company advertising in the very first edition of The Star on June 7, 1887.

Why not 17 minutes, we wonder? Or 18? Or a nice round figure like 20? Did fractions of a minute really make any difference to business in those days?

There were certainly plenty of businesses wanting to advertise on that first day but it looks as though you had to be strong to land a job…

"Wanted, a strong, active girl, as general servant, about 18…";

"Wanted, a strong young woman for the kitchen…"

"Wanted at once, a strong lad, to the Blacksmith Business…"

Or, if not strong, pushy.

"Wanted, a reliable and energetic salesman (married man preferred) of good address and pushing business habits…"

As well as being the financial lifeblood of newspapers, advertisements have always fascinated readers and this selection from The Star over the last 100 years or so is intended to show how lifestyles, tastes and, yes, prices have changed since 1887.

H.LAWSON, of Carver Street, Sheffield, claims in 1889 he was the only dentist in the city with a prize medal and, what's more, you could see it if you took your business there. AND you got a shot of cocaine before your teeth were pulled…

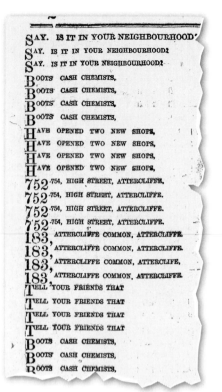

This is a small section of an 1897 Boots advertisement, which took up a whole column.

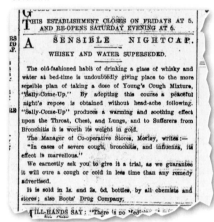

1897 and whisky and water at bedtime is OUT of fashion. "Sally-Come-Up" is IN.

WORN-OUT WOMEN

What greater strain could there be upon women's nerves than the never-ending cares of a household? None, unless it might be the exactions of Society. Four meals a day, seven days a week, and all different. Soft words and sweet smiles when husband is cross and children crying; wise talk on weighty subjects and witticisms on airy nothings. These things, and much more, are expected of women. It is strange that they are not always equal to the world's expectations.

OVERWORKED WOMEN

may find strength and vigour in

NERVO-VITA OR NERVE LIFE.

It is not a stimulant affording only temporary relief and followed by a corresponding depression, but a permanent renewer of life and vigour. Exhaustion, despondency, irritability, nervous headaches, and indigestion, and all ailments arising from nervous derangements and impure and weak blood are quickly relieved by this standard remedy. Sold in Bottles at 1s. 1½d., three and six times the quantity, 2s. 9d. and 4s. 6d., by most Chemists and Patent Medicine Dealers. Take no substitute.

No wonder 1899 women were tired and worn out if this was a typical day!

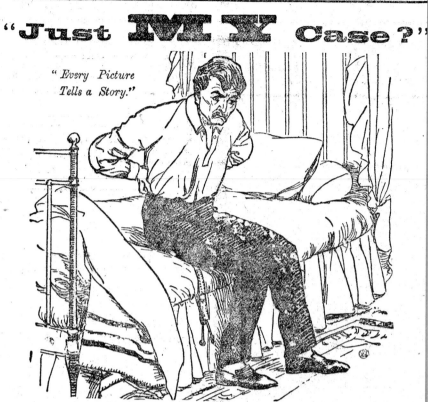

AND STAR, MONDAY EVENING, JULY 20, 19

"**Just MY Case?**"

"*Every Picture Tells a Story.*"

Tired in the Morning—Sleepless at night—Weak, Wasting, Wretched—Do you know the Reason?

Send 1d. Stamp for a FREE SAMPLE (See address below.)

Weak kidneys are to blame.

When they are ill, the back aches, there are urinary troubles, general weakness, rheumatism, gravel, stone, dropsy, etc.

The kidneys are not filtering all the uric acid and other poisons out of the blood, and you cannot be well until they do.

Doan's Backache Kidney Pills tone up the kidneys, drive out the uric acid poisons, cleanse the kidneys and bladder, stop inflammation and purify the blood.

They are safe for old and young, and their merits are proven by a neighbour's statement given here.

But you *must* get

A SHEFFIELD Example.

A year and eight months after telling of the benefit she had derived from Doan's Backache Kidney Pills, Mrs. S. E. Whiteley, Garrison Arms, 456, Penistone Road, Sheffield, said: "I have been in much better health since I first commenced using your pills."

Here is what Mrs. Whiteley said when describing her case: "I was ailing for about two years and a half. The trouble started with a shock I received ten years ago: there was a gale on, and one of our outhouses fell. We were up in the rain all night, I remember, and this brought on influenza. As the influenza left me my kidneys became in a bad state, which in time developed into serious kidney disease and dropsy. The doctor got me over this bad turn and cured the dropsy.

"For a long time, however, my kidneys were in a bad state, backache troubling me, and the urinary secretions were unnatural. I was sometimes unable to stoop; it was a nasty grating pain, and when I attempted to raise myself it caught me like a stab from a dagger.

"But Doan's Backache Kidney Pills cured me of this, and I've been free from it ever since. I have used the Pills twice since then—once, some months ago, when I thought my back was inclined to ache."

After 20 Months.

THE GENUINE

Of all chemists and stores, 2/9 per box; 6 boxes, 13/9; or post free, direct from Foster-McClellan Co., 8, Wells Street, Oxford Street, London, W.

What weak kidneys did to you in 1908.

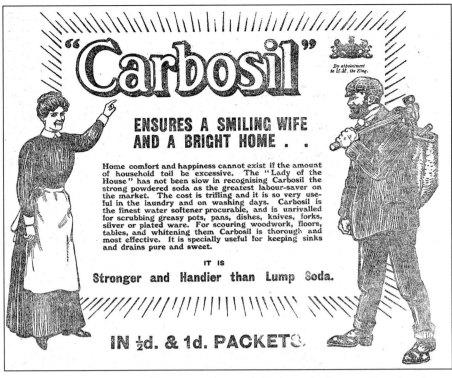

The husband being welcomed home to a clean and tidy house looks more like a burglar…

Who would have believed it? Shakespeare is used in 1912 to sell rubber heels!

Still going strong – Atkinsons of The Moor in 1908.

A First World War ad advertising hats to wear when the boys come home. Sadly, many of them never did.

How do you feel on Mondays?

THE "Monday morning" feeling is familiar to many of us. You feel little inclination to get up; your appetite for breakfast is not very keen; at the office, work seems to hold small interest for you. Yes, you recognise all the symptoms, don't you? Of course, there's nothing wrong with you, but still this Monday morning sluggishness is unpleasant.

Why let it continue?

Why not get up EVERY morning—Mondays as well—feeling refreshed by sleep, keen to be up and doing, in the full swing of health?

You can if you want to.

Monday mornings are no different from any other morning to the army of "Kruschen optimists."

"Every morning Kruschen Salts make a million optimists." You know the familiar phrase.

This feeling of alert, nimble health is very largely dependent on the efficient working of the body's eliminating system.

To feel really well, the liver and kidneys must be kept active, so that, in Nature's way, all impurities are cleansed from the system. Every man and every woman who cannot get REGULAR physical exercise needs Kruschen Salts.

Kruschen Salts are Nature's method of keeping the system clear of impurities. Under their tonic influence the liver and kidneys eliminate ALL waste matter. The whole body is braced and revived.

Get a 1/9 bottle at any chemist to-day. It will last over three months.

A farthing a day in 1922 would have stopped you looking and feeling like this.

What did you think when you . . .

Didn't you, when *you* were a kiddie, sometimes wonder, with puckered brow, why so many nice-to-do things were not "good" for you"?

So many things began with "Don't" or "You mustn't" . . . and, hateful thought, medicine time always began with "You *must*"—and ended with "It's good for you."

Remembering all this, you couldn't really be surprised if you found your Kiddies, in those strangely quiet moods, were pondering something like this :—

"Just wait until *I* grow up—I'll do all the things I mustn't do now. . . . And I won't *never*, *never* drink horrid medicine—an' things."

. . . there will be very little need for medicine if you show your Kiddies the Andrews way *now*.

A now-and-then morning glass of Andrews bubbles so fascinatingly for them, and tastes so pleasant that Kiddies love it.

. . . and it corrects the little ills ere they grow to "medicine-size."

Just try it! Hear the delighted shrieks when you say "Come on, you little rogue, it's bubbling Andrews' time!"

And see how clear-eyed, fit and happy Andrews will keep them. You too !

Andrews Liver Salt

is the Family Friend—time-tried and trusted. It cools, purifies and sweetens the blood and helps Man, Woman and Child to become—*and keep*—fit.

Try Andrews in your household—keep a tin on a handy shelf, always. The 4 oz. size costs 9d.; the 8 oz. 1/4 . . . both sizes are sold everywhere.

Clear-eyed, fit and happy with Andrews' Liver Salt in 1923.

The Charm of a Graceful Figure

Cole Brothers

Introduce the New

BELBON   SPÉCIALITÉ CORSETS   BELBON
100 Styles—5/11 to 70/-   AND BRASSIERES   100 Styles—5/11 to 70/-

AS corset specialists of many years' standing, we can present "Belbon" Spécialité Corsets with every confidence, being satisfied they embody all the qualities which a perfect corset should possess. Every model is designed on a perfect living figure and whether large or small, girlish or matronly, there is a suitable "Belbon" Corset.

BELBON
CORSETS AND BRASSIERES
Afford Distinctive Style for Women of Fashion.

"Belbon" Corsets are absolutely a new vogue in corsetry, and one which ensures grace, comfort and beauty of figure to every wearer. There are 100 styles —each one designed on a perfect living model.

Model B. Price 21/9
Low scalloped top, long hips. Strong Coutil, in White, Pink, and Dove. Elastic insets at front. Three pairs suspenders. Sizes 23 to 36.

Special Exhibition & Demonstration for one week— Commencing To-day, April 16th.

Model L.G. Price 42/-
A splendid model for well developed figures. Beautiful Pink Silk Brocade. Elastic insets at top, also at sides and bottom of back. Six silk suspenders. Sizes 25 to 36.

"Belbon" Front-Lace Corsets are made in a large range of fittings to suit every individual type of figure. There are models for every occasion, and whether large or small, girlish or matronly, there is a "BELBON" Corset to fit you "exactly." The convenience and support of the front lacing and the fascinating effect of the closed back will appeal to every lady.

Our New Corset Salon
has been much enlarged and we have placed this department under the direction of an **Expert Corsetiere** who will at any time be pleased to advise ladies on all matters of corsetry.

Write for Dainty Brochure of New Spring Styles. Sent post free.

Cole Brothers, Ltd., Fargate, Sheffield.

A 1923 Cole Brothers advertisement for corsets and brassieres (before bras were invented!)

That Kruschen Feeling

They didn't bargain for Grandpa !

"Great strength rings the bell, and you get your money back." But now they're wishing they hadn't egged the old boy on.

He always gets his full money's worth in life, because he's always in the high spirits that are the reward of overflowing health.

What keeps him so fit and jolly ? It's no secret. Each day he tips into his breakfast cup of tea just as much of the magic crystals as will lie on a sixpence—the little tasteless dose of Kruschen that means so much.

He knows that good health depends mainly on the clearness and virility of the blood stream. He knows that his

system needs something to counteract the ill-effects of insufficient fresh air and exercise, of worry, overwork, errors of diet, and so forth—something that will stimulate the liver and kidneys to a proper performance of their duty, clear all impurities from the body, and send new, refreshed blood coursing through the veins.

He knows, too, that that "something" is Kruschen Salts.

"That Kruschen feeling" makes true sportsmen of us all whether at work or at play. There are 96 morning "pinches" in a 1/9 bottle, a three months' supply. Get a bottle at once and your pleasures gladly when you take that daily dose.

Grandpa, all his muscles steeling, Knocks them with that "Kruschen feeling!"

If this is what Kruschen Salts did for you in 1923, why don't they bring them back?

They weren't called garages in 1923 – just motor-car houses.

Here comes electricity in 1926!

Swamp root did the trick.

Happy, robust womanhood in 1927? Not unless you take some of Dr Williams' pink pills.

These two clever Bass advertisements from 1929 were ahead of their time.

Just what the doctor ordered in 1930. Change to another brand of cigarettes!

HP sauce, 1936 style.

Handwritten note in the illustration:

... with Pamela for the weekend. Of course she's absolutely ga-ga about her engagement. Can't blame the girl either Don always had a way with him. He never turns up without a box of marvellous chocolates— same kind every time. They're called Black Magic. I tried them, of course— a never-to-be-forgotten experience, chérie I'm going to bully Paul into buying ...

This is melt-in-the-mouth Orange Cream, whose juicy tang comes from the fresh fruit and a secret blend of orange flavours.

Let us explain—

Black Magic are the wonderful chocolates which Society is preferring to the most expensive kinds. They are more popular than even 5/- a pound chocolates! And there's a good reason why. They contain the twelve delicious " centres " that were proved by test to be the most popular. How can Rowntrees sell these really superb chocolates for only 2/10 the pound? The answer is — by packing them in simple black boxes without any extravagant decorations or tinfoil.

Black Magic in 1936.

"Er ... well ... it's like this. Cars just don't grow on gooseberry bushes. With Fords, for example, it's mainly a question of *instinct* — or you might say a marriage of expert design and advanced production techniques. And when you've got it ..."

"*Got what, Mr. Harrison?*"

"The finest family of cars and commercials on the road, of course. As I was saying, when you've got it, it's got to be properly looked after. In Sheffield, Rotherham, Derby and district, that's where I come in."

"*What do you do, Mr. Harrison?*"

"That's easy. You could call me a sort of family doctor — I deliver the Fords around here and keep them all fit. When you get down to it, there are only two facts to remember — Fords for cars, Harrisons for Fords."

"*Is that all, Mr. Harrison? Sounds like ordinary common sense to me.*"

T. C. HARRISON LTD

A 1963 car advertisement.

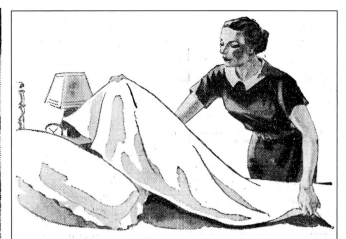

I was disgusted when I discovered mice in the linen cupboard . . . but I had experience with mice before, and knew just what to do. I put LIVERPOOL VIRUS down. It's wonderful stuff. In a short time all traces of mice had gone. LIVERPOOL VIRUS is the most hygienic method of extermination . . driving mice and rats into the open to die. And it is so safe to use because it cannot affect human beings or any domestic pets.

RAT - WEEK *NOV. 2—7.* BE SAFE—Use Liverpool Virus. Guaranteed non-poisonous to all except rats and mice.

LIVERPOOL VIRUS

The Safe Mouse and Rat Destroyer.

In tins from Chemists. For Mice 1/6 and 2/6. For Rats 2/6.

GUARANTEE : Liverpool Virus is guaranteed absolutely harmless to dogs, cats, birds, and all domestic animals.

EVANS SONS, LESCHER & WEBB LTD., Hanover Street, Liverpool.

November 2-7, 1936, was RAT WEEK...

 Launderette

A BENDIX LAUNDERETTE is now available to PARKGATE & RAWMARSH housewives at

BROAD STREET

(Opposite WOOLWORTHS)

WHAT IT IS:

The Bendix Launderette is a completely new form of laundry service designed to free you from washday worries and help solve your laundry problems.
At the launderette your weekly wash can be done in about half an hour using the famous Bendix automatic washing machine—and your hands never even touch water.

WHAT IT DOES:

The Bendix does all the work of washing by safe, thorough tumbling action; it rinses four times in fresh clean water and then damp dries by gentle spinning. As many machines as you need to do all your laundry work are available for your use while you shop, wait or visit. Your washing is done INDIVIDUALLY—no mixing. No articles are lost or mislaid since all are under your own control. Soap is supplied and only soft water used.

YOUR FAMILY WASH DONE AUTOMATICALLY while you wait or shop in 30 minutes.

2/6 per BENDIX load (up to 9 lb.)

OTHER BRANCHES :

SHEFFIELD 24, Ellesmere Road; 150, Crookes; 46, Firth Park Road; 202, Howard Road; 394, Langsett Road; 262, Staniforth Road; London Road, Heeley Bottom.

ROTHERHAM 85, Masbro' Street.

OPENING HOURS: MONDAY, TUESDAY and FRIDAY 9 a.m. - 8 p.m. WEDNESDAY & THURSDAY 9 a.m. - 6 p.m. SATURDAY 9 a.m.-5 p.m.

The launderette makes its debut in 1958.

Tommy makes the cricket first eleven in 1957…

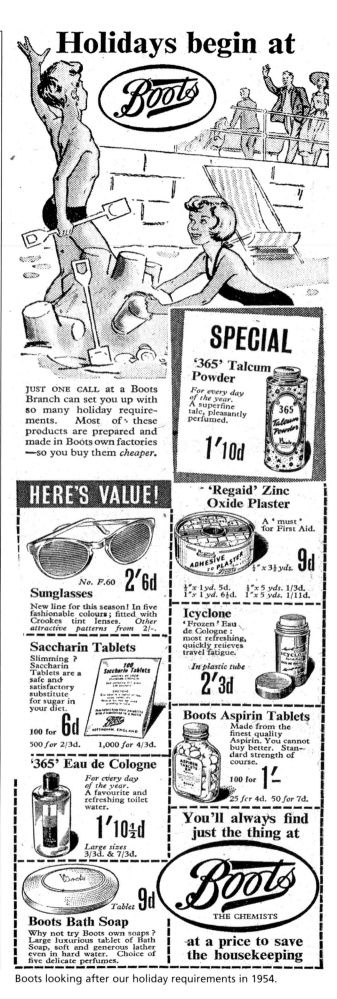
Boots looking after our holiday requirements in 1954.

HOLIDAYS for WIVES
No more washday slavery!

The 'ENGLISH ELECTRIC' Washing Machine takes backache and drudgery out of your washdays. Auto-washing, auto-wringing, auto-filling and emptying! **And** it pays for itself in laundry bills.

No more hot steamy kitchens! No more lifting heavy pails! No more washday raw hands! No more black worn-out Mondays! **'ENGLISH ELECTRIC' solves your whole laundry problem—the extra-easy way!**

14/2 a week

turns washdays into holidays—that's the weekly cost of the best household help there is—an 'ENGLISH ELECTRIC' Washing Machine.

£7.0.0. first payment and **24** monthly payments of **£3.1.3.** or **£69.10.0.** cash including P.T. Special Immersion Heater model **£8.4.2.** first payment or **£82.14.2.** including P.T.

See the 'ENGLISH ELECTRIC' Washing Machine at your local 'ENGLISH ELECTRIC' Dealer or Electricity Service Centre.

'ENGLISH ELECTRIC'
THE 'BIG CAPACITY' WASHING MACHINE

BRINGING YOU **BETTER LIVING**

THE ENGLISH ELECTRIC Co. Ltd., Domestic Appliance and Television Division, East Lancashire Road, Liverpool, 10

One of the early automatic washing machines, July, 1954.

He'd love a Gillette 'Rocket' Set for Christmas . . .

A really sparkling, exciting present and it only costs 6/6. This ' Rocket ' Set will bring him right up-to-date and give him all the benefits of Gillette Superspeed Shaving. An attractive blue case with transparent lid helps to make this razor set a very special gift.

8/6 value for 6/6

A 1955 shaving advertisement.

This Sporting Life – Our Area's a Real Winner!

CUP COMES TO SHEFFIELD FOR FIRST TIME

The day Sheffield Wednesday brought the FA Cup back to Sheffield for the first time, it was absolute bedlam...

So many people turned out during the early evening of April 21, 1896 – more than 100,000 according to The Star – that the players' tour of the city had to be abandoned halfway round.

Thousands of singing, swaying fans waited on The Moor for the arrival of the Cup victors – 2-1 winners over Wolverhampton Wanderers –but they never arrived.

The four-in-hand which had pulled the players from the Midland Station, stopping every two minutes because crowds were blocking the way, just couldn't get through the dense mass on The Moor so the team slipped into a city centre hotel for a meal.

When they reappeared later for a celebratory night out at the Empire Theatre, the crowds were still there in their thousands.

And inside the theatre, as the players filed into the stalls, "the vast audience rose and cheered with a will, drowning the strains of 'See the conquering hero comes'."

Not so happy the next morning were the reporters on our sister paper, the Sheffield Telegraph. They criticised the lack of organisation which had led to thousands of fans not having a decent view of the team and lambasted the Wednesday committee which they said was "not yet thoroughly imbued with a sense of what the public expect of them."

There had been "no method to the organisation, no local knowledge of what was to be done and the police were just as much in the dark as everybody else."

The report continued: "When Wednesday have won the trophy a few times more, perhaps we shall have a settled programme to work to and enthusiastic supporters of the club will have a better knowledge of where to go to see their favourites."

It was to be another 11 years before Wednesday were to win the trophy again, although the police had another Cup homecoming to handle when United won it three years later.

The first signs that Wednesday's Cup win would result in one of the city's biggest-ever crowds came well before the train carrying the players pulled into the Midland. Fans were surging round the station an hour before it was due and, when told they wouldn't be allowed access to the platforms, the clever ones bought tickets to Heeley, instantly becoming bona fide passengers and heading for the platform where the team was due to arrive.

This platform was "swamped to an uncomfortable degree" and when Inspector Bestwick's band, which was providing a musical welcome, tried to line up, the musicians couldn't square their elbows to hold their instruments and get in any kind of order around their conductor.

When the train pulled in, there was a surge to the carriage and each player was "forced to drag himself by sheer strength through the crowd." Outside the station, the scene was like nothing Sheffield had seen before.

"As far as the eye could see was a mighty throng, a serried mass of faces right away the length of the station approach, all along Station Road, on the roofs of the wooden sheds in their hundreds, up the iron supports of the covered space in front of the station and wherever standing room could be found."

And if you thought female fans were a newish introduction to the football scene, just listen to this...

"Favours were seen on every hand; women who had struggled down wore ribbons in extravagant profusion and blue and white-washed hats, umbrellas of the same fearful pattern and in fact ribbons and decorations of every character."

The four-in-hand eventually managed to leave the station "amid ringing cheers and in an almost indescribable uproar of hand-clapping and hurrahs."

The fervour was understandable. Wednesday hadn't won the Cup before and this was the ninth successive season they had reached the last eight, their fifth time in the semi-final and their second appearance in the final.

Hero of the day was 5ft 6ins outside left Fred Spiksley. The game, at Crystal Palace, was only 30 seconds old when he latched on to a pass from Archie Brash and beat Tenant, the Wanderers goalkeeper, in "splendid style".

The Wanderers equalised soon after but Fred popped up again before half-time to notch the match winner.

What follows next in the match report is a very clear indication of how verbal exchanges between players on the same side have changed over the years.

As the minutes ticked away, the Wolves defenders were heard to be encouraging their forwards with such phrases as "go on" and "look sharp".

Oh, really?

We've won the Cup! There were no newspaper photographs in those days but this 1896 drawing in the Telegraph, The Star's sister paper, captures the atmosphere of Wednesday's big day.

The Cup comes home "amid a scene of enthusiasm never excelled since there was such a trophy."

Wednesday's 1896 heroes.

NOW LET'S HEAR IT FOR UNITED!

Three years later, in 1899, another train was pulling into Sheffield with a Cup-winning team.

Both the locomotive and carriages were bedecked with red and white and, as the train clunked into Sheffield's then other station, Victoria, there was a "ringing cheer again and again repeated."

Great crowds thronged from the route from the station to Bramall Lane via Furnival Road, Sheaf Street, Commercial Street, High Street, Fargate, Pinstone Street, The Moor and Hereford Street.

As in 1896, fans were everywhere and the warmth of the reception matched that given to Wednesday three years earlier.

The players had dinner at the Bramall Lane pavilion and, as Wednesday had done three years earlier, spent the night at the Empire Theatre.

The day was noted for its excellent organisation. Said a local report: "Proof of the complete way in which the heavy duties which lay upon the police were carried out is to be found in the fact that, although the horses in the drags were never out of a walk, the whole extent from the Victoria Station to Bramall Lane was covered in just over half an hour.

"It was a triumph for those concerned in the arrangements, just as it was a magnificent reception on the part of the public to one of the most plucky and popular teams which has ever had its name inscribed upon the highly-valued English Cup."

One of the oddest stories to come out of the match surrounded United's right-back Thickett, Injured in a previous game.

One report said he had played in the final against Derby County "swathed in more than 50 yards of starched bandages interspersed with pads."

United were 1-0 down at half-time but, to deaden the pain, Thickett was allowed to sup a bottle of the champagne being kept on ice for the victory celebrations.

And guess what? It worked. Pain-free Thickett had a second-half stormer and United ran out 4-1 winners.

His half-time wonder cure made the headlines in at least one national newspaper the day after the match.

It was a great story. Only trouble was, it wasn't true!

When interviewed by a national newspaper reporter after the game, the doctor treating Thickett just couldn't contain his sense of humour and let his imagination run riot.

It was a wind-up of classic proportions. There had been no half-time champagne and probably no more than two feet of bandages. The good doctor said later he couldn't understand why the reporter had taken him seriously...

But there was Beer. Billy Beer...

His goal, together with those of Walter Bennett, Jack Almond and Fred Priest, ensured that the Cup came to Sheffield for the second time.

The match was the perfect stage for two of the greatest players of the time, United's Ernest "Nudger" Needham and Derby County's Steve Bloomer, to show their skills.

United managed to snuff out Bloomer which was no mean achievement. Earlier in the season, he had scored six in Derby's 9-0 defeat of Sheffield Wednesday, who, incidentally, were relegated to the Second Division on the very day United won the Cup.

1899... and this time it's United's turn to lift the Cup.

Fans are told the route their beloved Blades will take during the tour of the city.

Ernest "Nudger" Needham, United's captain. The final was the ideal showcase for his talents.

The triumphant United team. Back row, left to right: Hedley, Beers, Thickett, Foulke, Almond, Boyle. Front row, left to right: Bennett, John son, Needham, Morren, Priest.

SHEFFIELD'S CUP RUNNETH OVER

It's a good pub quiz question and one that many non-Sheffield football fans might just struggle to answer.

How many FA Cup Finals has Sheffield hosted? Just one, albeit a replay, in 1912, and, amazingly, the winners came from just 15 miles down the road.

It was the first and only time Barnsley have tasted FA Cup glory. They took West Brom to a replay after a 0-0 draw at Crystal Palace and won 1-0 at Bramall Lane.

There were some who said that the final should not go ahead because of the Titanic disaster ten days earlier.

But The Star argued against any postponement.

Our leader writer wrote forcibly: "It is a far cry from the tragedy of the Titanic to an event of the proportions of a football match, however big, but, after all, the everyday work

How The Star's cartoonist saw Barnsley's great day.

and even pleasure of the world must go on, and the cloud of tragedy must pass.

"It is necessary at such times to emphasise this, and, from that

point of view, we are glad that there has been no movement in the direction of postponing the Cup Final.

"We are not callous because we resume as early as possible the normal order of things. No one can accuse the people of Sheffield of having failed to respond to the call of the disaster upon their finer emotions."

The Star was jubilant that the final replay had come to Sheffield and reminded readers that Bramall Lane had now hosted an England v Australia cricket Test Match, international football matches involving Wales, Ireland and Scottish teams, FA Cup semi-finals and now an FA Cup Final.

Barnsley's fans were pleased, too, because a recent miners' strike meant money was short and few of them had been able to make the long journey to Crystal Palace.

On the day of the match, Barnsley "emptied itself in Sheffield."

There were a dozen special trains from Barnsley, as well as the ordinary services, and other fans went by road in a variety of vehicles, charabancs and waggonettes and on bikes.

Many colliers walked there and when asked by a Star reporter why they had gone on foot, one replied: "Thought we'd save a bob but it's cost us more'n that t'clear dust out of our throats."

Meaning, presumably, that they'd had a few pints on the way...

The game kicked off at 3.30pm and The Star historically captured Barnsley's extra-time winner in the Stop Press column of its late edition on April 24, 1912... "Tufnell got possession near the centre line and went clean through on his own. Pearson came out a few yards in order to narrow the angle but, taking steady aim, Tufnell put the ball past him. There was tremendous cheering and excitement."

There was a great reception for the Barnsley lads on the way home. As they passed through Birdwell and Hoyland Common in their charabanc, crowds lined both sides of the streets and in Barnsley itself Sheffield Road, from May Day Green to the borough boundary, was "black with a mass of people, headed by the band of the local Territorials, the crowd probably numbering about 30,000."

Outside the Clarence Hotel, the club's headquarters, wild scenes of enthusiasm greeted the players as they appeared on the balcony. Said The Star's report: "Although the crowd called loudly for Tufnell, it was only after much pressure that the hero of the game could be induced to disport himself.

"He was lifted shoulder-high by his colleagues and his admirers cheered wildly."

FOOTBALL GOSSIP.

Sheffield Gets its First Cup Final.

BRAMALL LANE'S RECORD.

Exciting Wind-up to the League Campaigns.

(By J. H. S.)

So Sheffield is to have a final tie after all. It doesn't matter very much whether it is a re-play

Sheffield's first and only Cup Final is announced in The Star.

SHIRE TELEGRAPH AND STAR, WEDNESDAY

MET ALBION

CUP FINAL PICTURES.

[Photo and Block: Lang, Ltd.

The upper picture shows a portion of the crowd at the Shoreham Street end at Bramall Lane to-day. The lower shows (on the left) a West Bromwich mascot, and (on the right) a Barnsley mascot being escorted off the playing area.

The quality leaves a lot to be desired but these pictures taken at the replay would have been regarded as quite special in newspaper production terms.

THE CUP-TIE.

Downs was responsible for another batch of very clever clearances, and so enthusiastic was he that he was seen over the half-way line. The Albion goal had a miraculous escape from Bartrop. Pearson was out of the way and beaten to the world, but Cook got his head to the ball, and saved.

From the corner which followed there was a similar incident, though in this case Pearson was ready the shot going just wide.

A free kick to the Albion taken by Pennington was mis-kicked by Bratley for a corner. This was cleared.

The referee awarded another corner against Downs, but the latter appealed, and on Mr. Schumcaher consulting the linesmen he reversed his decision.

Though Glendenning had made several attempts to get a fresh boot, he had been unable to do so, and his handicap in kicking with a broken-toed shoe was distinctly seen during an attack by the Albion.

Tufnell got possession near the centre-line and went clean through on his own. Pearson came out a few yards in order to narrow the angle, but taking steady aim Tufnell put the ball past him. There was tremendous cheering and excitement.

The Cup was presented to the winners immediately after the match by Mr. J. C. Clegg.

The stop-press item that made history...Tufnell scores the winner for Barnsley.

Barnsley's Cup winning team of 1912.

NOTTS COUNTY V. WOLVERHAMPTON WANDERERS.

REFEREE MOBBED.

This match was played on Trent Bridge Ground, at Nottingham, this afternoon, in severe weather. The visitors arrived very late, and the kick off was not made until 2.55. Notts early pressed their opponents, and forced four corners, without, however, bringing any definite result. Occasionally the visitors' forwards broke through, but at half-time neither side had succeeded in scoring.

After both sides had missed a goal Booth dashed along the left, and centring accurately, Wykes headed

Referees were having trouble with supporters as long ago as 1889.

THIS DAY'S FOOTBALL.

WEDNESDAY v. DERBY COUNTY.

These teams being left in for the English Cup, heralded a large attendance this afternoon at Olive Grove road, and it was estimated that 2,000 people were present. The weather was very fine, and although the ground was rather soft, it was better than expectation at this time of the year. Derby County were not well represented, but Wednesday were fairly so. The visitors won the toss, and Waller set the ball in motion in the direction of Sheffield. At the onset Wednesday had a corner, but Hudson's attempt was unavailing, and the game at once becoming interesting, both defenders having to utilise their capabilities. A most determined struggle in the Derby goal was marvellously saved. Excitement ruled the day and after Smith easily returned the ball, another melee occurred in Derby goal mouth, which all the home forwards had a hand in, and Ingram registered the first goal for Wednesday. The game had scarcely recommenced when Mosforth got away and waited while his compatriots got up and the result was another goal by Cawley. The play tamed down after this, but still the home team had the best of it, and it was only on rare occasions that Wednesday's defence was called upon. Again it was odds on the visitors' goal being captured while Marshall was out of his place, one of the backs just getting into the goal in time to save the ball from going through. Marshall's position was anything but a sinecure, as he was time after time called upon to save his citadel from falling. This was accentuated by three corners in succession, and which being grandly directed, occasioned the defenders a lot of trouble to repel. Wharmby, Rowlston, and Williamson stuck gamely to their work, and by dint of good hard work, relieved the pressure, and a final shot by Bingham went over the bar. The home team for a short time pressed, but they were ultimately compelled to fall back, and Cawley, who had no one to face, after a scuffle which Marshall did yeoman's work, added a third goal for Wednesday, immediately after which half-time was called, Wednesday three goals and Derby County none.

When ends were reversed play was recommenced with great vigour, more so on the part of the County. A foul was granted to the home team at mid-field, and some beautiful play by all the Wednesday forwards ended in Ingram registering a fourth goal. Again Ingram by a magnificent shot hit the top of the goal post, and before the backs and custodian could get rid of the ball Cawley placed a fifth success to Wednesday, which was followed immediately by another from a good corner by Dungworth. The County men now and again threatened the home fortress, and once Hall just missed the post. Cawley sent the ball over, and another time hit the post, but the defence prevailed. However, the visiting team could not stop their opponents, and Ingram by famous shot altogether beat Marshall, the seventh goal falling to Wednesday. It will be seen from this that Derby County had not a look in. Occasionally they forced the play, but the home back play was too good for them to overcome. Waller by a good fast shot, scored the eighth goal, and soon after time was called, Wednesday winning easily.

WEDNESDAY .... 8 goals.
DERBY COUNTY .... 0 goals.
DERBY COUNTY.—J. Marshall, goal; A. Williamson, W. Rowlston, backs; W. Cooper, W. H. Wharmby, C. E. Thorpe, half-backs; J. Hall, S. Ottewell, J. Lees, S. Willshaw, and A. Bingham. Umpire, Mr. J. Bulmer. Referee, Mr. H. Vessey.
WEDNESDAY.—J. Smith, goal; J. Hudson, F. Thompson, backs; J. Dungworth, T. E. B. Wilson, E. Brayshaw, half-backs; H. Winterbottom, W. Ingram, G. Waller, W. Mosforth, and T. E. Cawley. Umpire, Mr. H. Muscroft. Referee.

Now here's one for Wednesday fans! This report shows Ingram scoring the first goal against Derby County in a Cup game on Christmas Eve, 1887, in front of a "large attendance" of 2,000 people at Olive Grove, Wednesday's ground before they moved to their present site in 1899.

The good news is that they scored seven more and it finished 8-0. Then known as The Wednesday, they were eventually knocked out of the Cup, 3-1, by Preston North End in the sixth round.

Sheffield United were drawn against Heeley in the Cup in the 1880s. The game should have been played at Sheaf House, Heeley's ground, but it was moved to Bramall Lane to accommodate a 3,000 crowd. United won it, 1-0.

ENGLISH ASSOCIATION CUP TIES.

SECOND QUALIFYING ROUND.

HEELEY V. SHEFFIELD UNITED.

According to the order of drawing these teams should have met on the first-named club's ground at Sheaf House, but an arrangement was made whereby the contest took place at Bramall Lane this afternoon, in dull, threatening, but fair weather, before nearly 3,000 spectators.

The Heeleyites winning the toss elected to take advantage of what little wind there was, and at five minutes after the advertised time Donald started the ball in the direction of Shoreham street. The Heeley citadel was quickly besieged, but the goalkeeper relieved, and the United backs had all they could do to stave off a combined attack of the Heeley forwards. Both goals were in turn assailed, but the defence proved equal to the occasion, and although shots were directed they were resultless. The United vigorously attacked, got dangerously near, but the ball was eventually forced over the line, and subsequent efforts met with a similar result. Heeley changed the venue of play, and Stringer had to concede a corner, which was, however, got away. A visitation was made to the Heeley end, but the backs relieved the pressure. Two fouls occurred in the vicinity of the United goal, following which Heeley obtained another corner, which was unproductive. Heeley still attacked, and evoked enthusiastic cheers for their plucky play, but the siege was raised, and Donald, at the other end, had a chance of scoring, but shot very wide of the mark. United at length were conceded a corner from a smart attack, but Hudson directed behind, and a rush by the Heeleyites resulted in Sykes shooting over the bar, and immediately afterwards the United defence had to put in all they knew to save from another combined attack. Heeley obtained a foul close in, and the ball was steered through the posts from the free kick, but of course no point was allowed. Heeley were now having the best of the game, and kept the United defence busy, but the shooting when within range was very erratic. Good pressing by the United saw them in dangerous proximity to the Heeley goal, but the custodian cleverly saved. Howlett at the other end beat away a grand shot by Shaw, and M'Watt at the other end had to act similarly. Half-time arrived without either team having secured a point.

On changing ends United assailed, but were repulsed, and Himsworth headed an attack to the other end, but Howlett was on the alert, and beat away. The Heeley quarters were for a considerable time the scene of operations, and two unproductive corners fell to the United, followed by a foul close in the Heeley lines, but the ball was directed over the bar. Two more corners to the United were fruitless, and for some time the Heeley defence was severely tried, but the United forwards were slow and erratic, or would have scored. United continued to have all the best of the game, but lacked combination in the forward division, having repeated chances of scoring but for dilatoriness. Again the Heeley citadel was attacked, and Hobson from a fine chance shot over the crossbar. The Heeley forwards raised the siege, and Hemsworth hit the United bar, and from a subsequent corner the United backs relieved, and their forwards getting possession, a rush was made to the Heeley end, but the final effort was misdirected. Play ruled fast and furious, and both sides were cheered to renewed exertions by their partisans. The United resolutely assailed, and M'Watt saved just in the nick of time, whilst the backs showed fine form. A corner was conceded to the United, and from by-play there was some roughness in midfield, which the referee promptly dealt with. Another run by the United forwards gave them a chance of reducing the Heeley citadel, but Robertson shot just outside the post, and directly afterwards McWatt saved in grand fashion from a hot shot close in. A rush by the United saw the ball directed into the Heeley goal, and Stokes had the ill luck to put it through the sticks. The game eventually ended—

UNITED .... 1 goal.
HEELEY .... 0 goal.
Heeley.—Goal, M'Watt; backs, T. A. Tomlinson and H. Stokes; half-backs, R. Needham, I. Swallow, and D. Beach; forwards, W. H. Himsworth, G. Sykes, A. E. Shaw, H. Ward, and F. Roberts.
Sheffield United.—Goal, C. H. Howlett; backs, E. Stringer and Gilmartin; half-backs, Mack, Hobson, and Hudson; forwards, Galbraith, Robertson, Donald, Duncan, and Mosforth.
Umpires: Messrs. W. Deans and F. W. Madin. Referee: Mr. J. Darne.

FOOTBALL JOTTINGS

NO "NUDGER" BUT UNITED WIN THE BIG ONE

This was the crunch game that virtually decided the First Division Championship in season 1897-98. Sheffield United, just one point ahead of Sunderland, tried to have the match date changed because captain "Nudger" Needham was away on international duty.

But, said The Star, Sunderland had thought more of the championship than of their reputation for sportsmanlike conduct and refused to change, "an action for which they have been generally condemned in the sporting press of this country."

But justice was done. United edged it 1-0 and went on to win their first major honour, finishing five points ahead of second-placed Sunderland.

---

staggers number one for the crowd, which does not like the sensation, especially against the wind.

THE FOOTBALL LEAGUE.

LEAGUE NO. 1.

SHEFFIELD UNITED V. SUNDERLAND.

Few matches in this year's programme have been awaited by Sheffield United's supporters with more anxious eagerness than this. In many quarters during the last week or two it has been freely stated that the match would decide the championship, and it was indeed evident that the winner of the game would have a start which would need a good deal of catching on the part of the other. Prior to the match the teams were separated by only a single point, United having 36 for 27 matches played, while Sunderland had taken 35 for 26 matches. This was, of course, the return match of the season, the previous encounter at Sunderland having been won by the northerners by 3 goals to 1. The United team was by no means at its full strength, Needham, the captain, being away at Glasgow representing his country against Scotland. It was in consequence of the expected selection of Needham that the United Committee asked Sunderland to change the date

---

ing Lindley and his witnesses) would "get it" when she came out again.

A "FOOTBALL" VISITOR IN TROUBLE.—Thomas Dwyer, an Irishman coming from Liverpool, appears somewhat interested in the fortunes of the Everton football team. On Monday he came all the way to Sheffield to see the match between that team and Sheffield Wednesday. He must have been delighted with the result, for he apparently celebrated the victory of Everton by having a drink or two. He had, in fact, more than was good for him, for in Snighill at night he was seen by Sergt. Grannan and Detective Ibbotson very much the worse for drink. He was also shouting and using foul language, and in the end, instead of being allowed to return to Liverpool, he was locked up at the Central Police Station. At the Court House this morning Dwyer admitted his fault, and he was fined 5s.2 nd costs.

CORPORATION PROSECUTIONS.—At Sheffield Police Court to-day Joel Thorpe, cowkeeper, 21,

This Everton fan landed in trouble after his team had beaten Sheffield Wednesday in 1893.

(Right) Drawings were a popular way of enlivening football match reports in the early 1900s. The Star's cartoonist sums up the Wednesday v Middlesbrough game in September, 1912.

This was how The Star's cartoonist heralded the start of the 1912-13 football season. The Wednesday fan's optimism was justified. They finished third in the First Division, with United 15th.

RED LETTER NIGHT!

The New Programme of the

SPORTS SPECIAL

("GREEN 'UN")

COMMENCING

SATURDAY NEXT

Many New and
Attractive Features.

Something about every 1st, and 2nd, and Midland League Club.

Brightest and Best Football Paper ever issued on Saturday Night.

All the Matches
Specially Reported.

Comments Upon the Results.

AMUSING CARTOONS & SKETCHES.

If you want a real live up-to-date account of Next Saturday's Football, see that you get the

SPORTS SPECIAL

Enormous Demand--Order at Once.

And this is how the Green 'Un, The Star's famous sports paper, promoted itself at the start of the 1912-13 season. It has always been regarded as one of the best, if not THE best, Saturday sports editions in the country and has proved it by winning several national awards.

THE UNPARALLELED CUP FINAL.

WHO IS TO BLAME FOR THE SCENES AT WEMBLEY?

QUESTION IN HOUSE OF COMMONS.

HOW LARGEST CROWD ON RECORD RUSHED THE BARRIERS.

for the unprecedented scene

April, 1923. The first match at Wembley Stadium and the most famous Cup Final of all. And The Star had strong words for the Stadium authorities after 200,000 fans, including train and bus loads from Sheffield, managed to get into the 125,000 capacity spanking-new ground, many of them by climbing over gates.

More than 1,000 were injured and The Star said: "The remarkable fact is that no person was killed on the spot or injured fatally."

UNITED'S CUP WIN OF 1925

TRAINLOADS O...

Bright Sunshine Greets the Crowds on Arrival in London.

NO RUSH TO GROUND.

Sheffielders Take a Trip Round in Ancient "Growler."

'TELEGRAPH' TRAIN COMFORT

Ticket System Prevents Repetition of Fiasco.

"I am going to assist the mascot who has already arrived in his efforts to help the United win. It will be the first football match I have ever seen, and I think my attendance on this historic occasion will mean a success for our team. We are all full of hope."

This message was given to a "Star" man this morning by the Lord Mayor of Sheffield (Alderman A. J. Bailey) just before he took his...

We're off to Wembley! The Lord Mayor of Sheffield and party go to the 1925 Cup Final.

And as he boarded a special train at Sheffield Victoria, the Lord Mayor, Ald A.J.Bailey, told a Star reporter: "It will be the first football match I have ever seen and I think my attendance on this historic occasion will mean a success for our team."

Fancy that! You go to your first ever football match and see Sheffield United win the Cup! Many football supporters have to wait half a lifetime to see their team lift a trophy – and for some it never happens at all.

United Ahead at Half-

100,000 SEE SHEFFIELD TAKE THE LEAD.

LORD MAYOR OF SHEFFIELD ADDS HIS INSPIRATION TO THE TEAM'S MASCOT.

TUNSTALL SCORES HIS FOURTH CONSECUTIVE CUP TIE GOAL.

HASLAND EXCURSIONIST KILLED ON JOINING TRAIN FOR THE FINAL.

THE exceptional attractiveness of the Jubilee Cup Final at the Wembley Stadium to-day—the success of Cardiff giving the meeting an international flavour—began to crystallise in the form of great crowds of partisans arriving in London from an early hour this morning. Sheffield United and Cardiff City arrived in the Metropolis overnight, with vanguards of optimists, and from shortly after midnight trains from England and Wales landed their packed companies in rapid succession. Happily the later morning arrivals had the satisfaction of sunny weather, and with this as an aid, were able to pass the spare hours in pleasures of their own choice.

The Lord Mayor of Sheffield (Alderman A. J. Bailey) journeyed to London to add his inspiration to the team's mascot, and before his departure expressed a sound belief in a victory for the United. In that event a civic welcome to the winners on their return with the Cup is assured. The many trains from Sheffield were all crowded, and there was a great display of red-and-white favours—one enthusiast adding to his outfit the semblance of a huge Sheffield "blade."

The Welsh contingents arriving in London also evidenced the tremendous enthusiasm and confidence extending throughout the Principality, and, with the recognised "glorious uncertainty" of Cup-tie form, especially with teams so well matched, excitement throughout the ranks of the armies intensified as the sides made their way to the vast amphitheatre.

The views of the men directly concerned are interesting. The captain of the Sheffield team, on arrival in London, said: "We are all well and ready, and are confident we shall win the Cup." The Cardiff captain said: "We are confident, but not over-confident. We do not know whether we shall win until the match is over."

It is no novelty for the Sheffield team to participate in the Cup Final. The United have won the trophy on three occasions—in 1899, 1902 and 1915—and once they lost to Tottenham Hotspurs, in 1910. The Stadium has accommodation for 95,000 people. The gates were opened at noon, and the kick-off took place at three o'clock.

The attendance was reported in the neighbourhood of 100,000—97,000 being in the gr... by 2.30... and it is stated...

W. GILLESPIE,
Captain, Sheffield United.

J. BLAIR,
Captain, Cardiff City.

THE MEN WHO BROUGHT THE CUP TO SHEFFIELD.

CHARLES SUTCLIFFE: goalkeeper, born at Bradford, stands 5ft. 11½in., and weighs 11st. 6lb. Obtained from Rotherham County this season to replace Gough. Young brother of the great "J. W." Did he ever dream of a Cup medal at Millmoor?

W. COOK: right back, 5ft. 9in., 11st. 2lb. Born at Unsworth. The solitary link with the 1915 Cup-winning side. Happy and unconventional, and played finely at Wembley. An acrobatic kick.

E. MILTON: left back, 5ft. 8in., 11st. 7lb. (Kimberworth), one of three well-known brothers, all left-backs. Sturdily built and robust. Has played in minor representative games.

H. PANTLING: right half, 5ft. 9½in., 11st. 6½lb. (Leighton Buzzard). Played for England against Ireland, and also was in International trial. Learnt his football at Watford. A big-hearted player.

S. KING: centre half, 5ft. 8in., 11st. 5lb. (Penistone). Was obtained as a back, and developed in his present position when Waugh got hurt. Very fast and keen tackler. Good all-round sportsman.

G. GREEN: left half, 5ft. 10½in., 11st. 13lb. (Leamington). Really a right-half, but could play anywhere. A great United "find" for last season. Twice on International trial, and picked to play against France.

D. MERCER: outside right, 5ft. 7in., 11st. 6lb. (St. Helens). An artist with the ball, though no longer a sharpshooter. Cost £4,500, of which United have never regretted a penny. International and toured South Africa.

T. BOYLE: inside right, 5ft. 9½in., 12st. 1lb. (Sheffield). Certain to make a big name if all goes well; a craftsman with the Buchan touch. Son of Peter Boyle, a former famous United back.

H. JOHNSON: centre-forward, 5ft. 7½in., 10st. 6lb. (Ecclesfield). Plucky, fast, hard-charging; often causes defensive disturbances as he did at Wembley, and scores plenty of goals.

W. GILLESPIE: inside left, and captain, 5ft. 8½in., 11st. 2lb. (Ballintrae). One of the truly great figures in the game; a superb artist with the ball, a real leader, and the mainspring of the United attack. Ireland's captain.

F. TUNSTALL: outside left, 5ft. 7½in., 11st. 8lb. (Low Valley). The man who scored the Cup-winning goal. Brilliant winger who has been compared with Spiksley; often cuts in and wins matches by his fierce, accurate shooting. English International.

GEORGE WALLER: The prince of trainers, who has been actively connected with eight Cup finals (including replays). Played for Wednesday in one. A Yorkshire cricketer in the '90's. Regarded as a splendid friend by all the team, to whom he acts as coach.

The Star's match report on the first half of the final. The score stayed that way and England international Fred Tunstall's 31st minute goal was enough to send half of Sheffield delirious.

Fred, a former miner, had been signed from Scunthorpe in 1920. United first had him watched when he was playing for a team at Darfield, Barnsley – his birthplace – but had not been impressed!

Here they are... the conquering heroes.

On their way to final they had beaten The Wednesday 3-2. It was the fourth time United had won the Cup and they haven't done it since.

The News in Pictures

The Star's picture coverage of the game.

THE CUP COMES TO SHEFFIELD.

United's Return with the Famous Trophy.

CHEERING CROWDS.

A Magnificent Welcome for the Triumphant Players.

The home-coming of the Sheffield United, the Cup-winners, this afternoon, was marked by scenes of tremendous enthusiasm.

Usually, Sheffield citizens are a stolid lot who take their ups and downs dispassionately; but there are occasions when they "let themselves go" and give vent to their feelings. This afternoon was one such. And what an outburst! For weeks the question which had been

slapping and handshaking. The members of the team, all smiles and in the best of good spirits, were overwhelmed. They had expected a warm welcome, but in their most fanciful moments perhaps nothing like that to which they were being subjected.

Sheffield was in a joyous mood, and the men of the United team were being taken to her heart. It was a welcome an Emperor might well have envied.

But the best had yet to come. The station premises were all too small for

The Star's headlines of April 28, 1925, sum up a great day for Unitedites.

Warriors all...the 1925 Cup winning side.

Star

COLE'S "ALTERATION S.."
DUE to our constantly increasing business (up to this date also showed an enormous increase over the previous one) we have handicapped by lack of sufficient floor space. Structural alteration are therefore to be carried out which, when completed, will give *3,000 MORE SQUARE FEET OF FLOOR SI*

Sheffield United 11 ; Cardiff 2

United Put Up a Record Victory.

LEAGUE SCORING FEAT

Cardiff City Swamped and Blotted Out.

TWO "HAT=TRICKS."

Now here's a headline every Unitedite should have framed and hung over the fireplace – or even the bedhead.

The club's record win, which still stands, was on New Year's Day, 1926. Considering what United had done to them in the 1925 Cup Final, Cardiff must have been as sick as a parrot.

United finished fifth in the First Division that season and Wednesday were promoted from the Second Division.

Can you believe it? The Wednesday are training on the beach at Scarborough in collars and ties! But they had the last laugh. This picture appeared in The Star on March 18, 1926, and a few weeks later, the smart-looking Wednesday lads had the Second Division championship all buttoned up.

Telegraph & Star

PRESTO TOYS.
New Action, No Clockwork, from 1/-
OVER THE TOP.
Ingenious MECHANICAL TOY, 1/6.
ADANA Printing Machine.
THE REAL THING. - - - 10/6.
Wilson, Gumpert & Co., Ltd.
57. FARGATE.

SHEFFIELD: TELEPHONE 22055 (FOURTEEN LINES.)
No. 13,533.   SHEFFIELD, WEDNESDAY EVENING, MARCH 5, 1930.
[12 PAGES.]
ONE PENNY.

Sheffield Wednesday Again Tackle Notts Forest in the F.A. Cu[p]

"Star" photograph of the huge crowd on "Spion Kop" at Hillsborough to witness the Nottingham Forest-Wednesday replay this afternoon.

TO-DAY'S REPLAY | PODMORE'S ALLEGED PRISON T[ALK]

Flat caps galore as Wednesday and Notts Forest meet in an FA Cup Sixth Round replay on March 5, 1930. Wednesday won 3-1.

If you look closely, you'll see the odd trilby or two. Wednesday were knocked out in the semi-final, 2-1, by Huddersfield but their consolation that season was the First Division championship.

In the process, they scored 105 goals and conceded 57.

Wednesday had also topped the First Division the season before.

Wednesday… the very best in English football in both 1929 and 1930.

SHEFFIELD PLAYERS IN NEXT MONDAY'S INTERNATIONAL.

GILLESPIE. (IRELAND.) BLENKINSOP. (ENGLAND.) STRANGE. (ENGLAND.) LEACH. (ENGLAND.) BURGESS. (ENGLAND.) DUNNE. (IRELAND.)

Players from Wednesday and United who were representing their countries in the England v Northern Ireland international at Bramall Lane on October 20, 1930, made ideal subjects for The Star's artist. It had been 27 years since an international game had been played at Sheffield United's ground and ten years since an England v Scotland match at Hillsborough.

  This was England's day. They ran out 5-1 winners.

This is how Harry Heap, The Star's famous cartoonist, saw the game.

All smiles as manager Billy Walker gives his Wednesday players a briefing before the 1935 final against West Brom. It worked. Wednesday romped it 4-2. United reached the final the following season but were beaten 1-0 by Arsenal.

86—HOTTEST FOR 14 MONTHS

THE temperature in Sheffield this afternoon soared to 86 degrees in the shade, breaking last August's record.

It is the hottest day since June, 1947, when 88 degrees was recorded.

Air Ministry experts said today there was no sign of a break in the weather, and the outlook was fair or fine everywhere.

Swimming pools were filled with bathers, and holiday crowds basked in the parks and on the moorlands.

After eight bus-loads of people had left for Manchester the queue was told no further buses could be spared for that route.

HOTTER STILL

By early afternoon the temperature in Rotherham was 81 and at Barnsley 84 — only two degrees below yesterday's record.

Afternoon temperature at Mansfield reached 85 degrees in the shade—three degrees hotter than yesterday.

Shade temperature in Doncaster reached 86, the highest of the year.

From holiday resor~~~ ~ame

SHEFFIELD UNITED players found it warm work when they reported to trainer Doug Livingstone at Bramall Lane today—but there's a shower to look forward to.

* * Latest football news on Back P~

July 27, 1948, was, at 86 degrees, the hottest day of the year. What a day for United to start training. The heat was on them all season and they were relegated from the First Division.

DOOLEY, DOOLEY, HALLELUJAH...

He's terrific...he's colossal...he's – oh, skip it.

That was how a front page report in the Green 'Un started on December 29, 1951, in a tribute to Derek Dooley, Sheffield's greatest football legend.

Derek had just banged in another two for top-of-the-table Wednesday in a 4-1 win at Southampton and local and national newspaper sports writers, proud of their word power, were finding it hard to come up with adequate adjectives to describe a footballer who could find the net almost at will.

The previous month, two days before Bonfire Night, Derek put on his own personal display of fireworks by scoring five against Notts County.

He ran Leon Leuty, County's highly regarded centre-half, ragged and completely overshadowed the centre-forward at the other end of the pitch...Tommy Lawton!

In that amazing 1951-52 season, rampaging Derek scored 47 goals, taking Wednesday back to the First Division almost single-handed.

The lanky, tousle-haired Derek, who played his football just like a soccer hero from a boy's comic, was manna from heaven for The Star's cartoonist Harry Heap who regularly featured him on the front page of the Green 'Un.

But one of the biggest success stories in Sheffield's sporting history was to take a tragic turn, so tragic that the young lad of 23 with the strength of a sturdy pit prop and years of football ahead of him, was to find himself at death's door.

A leg injury in a match against Preston in February, 1953, went terribly wrong when gangrene set in and the leg had to be amputated to save his life.

When Derek proudly and defiantly hobbled into Hillsborough to see his teammates a few weeks later before the match against Manchester City, the crowd went wild.

And two years later, 55,000 packed into Hillsborough for his benefit game – surely the biggest "thank-you" Sheffield has ever given to one of its soccer heroes.

But the remarkable Dooley story didn't end there. He was appointed manager of the club he loved in 1971, sacked two years later on Christmas Eve and then offered a job across the city with United.

After a spell as commercial manager, he became a director and then managing director.

Derek, a freeman of Sheffield, was still in the hot seat when he celebrated his 70th birthday in 1999 and helped to negotiate the signing of new manager Neil Warnock.

He's terrific...he's colossal...he's...oh-skip it.

November fireworks as Derek bangs in five.

Derek was manna from heaven for The Star and Green 'Un cartoonist Harry Heap.

Dangerously ill and fighting for his life...

Before the game against Stoke, Wednesday's vice-chairman, Coun. James Longden, reads out a special message to be sent to Derek.

Re-united with his teammates.

Sacked on Christmas Eve, 1973.

Think of Wednesday greats, think of Dooley. Think of United greats, think of Tony Currie who broke 40,000 plus hearts in June, 1976, when he moved to Leeds.

Sheffield United, who had paid Watford £27,500 for him, sold him for £275,000. But there probably wasn't a single United fan who thought the deal represented a shrewd bit of business.

Happily, after an illustrious career which took him on to an international stage, Tony is now back where he belongs, at Bramall Lane, heading United's Football in the Community programme. This picture is from 1990.

No. 32,384 Sheffield, Monday, April 22, 1991 22p

WE WON THE CUP

Glory, glory day for Owls and Big Ron's Barmy Army

By Mike O'Sullivan and Tony Pritchett

BIG RON'S army had every reason to go barmy . . .

And jubilant Owls fans today banished that Monday morning feeling to start the week in ecstatic mood after Sheffield Wednesday's 1-0 League Cup Final triumph over Manchester United.

Fans who made the long trek back from Wembley yesterday were expected to begin their celebrations in earnest tonight.

We did it for you: P16

They'll be looking forward to Wednesday evening, when the promotion-hunting Owls are expected to show off the silverware before the match against Leicester City at Hillsborough.

Ron Atkinson's Second Division underdogs covered themselves with glory and scored Wednesday's first Wembley success in 56 years.

And, off the field, Owls supporters helped turn the day into the friendly final — with police praising fans and reporting no arrests among the 77,612 crowd.

'BETTER THAN DISNEYLAND'

Wednesday supporters — who call themselves "Big Ron's barmy army" — rose to the occasion with magnificent backing for their heroes.

Sheffield's last big football triumph. Big Ron's Barmy Army really did go barmy when Wednesday came home with the League Cup on April 22, 1991. It was their first Wembley success in 56 years.

And the fact that they were in the Second Division at the time and the team they beat 1-0 was Manchester United made the victory that much sweeter...

SHEFFIELD WINS THE BIG WEMBLEY SEMI-FINAL

Even United fans, who saw their team lose 2-1, have described the United v Wednesday FA Cup Semi-Final at Wembley on April 3, 1993, as the most momentous match in the history of Sheffield football.

For our two clubs to meet in the semi-final was the stuff of dreams.

The real winner, though, was Sheffield. The city went to London, had a great, great day and showed the rest of the country what sportsmanship and camaraderie between rival clubs was all about.

Sheffield was, justifiably, so proud that day. The city where football had its beginnings had proved that the game did have a sunny side to it after all.

For the record, Wednesday met Arsenal in the final, drew 1-1 after extra-time and then lost the replay 2-1, also after extra-time.

All mates together...

Front page of The Star's Sheffield At Wembley supplement. United's Dave Bassett and Wednesday's Trevor Francis in bubbly mood before the game.

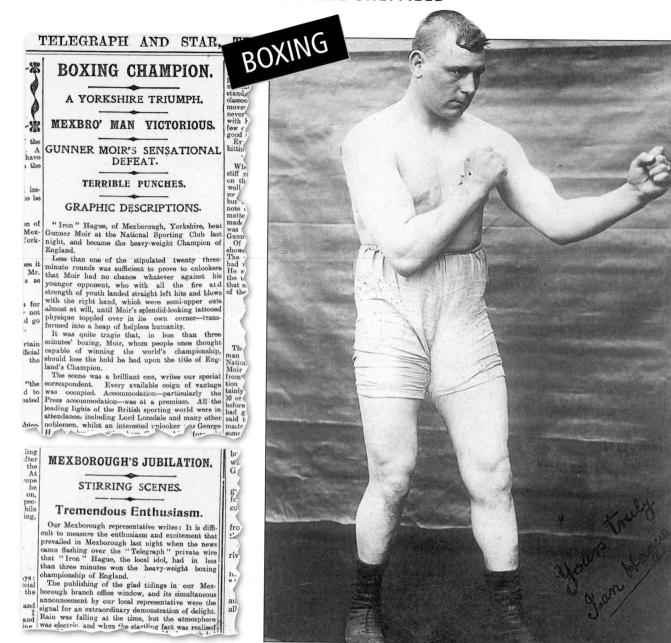

BOXING

TELEGRAPH AND STAR,

BOXING CHAMPION.

A YORKSHIRE TRIUMPH.

MEXBRO' MAN VICTORIOUS.

GUNNER MOIR'S SENSATIONAL DEFEAT.

TERRIBLE PUNCHES.

GRAPHIC DESCRIPTIONS.

"Iron" Hague, of Mexborough, Yorkshire, beat Gunner Moir at the National Sporting Club last night, and became the heavy-weight Champion of England.

Less than one of the stipulated twenty three-minute rounds was sufficient to prove to onlookers that Moir had no chance whatever against his younger opponent, who with all the fire and strength of youth landed straight left hits and blows with the right hand, which were semi-upper cuts almost at will, until Moir's splendid-looking tattooed physique toppled over in its own corner—transformed into a heap of helpless humanity.

It was quite tragic that, in less than three minutes' boxing, Moir, whom people once thought capable of winning the world's championship, should lose the hold he had upon the title of England's Champion.

The scene was a brilliant one, writes our special correspondent. Every available coign of vantage was occupied. Accommodation—particularly the Press accommodation—was at a premium. All the leading lights of the British sporting world were in attendance, including Lord Lonsdale and many other noblemen, whilst an interested onlooker as George H...

MEXBOROUGH'S JUBILATION.

STIRRING SCENES.

Tremendous Enthusiasm.

Our Mexborough representative writes: It is difficult to measure the enthusiasm and excitement that prevailed in Mexborough last night when the news came flashing over the "Telegraph" private wire that "Iron" Hague, the local idol, had in less than three minutes won the heavy-weight boxing championship of England.

The publishing of the glad tidings in our Mexborough branch office window, and its simultaneous announcement by our local representative were the signal for an extraordinary demonstration of delight. Rain was falling at the time, but the atmosphere was electric and when the startling fact was realised...

NO-NONSENSE MEXBOROUGH MUSCLE

Just about the whole of Mexborough turned out on April 19, 1909, to cheer local lad Iron Hague, 14-stone of no-nonsense Mexborough muscle, as he left for the National Sporting Club, Covent Garden, and a date with Gunner James Moir for the heavyweight boxing championship of England.

The Bull's Head Hotel, his training headquarters, was besieged with fans and High Street, Station Road, and Mexborough station itself were almost impassable.

The Star's Mexborough correspondent wrote: "When Iron came out of the Bull's Head, a typical Yorkshire roar rang through the streets, renewed again and again when it was seen that the boxer and his party were wearing red and blue rosettes, the Mexborough Town football club colours.

"Caps were flung high in the air and as Hague, with difficulty, made his way along, scores and scores of rough hands that told of long association with hard work were thrust forward for a friendly shake with that 'terrible right' from which so much is expected tonight. "

In London, excitement was mounting. The Star's London correspondent, describing the arrival of Iron's fans, wrote: "Certain types of the provincial are easily recognisable in London

and the hardy Northerner soon adds the leaven of his presence to The Strand and The Embankment, the two most favoured spots of all. The cap betrays them."

Meanwhile, Iron himself, "the picture of health and condition, his face and brawny arms bearing the bronze of the Yorkshire sea breezes", arrived at his hotel and went to bed.

The arrangements were for the Mexborough hard man to rest until 8pm and then "betake himself to the scene of the action."

Betake himself he did and in two minutes 47 seconds, Iron was the heavyweight champion of England. He had won with three of his "terrible rights" and had "planted himself on the pedestal of fame."

Amazingly, the news reached The Star's Mexborough branch office by private wire only four minutes after the start of the fight at 10.51pm.

It was pinned up in the window and, although rain was falling, the atmosphere was electric as crowds gathered to read the news for themselves.

Said The Star's man in Mexborough: "The scenes were stirring in this hour of Iron's victory and many beds in Mexborough were not occupied until daylight came."

RAILMAN BRUCE STEAMS TO TITLE

Many years later, another South Yorkshire boxer was to become a household name.

Bruce Woodcock landed the British and British Empire Heavyweight Championship in July, 1945, and said after the fight that all he wanted to do was to get away from the thud of the punchbag and the smell of the rubbing bottle and go away for a few days with a few of his mates.

But that wasn't possible so, instead, he was going back to work with the London and North Eastern Railway Company at Doncaster Plant Works!

Bruce, who became landlord of the Tumbler pub in Edlington, Doncaster, in later life, died in 1997.

Bruce Woodcc

GLITTERING AMERICAN OFFERS LIKELY

BRUCE WOODCOCK, of Doncaster, the new British and British Empire Heavyweight Boxing Champion, plans to restart work on the L.N.E.R., at Doncaster, next Monday.

His one desire, he told "The Star" to-day, was to get away from the thud of the punching-bag and the smell of the rubbing-bottle, and take a short holiday with half-a-dozen pals. This was not possible, so he intends to go to work at Doncaster Plant Works instead.

Woodcock motored to Manchester to-day for consultation with Tom Hurst, his manager. After driving through the night with his brother, he reached Doncaster early this morning and had plenty of tea, while discussing with members of his family, the fight and the bigger-still "fight" to get from the ring to his dressing-room.

Bruce said that the supposed cut on his nose was nothing of the sort; it was just nose-bleeding which any boxer might have after receiving a hefty punch.

CONGRATULATIONS

To-day, shoals of telegrams, congratulating him on winning the championship, came from all over the country.

One of the first to ̶ ̶ ̶ ̶ from the Mayor ̶ ̶

What a belter!

Bruce is a real knock-out...

SHEFFIELD'S PRINCE IS POETRY IN MOTION

Then along came the incomparable Naseem Hamed, the first boxer to bring a recognised world championship belt home to Sheffield.

He talked, swaggered and punched his way to the WBO featherweight crown against Steve Robinson in October, 1995, and Sheffield realised that here was a boxer on his way to becoming a legend.

His then manager Brendan Ingle, ever astute and a boxing scholar with a wily way for words, told The Star after the fight that he had a feeling Naz would one day be as good if not better than Ali.

And who would argue with that? As the start of the new millennium came and went, fight fans were asking the obvious question: "Is he unbeatable?"

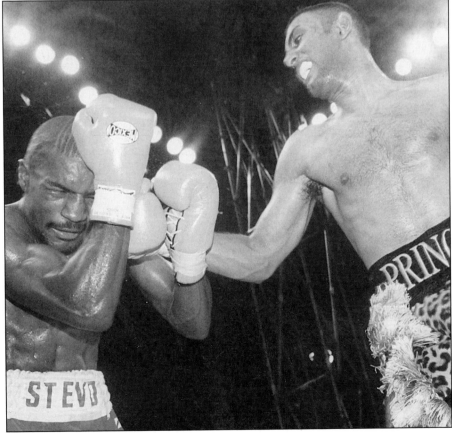

Ouch, says Steve Robinson as a right goes in.

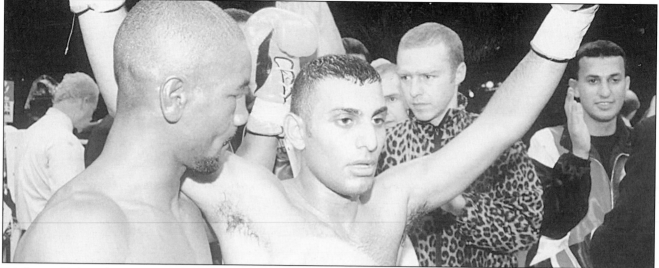

He's the world champion!

DOG RACING

SHEFFIELD GOES TO THE DOGS

Sheffield went to the dogs in May, 1927, and the new sport caused great excitement.

A reporter from The Star, sent to cover the first night at Darnall Wellington Cricket Ground, was very impressed. He wrote: "The parading of the dogs prior to each race was a very pretty spectacle, the attendants wearing white coats and scarlet jockey caps."

His report continued: "When the dogs for the first event had been put in the starting trap (a machine which ensures an equitable start) the "hare" makes its appearance from its "hide" and encircles the track at terrific speed, and when it emerges from the back of the trap and the dogs have sighted it, they are released and for a few fleeting seconds one has all the excitement of a horse race, for there is no doubt the dogs are all triers and, moreover, put all in."

And a noticeable feature of the gathering was "the large number of ladies present and they seemed to enjoy the racing equally with the men."

But it didn't find favour with the Primitive Methodists who thought that the sport was being made respectable and that the bookmaker, "the parasite", was making use of the greyhound course as a happy hunting ground."

YORKSHIRE TEL[

COURSING THRILLS.

ELECTRIC HARE RACING

IN SHEFFIELD.

A GREAT SEND-OFF.

Having had some small experience of whippet racing and coursing proper, says a correspondent, it was with some doubts that I wended my way last evening to the Darnall Wellington Cricket Ground to witness the Sheffield inauguration of the latest sport—electric hare racing.

I must say that my doubts were quickly dispelled for the sport proved all its enthusiasts had claimed for it, and despite the fact that the weather was inclement a company of I should say 6,000 thoroughly enjoyed the fare provided.

A noticeable feature of the gathering was the large number of ladies present, and they seemed to enjoy the racing equally with the men.

The parading of the dogs prior to each race was a very pretty spectacle, the attendants wearing white coats and scarlet jockey caps. The dogs wore light muzzles, which however do not actually keep their mouths closed and so interfere with free indrawing of breath, but ...fashioned as to prevent the indulging

Sheffield's new sport is off the blocks.

"ALL REIGHT."

THE GREYHOUND RACING

AT DARNALL.

(By " Split Second.")

At the greyhound racing in Darnall last night I met an old friend, who used to be a good professional runner, and knows a lot about the inside of speed work. I asked him what he thought of the new sport.

"It's all reight," he said, meaningly. "Ah'm satisfied. Ah've watched it, and found two winners. It'll go."

So that's that, from a good judge of sport; an opinion on something new, from one of a shrewd crowd.

We are well used here to foot-running. The difference between that and greyhound racing is that a man runs with judgment, and these dogs do not. They are "bang out" every time. It is inborn in them that they must have that thing which they see flying in front of them, and going all out they should run true to form every time, if they are put down fit.

Later on I shall make some detailed observations on the racing in the "Star." For the first meeting it was a case of moving in the dark, as many of the dogs were almost untrained, except in actual coursing, which is a different thing.

Meanwhile I have been asked to say a word or two about weighing up form in the game.

Time the Vital Matter.

Well, the vital thing is time. A man doing "evens" runs two yards in a fifth of a second. But in greyhound racing a fifth of a second means considerably more than that; say two lengths. The official times run to fifths, but ...

One fan sums it all up perfectly. Greyhound racing is "all reight."

The News.

For the record, the winner of the first race at the first meeting was a greyhound called Mission. His proud pose seems to indicate that he knew he was top dog.

SPEEDWAY

THE STAR SUPPORTS NEW SPORT

Two years later, speedway racing arrived in Sheffield and The Star's verdict was that it would fill a gap during the summer months "and do a good turn to the Sheffield business people in bringing visitors into the city."

And The Star was quick to support the new sport by offering a silver shield for one of the races. The paper said they "frequently encouraged new sport by gifts of splendid trophies."

However, the newspaper warned in an article published on the day speedway – they called it dirt track then—was to start that the sport was not one for old ladies or for those suffering from weak hearts.

"Full of thrills and excitement, it depends upon the spectacular effect of broadsiding and full-blooded racing of fearless riders."

The first meeting, at Owlerton Stadium, had Dare-Devil Beckett and Smoky Stratton racing against each other for the British Dirt Track record.

G, MARCH 30, 1929.

DIRT TRACK RACING.

Sheffield's First Thrills This Evening.

To-night the Sheffield public is to be given an opportunity of witnessing the new motor-cycle sport of dirt track racing.

What will be its verdict? The opinion of enthusiasts is, that the racing will become as popular in Sheffield as it has in other large towns where this form of sport has been in progress during the last two years.

It will certainly fill a gap during the summer months and do a good turn to the Sheffield business people in bringing visitors into the city.

The sport is not one for old ladies or those suffering from weak hearts. Full of thrills and excitement, it depends upon the spectacular effect of broadsiding and "full-blooded" racing of fearless riders.

One particular point the spectators may rely upon—there will not be any "squared races." Every race will be one of competitive skill and brains, and the youngsters who take part in these events are full of keenness and enthusiasm to do their "darndest," for to them it means everything.

The Auto-Cycle Union take an active part in controlling the new sport. Their attitude is strictly clean, and betting is *de trop.* The A.C.U has an official at every meeting to look after their interests and those of the riders.

DIRT TRACK RACING!

STARTS ON SATURDAY.
7.30 p.m.

EVERYONE ON TIP-TOE

GREAT OPENING MEETING will take Sheffield by storm!

FIRST MEETING, SAT., MARCH 30, at 7.30
Terrific Pace. Enormous Hazards. Thousands will be thrilled and thrilled again. These wonderful lads will give you the thrill of your lives, and

DARE-DEVIL BECKETT,
the spectacular star of 1928, unapproached for daring.

SMOKY STRATTON,
the brilliant New Zealand Star, will make an attempt on the BRITISH DIRT TRACK RECORD,
which is at present held by C. H. Beckett, who is being presented with a *d—ous trophy* to commemorate his great achievement. THESE STARS WILL ALSO BE RACING—
JOHNNY BROUGHTON, of CROYDON.
WIGFIELD, of BARNSLEY.
CUMMINGS, of EDINBURGH.
SHERLOCK, of LEICESTER.
and dozens of local lads who have developed amazingly, and who will be "all out" to reach the top in this clean, vigorous and sensational sport.

RACES for the GOLDEN HELMET,
and Cash Prizes totalling £50 at each Meeting.

GRAND MEETING
EASTER MONDAY,
at 7.30 p.m.
Admission - 1/2, 2/4, 3/6.
Everyone can see. Excellent stands
CAR PARK FOR 1,000 CARS

SHEFFIELD SPEEDWAY

THE STADIUM, PENISTONE ROAD, OWLERTON MEADOWS.

The great opening meeting will take Sheffield by storm, says the advertisement in The Star.

1, BALLYRAGAN; 2, Cruxty Finn. Won by a distance. Time, 32.95sec.

"STAR" SHIELD.

Valuable Trophy for Dirt Track Riders.

A feature of the Dirt Track Racing at Owlerton on Easter Monday will be the first contest for a magnificent silver shield to be known as the "Star" Shield.

This trophy has been presented to the track by the "Yorkshire Telegraph and Star," which has frequently encouraged sport by gifts of splendid trophies.

The "Star" Shield, intended to encourage the new form of popular sport, is specially designed. The public will get a good view of it when the winner rides round the track, as the beautiful specimen of Sheffield silversmiths' work will be borne on his arm.

There is no doubt that the "Star" Shield will be one of the most keenly contested prizes in the valuable collection at the Owlerton Stadium.

DERBYSHIRE MEDALS.

Hathersage meet Friddon Sports in the final
Bakewell

The Star puts up a new shield.

Speedway racing arrives in Sheffield.

TENNIS

BARE LEGS BIG TALKING POINT

The main story on The Star's sports page on June 6, 1929, might not have been local but it was a big talking point.

Up for discussion at the All-England Club, Wimbledon, was the question of bare legs on the court.

The fashion of playing stockingless had been started by Miss "Billy" Tapscott, the South African player. Helen Willis, the current champion, had not worn any in the recent French championships and many of the leading British, American and French players were playing bare-legged on the Continent.

The All-England Club championship committee issued a statement after the meeting which put the ball back in the players' court by saying they would prefer to rely on the good taste and good sense of the players.

The Star pointed out that neither the Lawn Tennis Association or the All-England Club had anything in its rules governing what players of either sex should wear on court and rather than pass a hurried rule giving the authorities power to dictate as to the clothing of the players, the Championship Committee had come to a wise decision in leaving the matter in the hands of the competitors.

TASTE AND SENSE.

TENNIS AUTHORITIES AND BARE-LEG CONTROVERSY

POPULAR DECISION.

Representatives of the Lawn Tennis Association and the All-England Club, Wimbledon, where the lawn tennis championships are held, met yesterday in committee, one of the subjects which came up for discussion being the question of bare legs on the court.

The following statement was issued by the Championship Committee after the meeting:—

"It has been suggested that the Championship Committee should express an opinion on the nature and extent of the clothing suitable for competitors at Wimbledon. The circumstances attendant upon the championship meeting have a quality of their own, and the Committee would prefer to rely, as heretofore, on the good taste and good sense of the players, whom the Committee wish to regard, so far as possible, as their invited guests."

The decision was in accordance with the expectations of everyone who had followed the so-called "controversy" through its various stages.

A Modern Fashion.

Neither the Lawn Tennis Association nor the All-England Club had anything in its rules governing what players of either sex should wear on court, and rather than pass a hurried rule giving the authorities power to dictate as to players, the Cham ionshi

MacClennan.

Roger in another 5-set battle

Roger Taylor thrilled Wimbledon and shocked the German star with an exciting comeback in this afternoon's semi-final.

The German started off in terrific style, cool and efficient while the city player looked under pressure.

Taylor double-faulted six times in first set and Bungert took it 6-4.

With Bungert appearing in full control, Taylor's dramatic bid to reach Friday's final was in danger. Then midway through the second set the Taylor rally opened up.

RACED AWAY

Playing with more fire than his opponent, the Sheffield ace suddenly altered the whole trend of a tense battle.

Bungert's service cracked and Taylor was on his toes in battling mood to exploit the situation.

He won the second set 8-6 and then raced away with the third 6-2 to thrill the centre court crowd.

LATER: Bungert twice broke Taylor's service to lead 3-2 in final set.

**FULL REPORT —BACK PAGE

ROGER...AND OUT!

Nearly 40 years later, a Sheffield tennis player called Roger Taylor was a sensation at Wimbledon – and it was nothing to do with his bare legs.

Roger, son of a steelworker, made it to the Wimbledon semi-finals in July, 1967, the first British player to reach that stage since Mike Sangster in 1961.

Thousands of fans, most of whom were unable to get tickets for his centre court match against Germany's Wilhelm Bungert, swarmed into the All-England Club and paid 7s 6d to watch the progress of the game on an electronic scoreboard outside the centre court.

The queues for the game were the biggest on record for a semi-final and a Wimbledon official said: "This tremendous crowd must only be put down to the fact that Roger Taylor is playing." Roger's mum and girlfriend were there but dad Mark was doing his normal day's work in the steel melting department of English Steel Corporation's Tinsley Park Works.

Sheffield – indeed the whole country – could hardly bear the tension as play got under way. But The Star's readers were devastated by the headline over the item in the stop press column in the late edition of July 5, 1967: DEFEAT FOR ROGER TAYLOR.

Having lost the first set against Bungert, Taylor stormed back to lead 2-1 but the German then took the next two sets.

It was heartbreaking. But at least Taylor had the comfort of knowing he had brought a tremendous honour to his home city.

DEFEAT FOR ROGER TAYLOR

Bungert won final set 6-4 to clinch place in final. He beat Taylor 6-4, 6-8, 2-6, 6-4, 6-4.

PAY ROW PILOTS SUING AIRLINES

British Airline Pilots' Association decided today to continue legal action against BOAC, BEA and BUA for salary increases due under three-year agreement which association maintain have been illegally withheld. Writs in test cases served. Total affected

CRICKET

Clever little drawings were used to illustrate cricket reports in The Star. Haigh's bowling feat for Yorkshire (3-22 from 20 overs) helped them overcome Lancashire on August 9, 1905, and also ensured that he was the artist's subject on that particular day.

YORKSHIRE v. LANCASHIRE.

A THRILLING FINALE.

Brilliant Yorkshire Victory

THE LANCASTRIANS MASTERED.

Last year's result:—A draw. Score:—Yorkshire, 403 (E. Smith 98, Hirst 65, Tunnicliffe 55, Lord Hawke 54). Lancashire, 173 (A. H. Hornby 59) and 163 for three wickets (Tyldesley 108 not out).

A brilliant recovery by Yorkshire yesterday completely altered the outlook at Bramall Lane, and to-day's play was invested with a great deal of interest.

After being 101 behind on the first innings, Yorkshire, owing to excellent batting by Denton, Rhodes, and Jackson, set Lancashire 185 to get to win. Of this number 50 were obtained before the end of yesterday's play.

This morning the weather opened dull, and about nine o'clock there was a slight shower. Whether the rain has affected the wicket remains to be seen.

There was a fair crowd this morning when at half past eleven the Lancashire innings was re-

HAIGH'S TROUBLESOME BOWLING

sumed, Tyldesley (14) and Poidevin (1), the overnight not outs, being opposed by Jackson and Rhodes.

Off Jackson, Tyldesley, who was far more active than Poidevin, obtained four to leg and three through the slips, but when Haigh went on for his captain at 66 the crowd became exceedingly jubilant as the fifth ball knocked back Tyldesley's off-peg.

The last day of cricket at Bramall Lane.

STUMPS UP FOR LAST TIME AT BRAMALL LANE

August 7, 1973...and the last day of cricket at Bramall Lane. After that it was to be football only on a ground whose hallowed turf had, at one time or another, felt the footprints of the famous.

It was a pity that rain spoilt the big day.

It was a shame, too, that the illustrious Geoffrey Boycott was out for just six. Why didn't fate decree that, on such an historic occasion, the master batsman would craft one of his many centuries?

What fate did decree four years later was that Boycott would make the most famous of his centuries on Yorkshire soil.

His 100th hundred came at Headingley on August 11, 1977, during the England v Australia game. What's more he achieved it after a bad night's sleep because the hotel was too warm. What must have tickled the dour Yorkshireman as much as his historic ton was the banner held aloft at Headingley: "BEETHOVEN, BACH...AND BOYCOTT."

When his career ended, he had scored 125 hundreds and amassed more than 40,000 runs in first-class cricket.

Beethoven, Bach...and Boycott! And no, he isn't suffering from a bad back. He's just limbering up before the start of a 1982 benefit match in Rotherham.

ENGLAND DECLARE AT 658 FOR 8 WICKETS

Compton playing McCormick on the resumption of play in the Test match at Trent Bridge to-day.

STAGGERING DAY OF RECORDS

Wright Strikes an Early Blow by Bowling Fingleton

ENGLAND staggered the Australians with records galore to-day and a declaration at their highest score ever in "Ashes" games left Bradman and Co. with over 500 to get to save a follow on.

Eddie Paynter shared in many of the feats in scoring a brilliant double century.

Then followed another shock, for Wright, the young Kent player, clean bowled Fingleton with only 34 scored. Don came next.

TEST NEWCOMER GETS THE MIGHTY DON

Middlesex Back a Loser

SKITTLED BY YORKSHIRE ON DOUBTFUL WICKET AT HEADINGLEY

AS things went the Middlesex captain must have felt a little sorry for himself in not having taken the risk of putting Yorkshire in at Leeds to-day, for his side was out in 110 minutes for 105 runs.

Yorkshire supported some hostile bowling with some remarkably good fielding. Robinson, Sellers an...

SCORES IN THE COUNTY GAMES

SOMERSET v. NOTTS
Sensational cricket was seen at the start of the Nottinghamshire innings against Somerset at Taunton. Batting first on winning the toss the visitors lost six wickets in 45 minutes for 29 runs. Andrews took five of these for 20 runs in six overs and one ball.
At 123 Larwood mistimed Wellard and was clean bowled, the eighth wicket having added 62 in threequarters of an hour.

NOTTS—1st Inns.
Harris, b Wellard ...
Keeton, lbw b Andrews ...
Gunn b Andrews ...

THE TEST SCORE BOARD
ENGLAND—1st Inns.
Hutton, lbw, b Fleetwood-Smith 100
...Cormick ...19...

NOT AT EASE NOW!! With over 658 runs in arrears our Australian friends sit down and discuss the problem at Trent Bridge this afternoon.

TO-DAY'S SPORT RESUME

LANCASHIRE CATCHES THE TEST FEVER!

THERE was some thrilling play in County Cricket to-day. Lancashire passed the 270 mark for the loss of one wicket against Glamorgan at Manchester. Washbrook and Hopwood, each of whom scored centuries, making 188 for the opening stand.

There are two reasons for reproducing this page from June 11, 1938. Yorkshireman Len Hutton scored a century against Australia at Trent Bridge and England ran up a score of 658 for 8...

Sheffield-Born Jockey's Great Treble

Harry Wragg Has Pleasant Surprise on Bistolfi

Specially Contributed

IT was a gala day for the Sheffield-born brother jockeys at Epsom yesterday, for they won between them four out of the five races in which they were eligible to ride.

HARRY WRAGG WINS AGAIN

THE Cesarewitch Stakes at Newmarket this afternoon resulted as follows:—

1. Monsieur l'Amiral
   H. Wragg 33-1
2. Ford Transport
   T. Weston 100-7
3. Geoffrey's Lady
   A. Carson 100-6

The winner is trained in France, but owned by an Englishman, and continued the astonishing run of French triumphs in big races this season.
Sheffield-born Harry Wragg was the successful jockey. This is Wragg's last season before he takes over as a trainer next year.
* * *Full racing details. See back page.*

Harry Wragg, born in Sheffield, was one of the most famous jockeys of all time. Known as "The Head Waiter", he won 13 classics, including the Derby three times in 1928, 1930 and 1942.

Harry also won the Oaks four times and was Champion Jockey in 1941.

After retiring as a jockey, he turned his hand to training and was just as successful.

ATHLETICS

FAST TRACK TO FAME FOR SEB COE

Over the years, many South Yorkshire athletes have legged it to glory, none more so than Sheffield's Seb Coe.

Prominent as a youngster in local schools athletics, he became one of the finest Olympians this country has produced, winning a 1,500 metres gold medal in successive Olympics (Moscow and Los Angeles).

Breaking world records in the 800, 1,000, 1,500 and mile became a habit and he was a splendid ambassador both for athletics and Sheffield.

The super runner who lorded it over his opponents in the nicest possible way was made a real Lord in the spring of 2000.

The former MP for Falmouth and Cambourne who lost his seat when Labour swept to power became William Hague's private secretary and also his judo partner.

Oh, baby! Like all parents, Seb's mum and dad thought their little boy was the best in the world...and eventually he was.

The background to this photo of young Seb is blurred. Is that because he was running so fast?

Coe wins his third title

Sheffield's Sebastian Coe trimmed his previous best 1,500 metre time when he captured the A.A.A.'s under-20 title at Kirkby, Liverpool on Saturday.

Eighteen-year-old Sebastian who is coached by his father, won in 3 minutes 47.1 seconds to collect his third title of the season.

In the discus event the St. Bernard's, Rotherham schoolboy Dave Allen also scored a victory with a throw of 45.94 metres to add to his senior schools title he captured a fortnight ago.

Coe is on his way. The 18-year-old wins a 3A's title in 1975.

Coe 'thrilled and proud' after smashing world record

BILL ARTHUR REPORTS

could not believe I had done it. But now I feel thrilled and proud.

"Everyone thought the clocks had gone wrong. Then, when it was finally clarified, I

Top of the world! Coe breaks the 800 metres record in Oslo in 1979 and receives a telegram from The Star and its readers.

Yet another cup for Coe in 1980. This one, though, has tea in it, poured by proud mum Angela.

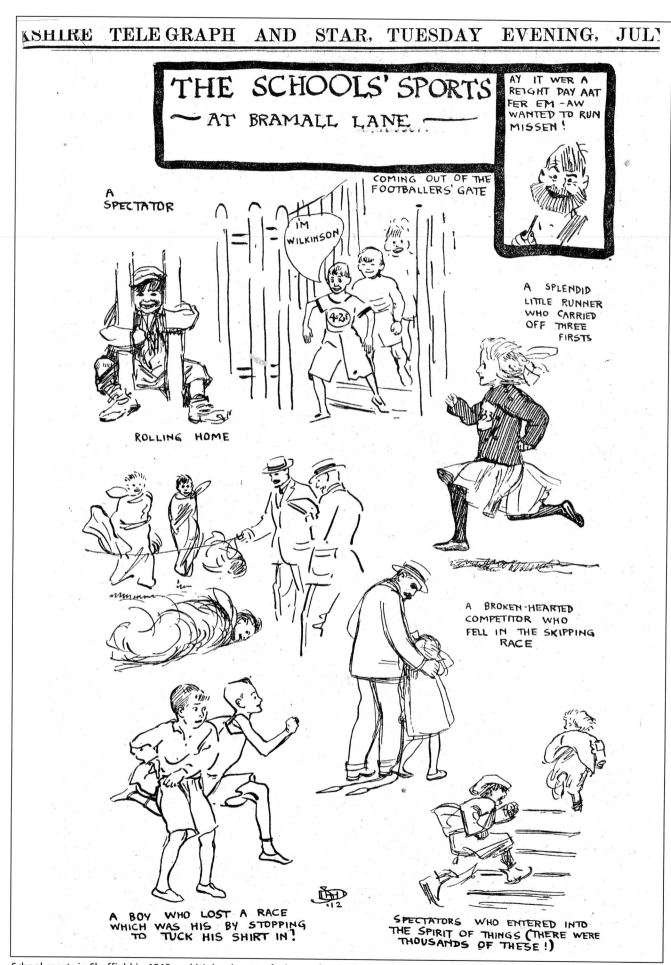

School sports in Sheffield in 1912 and it's hard not to feel sorry for the little girl who fell in the skipping race.

AT THE CALFFIELD SCHOOL SPORTS.

More school sports...July 1, 1929.

THE GREAT "STAR" WALK.

WALKING

The famous Star Walk, which started in 1922, is still going strong but doesn't attract the really large crowds it once did. Throughout the 1920s, 30s and 40s, as many as 150,000 turned out annually to watch all the huffing and puffing. These pictures were taken at the third Star Walk in June, 1924.

SUBSCRIBERS

1 Michelle Jackson
2 David Edmondson
3 Gary Grimes
4 Peter Charlton
5 Mark Rodgers
6 Richard Sharp
7 Terry Morris
8 Amanda Bagnall
9 Kenneth Slinn
10 George W Revill
11 Jean Frances Wood
12 Richard Hobson
13 Paul Watson
14 James Larkin
15 David Fletcher
16 Keith Cotterill
17 G A Plumtree
18 I A Nuttall
19 Esther Crawshaw
20 Charles Ronald Rawlings
21 Mavis Lem
22 Dorothy Holland
23 Gary Bartram
24 John Barrett
25 Kathryn Dumelow
26 Steven P Goulding
27 Simon David Statham
28 Betty Gallacher
29 Brian Thompson
30 Raymond Keith Longden
31 Mary Haigh Glover
32 Mrs Dorothy Wright
33 Joanne Taylor
34 Tom Bromley
35 David James Gains
36 Raymond Allwood
37 John Michael Naylor
38 Doreen Speight
39 Ronald Ernest Goodyear
40 Gordon Frederick Wakefield
41 Nancy Grayson
42 Mrs B A Hossell
43 Gordon Gregory
44 Brett Griffin
45 Jack Birch
46 Roy Young
47 Harry W Leaper
48 Raymond Brown
49 Bryan Pearson
50 Patricia Jukes
51 Alan Thornton
52 Mrs Beryl A Johnson
53 John Wilfred Deane
54 I N Thorpe
55 Melissa Thorpe
56 Sandra Gillott
57 Audrey E Bark
58 Margaret Wedgewood
59 Jane Nashvili
60 Margaret Carr
61 George Samuel Millhouse

62 Robert Michael Prestwood
63 Shirley Mitchell
64 Kenneth Crooks
65 Geoffrey Ward
66 Peter Bryan Conway
67 Ronald Pearce
68 Fred Vine
69 Trevor Vine
70 Mr Gordon Hodgkinson
71 Gilbert Perkins
72 James Wainwright
73 Michael John Bolsover
74 Susan Williams
75 Joan Giles
76 Sylvia Houghton
77 William Richardson
78 Michael Richardson
79 Robert Whitham
80 Kathleen Sharman
81 Edith Godbehere
82 Jack Matthewman
83 John Waller
84 Keith Machin
85 Joseph William Goddard
86 Brian Molloy
87 David V Miller
88 John B Mosley
89 Shaun Redford
90 Denis Thompson
91 John Henry Hague
92 Roger Shepherd
93 Kathleen Lilian Smith
94 Anthony W Rider
95 Alice Mary Brothers
96 Daisy Avena Toothill
97 Jennifer Mary McDermott
98 Mr Brian Gregory
99 Wendy Bell
100 Lynne M Howsam
101 Jason Lee Murray
102 Michael Peter Brookes
103 Terry George Yeardley
104 Patricia Ann Chapman
105 Betty Roe
106 Janet Crawford
107 Philip Perry
108 Brian Woodward
109 John Richardson
110 William Shaw
111 Darren Hayes
112 Mr Tony Medlicott
113 Ray Monica Bond)
114 Rosa James
115 Raymond Anthony Summers
116 David Norman Storey
117 Sheila Pasley
118 Allan G Podoski
119 John D Aldam
120 Mrs Elsie Pownall
121 J Barry Swift
122 Maureen Owen

123 Mark C Priestley
124 G W Bell
125 Eric Shipley
126 Derek Tingle
127 Roy White
128 Irene Eastwood
129 Adrian Ralph Carr
130 J B Sutcliffe
131 Roger Stevenson
132 Kev Briggs
133 Robert William Spencer
134 M J Crossland
135 Edward Blagburn
136 David John Blagburn
137 Brian Dukes
138 Mr Peter E Bradshaw
139 James S Eccles
140 Cyril Spooner
141 Trevor Wilson
142 Jack Birkinshaw
143 Alan E Barber
144 Frank Douglas Stocks
145 George Whitehead
146 Renee Jakes
147 Eric Teigh
148 Michael Anthony King
149 Richard Gilson
150 Christine Heriegel
151 Norman Gilson
152 Victor Malcolm Smith
153 Brian Thompson
154 Ernest Green
155 Mrs Connie Sweet
156 E J Edwards
157 Mrs S M Owen
158 Maurice E Bellamy
159 Graham Marshall
160 Hayley Mae Lewis
161 Dennis Rooke
162 Mrs Hilda Evans
163 Mrs E M A Claypole
164 Mrs Dorothy Ford
165 Albert Edward Sparkes
166 Charlotte Rose Butler
167 Ernest Marshall
168 Kathleen Hill
169 N P Goodison
170 Leonard Brooks
171 Graham Ernest Simpson
172 Thomas Surr
173 Brenda Jean Rose
174 Mrs Mavis Maureen Bradbury
175 Gregory Chapman
176 Leslie Waller
177 Charles E Parkin
178 Marjorie Grayson
179 Raymond Howard
180 Connie Fox
181 Kevin Vine
182 Steven P Goulding
183 John William Earnshaw

184 Derek Anderson
185 Mary Cooper
186 Mary B Tong
187 Edna Young
188 Marc Eagle
189 Mrs Joan Naylor
190 Brenda May Brown
191 Frederick Taylor Pontefract
192 Anne Jessop
193 David Turton
194 Leonard Forrester
195 Desmond Brown
196 Brian Quincey
197 Frank Pashley
198 John Guest
199 Terry Jackson
200 Nigel T Whitham
201 Beatrice Marjorie Kay
202 Barry Buckmaster
203 Kenneth Latham
204 Mrs Joan Newland
205 Brian Colgrave
206 Brian Pilkington
207 Jayne Allyson Cheetham
208 David Barker
209 Jack Bingham
210 Arthur Cooke
211 VIncent Ward
212 Charles William Daniel
213 Douglas Stuart Happs
214 Anthony David Baker
215 Mrs Iris Morton
216 A E Wade
217 Kathleen Wright
218 Peter Marrison
219 Desmond Pass
220 Janet Froggatt
221 Philip William Baxter
222 Joan Marsden
223 Bryen David Hillerby
224 Alan Bell
225 Marie
226 John S Damms
227 Joyce L Jenkinson
228 Raymond Clarkson
229 Barrie H Rowding
230 W E Spooner
231 Ernest Rotheram
232 Mrs Annie Maria Weston
233 Victor Roy Hellewell
234 Mac Millard
235 Marie Elizabeth Kate Mulvey
236 Sharon Popplewell
237 G Cottam
238 Anthony James Cawthorne
239 Walter Gill
240 Frank Butler